# CORVETTES

First published in 1989 by Motorbooks International Publishers & Wholesalers Inc, P O Box 2, 729 Prospect Avenue, Osceola, WI 54020 USA

© Henry Rasmussen, 1989

Motorbooks International is a certified trademark, registered with the United States Patent Office

Printed and bound in Hong Kong

The information in this book is true and complete to the best of our knowledge. All recommendations are made without any guarantee on the part of the author or publisher, who also disclaim any liability incurred in connection with the use of this data or specific details.

We recognize that some words, model names and designations, for example, mentioned herein are the property of the trademark holder. We use them for identification purposes only. This is not an official publication

Library of Congress Cataloging-in-Publication Data
ISBN 0-87938-362-3

Motorbooks International books are also available at discounts in bulk quantity for industrial or sales-promotional use. For details write to Special Sales Manager at the Publisher's address

First published in 1984 as *Corvettes For The Road*

# FOR THE ROAD

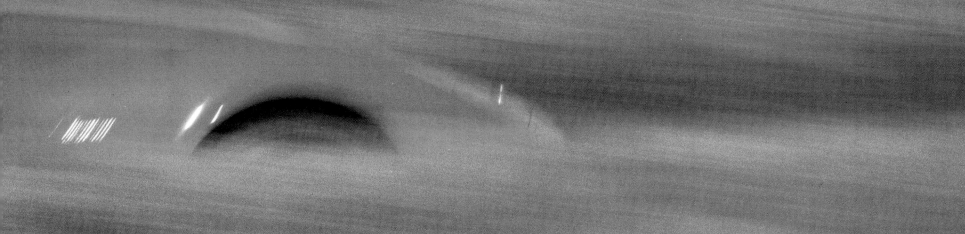

Beginning of it all! General Motors' chief stylist, Harley Earl had the dream. Bob McLean put the shape on paper. Stylists even decided location of axles and engine. Then came engineering, by Maurice Olley, under Ed Cole, chief engineer.

Power source was a 235 cubic-inch, over head valve, straight six. Basically a prewar truck engine! But new manifolds, higher compression ratio (eight to one), plus other improvements, raised output to 150 bhp. Three sidedraft Carter carburetors were used. Zero to 60 took 11 seconds. The quarter mile took almost 18. Zero to 100 took 39. Top speed was 108 mph.

The frame was new. Front and rear suspension (rigid axle), brakes (11-inch drums) and steering were adapted stock Chevrolet components. The body was fiberglass—a first for a production car! Overall weight of the 167-inch long, 72-inch wide, 52-inch low car, was 2900 pounds. Price was $3250. Only 300 were made, all white roadsters with red interiors.

Although the Corvette concept was well accepted, Powerglide—a two-speed automatic—coupled with the lack of performance, dampened the enthusiasm. The Corvette was off to a slow start!

Classic of the second-generation Corvettes! Changed styling had come in 1956. No rear fins now. Conventional headlights. Sculptured side panels. Roll-up windows. Exterior door handles. Clean and mature lines. But in 1957, came the clincher, fuel injection! A first for an American car.

European-born engineer and race driver Zora Arkus-Duntov, who had come aboard in 1953, began to make his marque, gradually improving both performance and handling.

Underneath the new body, things were basically the same as before (except for Zora's subtle changes), as were overall weight and dimensions. Performance wise, Chevrolet's new small block V-8 made a difference. It was first used in 1955 models, 235 cubic-inch then; now 283. Four tuning stages were available. The strongest had 283 bhp. And fuel injection! And optional 4-speed! Compression was 10.5 to one. Zero to 60 took 5.8 seconds; the quarter mile, 14. Top speed was 133 mph.

After a slow start, the Corvette was off and running. Production was 6,339 (1,040 fuel-injected). Price was $3427, (higher with options). V-8 power with fuel injection saved the Corvette. Nothing could stop it now!

## 53

## 57

The styling race was on! In 1958 the Corvette grew nine inches longer and two inches wider (due to bulging grille and bumpers). It had been adorned with twin headlights and two extra grille openings, as well as more chrome and fake louvers. The louvers on the hood were all gone by 1960. So were the chromed bars on the trunk lid. For the better!

For 1960 Zora Arkus-Duntov reworked the suspension, improving both handling and ride comfort. For the first time, an anti-roll bar was fitted at the rear. The one at the front was up-sized. The steering now became closer to neutral.

If the styling-race was on, so was the horsepower race. For 1960, Duntov squeezed 315 bhp (most of four options) from the 283, mainly by increasing compression to 11 to one and enlarging the plenum chamber of the injection unit.

In spite of the increased use of aluminum over the years, weight of the 1960 was 3,100 pounds. Price was $3872. Incredibly, the Powerglide had survived, and was a $199 option. For comparison, the 4-speed manual was a $188 option.

For the first time, production topped ten thousand (10,261). The Corvette was really flying now!

Last year of the second-generation Corvettes! Styling had been modified in 1961, a result of Bill Mitchell having taken over as chief stylist. No teeth in the grille. New rear. For 1962 the cove in the side panel had no chrome molding. The cove was therefore always the color of the car.

The 1962 was last in many ways. Last with rigid rear axle. Last with optional power top. Last with exterior trunk opening. Last with exposed headlights.

Under the hood, the 1962 sported a bigger engine, a 327. It came in three performance options. Top of the trio was the 360 bhp version. In spite of the increase in power, performance was equal to that of the first fuel-injected 1957; the weight had crept up with another 150 pounds.

Sales skyrocketed! Total production, 14,531. Price, also up, was $4227, base. The Powerglide was still hanging on; price, unchanged. Four-speed, also unchanged. But things could not stay as they were, in spite of sales records. The Corvette had been around for almost a decade. It was time for a radical change. And, Duntov and Mitchell had a winner waiting!

## 60

## 62

Classic year of the third-generation Corvettes! Controversial then, the split-window coupe now stands out as the most representative of all Corvette designs. Mitchell and his team had created a bold, beautiful new look, available in both coupe and convertible. The new car was three inches lower, and slightly shorter, on four inches shorter wheelbase.

New exterior covered new interior, except engine and transmission and their various options, which were carry-overs. The frame was new, and, most notable, the Corvette now had independent rear suspension. Arkus-Duntov's efforts in engineering were just as succesful as Mitchell's in styling, producing a car with vastly improved ride and handling. Brakes were also improved, but were still drums. Power-assisted brakes and steering were available as an option for the first time.

Although weight was up, performance was unchanged, thanks to improved aerodynamics. Price was $4394, base. Production was up drastically, 21,513 units. The creators of the new Corvette had reason to be satisfied; they already knew how well their creation looked, and how well it performed, but now they knew the buying public also agreed.

The convertible Sting Ray was it! The convertible and the coupe had sold equally well in 1963. Now the convertible pulled ahead. Almost twice as many were sold. The trend began in 1964, when the split window was removed. Vision considerations had won out. The convertible was indeed very well-balanced, very clean-looking, very European-looking.

Most years have features that make them unique. The 1965 was the first with disc brakes. And the last with fuel injection! The discs were fitted all around, standard. But drums were still available. Opting for them saved $64!

In the engine compartment, there was a wide choice. No less than six tuning stages! The 250 bhp and 300 bhp used four-barrel Carters. The 350 and 365 featured Holleys. The 375 used fuel injection. All these took their power from the 327. Add to these the real brute! The 425 bhp option. This was the new 396 cubic-inch engine, fitted with a four-barrel Holley. A special hood bulge had to be created! Added to this could be another new option. Side-mounted exhaust pipes! It cost a mere $134 to attach this sure attention-getter.

Base price was $4106. Total number produced, 23,562.

 **63**

 **65**

Last of the third-generation Corvettes. The 1967 almost never happened, that is, the new Corvette was supposed to have come that year, but final testing revealed that the car was still not ready. So, the old style was carried on yet another year. In a sense it made the car better. The body was further cleaned up; certain trim and emblems were removed and the fender vents, functional since 1965, became five angled slots and the best looking yet.

In the engine compartment, things had also received attention; there was the basic 300 bhp engine, plus four options; the L71 was the 435 bhp 427, top of the line. Fuel injection was no longer used. Instead three two-barreled Holleys were employed. A hood bulge had been designed for that option. True, there was another option, the now famous L88. But with aluminum heads and a reported output of 560 bhp, it was really someting just for the racing minded.

Safety concerns had eliminated the knock-off wheel; the new bolt-on cover looked the same, but had a wingless cap covering the nuts. Base price was $4327. Total production was 22,940, down from the 1966 figure of 27,720.

Second year of the fourth generation! In 1968, the new car met with mixed reactions, due to lack of development.

The new Corvette took its inspiration from Mitchell's Mako Shark experimental cars. Stylists Larry Shinoda, David Holls and Henry Haga worked out the production look. It was two inches lower and seven inches longer than the first Sting Ray, but kept the same wheelbase. Width was about the same, but track a little wider. Rims were 7-inch; in 1969, 8-inch.

Under the new shell, things were basically the same as in 1967. Due to organizational changes at GM and a long illness, Duntov had not been all that involved with the new car. In 1969, he was back again, and his touch was again apparent; the Sting Ray badge reappeared, now spelled Stingray.

Engine options were spectacular: seven, in addition to the basic. The small block was reintroduced, now 350 cubic inches. The L71 option 427 had 435 bhp. But its zero to 60 time did not creep below six seconds; the new body was heavier.

Price was $4400. Production numbers show that the trend had turned in favor of the coupe, 22,154 compared to 16,608, for a total of 38,762. A new record!

67

69

After seven years, it was really time for a new design. But the 1975 Corvette still looked the same. Of course, the climate was not all that healthy in the marketplace. Not for sports cars! Smog rules. Safety laws. World wide depression.

The 1975 lacked many of the features that had made the Corvette! There was no Mark IV engine. No genuine dual exhaust. And it was the last year of the convertible!

Adding to all the other negatives, 1975 was the first year for the catalytic converter; unleaded fuel had to be used. The front and rear by now sported impact-resistant designs that added weight, now up to 3,660 pounds.

On the engine front, the decline of the Corvette as a purist car showed clearly. There was only one option, a 205 bhp, 350 cubic-inch small block. The base version developed 165 bhp. Zero to 60 took almost 10 seconds. The quarter mile, almost 17. Not much better than 20 years earlier!

The price did not decline, however. Base was $6810; more with necessary options. Total production was 38,465. Convertibles accounted for 4,629 of that total.

Year of the Silver Anniversary! Year of the Pace Car! Both exterior and interior had received a facelift. The rear had become a fastback, with a large window. Instruments and armrests had been redesigned and the fastback style allowed for a somewhat larger luggage space.

The Corvette performed the honors of pace car at the 1978 Indianapolis 500. Thus the limited edition. According to initial plans there would only be one thousand units made. In the end, 6,502 were assembled, approximately one car for every Corvette dealer in the country. The Pace Car featured prominent front and rear spoilers, and two-tone paint; black on the upper half of the body, and silver on the bottom half. There were also special decals included with the Pace Car, but most owners let them stay in their wrappers.

There was still not much to brag about under the hood. Still only one option, now producing 220 bhp—15 horses more. The base price was $9351. Base price for the Pace Car was $13,653; that still did not include the stronger engine. It was another $525. Demand was so great that many a Pace Car went for upwards of $20,000. Total production, 46,776.

**75**

**78**

The old body style was still hanging on. By now it had been drastically updated. For 1980 there were new front and rear bumper assemblies. Front and rear spoilers were built into these. Those spoilers definitely improved the aerodynamics. And looks!? It had become quite "awesome", to use a word popularized by another manufacturer.

In the engine compartment things looked only a little brighter than before. There were two performance levels, but not in California, where tight emission restrictions caused GM to offer only the 305 cubic-inch, 180 bhp unit, while elsewhere L82 was the most powerful option, giving 230 bhp. The fact that GM engineers had managed to lighten the car by 250 pounds, was commendable, but did not improve performance to the level of the good old days.

If things looked bleak on the performance front, they looked much brighter in the area of creature comfort; there were no less than seven options that had to do with sound equipment. Stereo with CB and power antenna cost $391 (same as removable roof panels of glass). Base price was $13,140. The total number of cars produced was 40,614.

The old Corvette had been around for fifteen seasons. There had been many experimentals. And much talk. But with the old selling so well, wishes of stylists and engineers did not count. But, finally, in 1983 there was a new Corvette!

The new frame and suspension got highest marks. Responsible was Dave McLellan. He had worked with Duntov before taking charge, starting with the 1976 model. The styling was clean and beautiful, on a par with the best from Europe, but still unmistakably Corvette. Responsible was Jerry Palmer, working under Charles Jordan and Irv Rybicki.

Length was down nine inches, to 176.5. Width was up two inches, to 71. Height was down over an inch, to 46.7. Wheelbase was shortened to 96.2. Weight was down over three hundred pounds, to 3,200. The engine was about the only carry-over. The 350 cubic-inch put out 205 bhp. Zero to 60 took just over 7 seconds. Top speed was 140 mph.

Price was $24,600. A drastic jump. But it was very much car for the money! There are no 1983's. All are 1984's. Total units produced, to the end of March, is 37,389. The present assembly line pace works out to three thousand a month.

**80**

**84**

# The Beauty of the Beast...

Few sports cars, if any, have had as much printed about them as has the Corvette. There are uncountable articles, numerous specialty magazines, a variety of club publications, and scores of books... In spite of this abundance, there always seems to be room for more; there always seems to be talk of that final, definitive book... Well, this is not the one!

In fact, none of the books in The Survivors Series claim to give a comprehensive documentation of the technical and historical aspects of a marque in question. The emphasis of The Survivors Series has always been on the beauty of the cars...

In this new volume, ninth in the series, this emphasis is even more obvious. For two reasons. First, the Corvette is a photographer's dream, so incredibly flamboyant... I simply couldn't resist being carried away by its appearence! Second, as a favor, General Motors Design allowed special access to their long-stored-away photographic files, making it possible to document the styling aspect of the creation process as seldom before.

So, don't look for information on the location of serial numbers, or complete listings of options, or explanations of fuel-injection systems... Instead, lean back in your favorite chair and open the pages to the beauty of the Corvette, seen from a variety of perspectives. For a Corvette is much more than just suspension geometry, gear ratios, and gas mileage... A Corvette also deserves to be looked at, driven, remembered... That's the beauty of it... The beauty of the beast!

**S**omewhat pretentious, the emblem of the first Corvette carried an aura of racing distinction; there was no involvement in racing until the introduction of the second-generation Corvette. But from then on it more than made up for the initial innocence; over the years Corvettes were perennial class winners at Sebring and captured a long string of regional and national SCCA championships. Best of all, its eminent career is far from over yet!

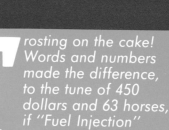 **F**rosting on the cake! Words and numbers made the difference, to the tune of 450 dollars and 63 horses, if "Fuel Injection" adorned the cove of a 1957. On the bulging hood of a 1967, the "427" could mean a difference of 437 dollars and 135 horses. The "Limited Edition" decal on the side panel of a 1978, meant 4302 dollars, but it did not buy any extra horses!

**S**ingle is all right, but double is better! That seemed to be the reasoning among automotive stylists in the mid-fifties. Naturally, the Corvette received its share too. The single light was last seen on the 1957, its simple "sugar scoop" rear unit pictured on the opposite page. From 1958 on, Corvettes were stuck with the double lights. The double rear lights became something of a trade-mark, carried on to the 1984.

**W**heels of fortune! Pictured on this page, the 53-55 wheel cover (right), and the 56-62 (far right and above). Shown on the opposite page, the 63-66 optional alloy wheel (top left), the 68 and on standard wheel cover (top right), the 76 and on optional aluminum wheel (bottom left), and the new 84 wheel (bottom right).

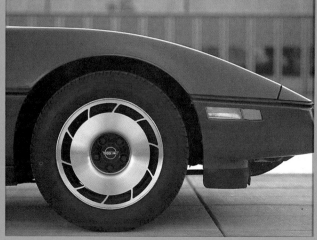

**D**ash design remained the same after the new body came in 1956. Shown above, the 1953 interior, the 1957 to the right. Restyled dash was introduced in 1958. It stayed until 1963. A 1960 is pictured on the opposite page (far right). Shown below it, the controversial Sting Ray dash as it appears on a 1965 roadster. In 1968 it was again time for a restyling. A 1969, minus roof panels, is pictured in the middle.

*Overembellished? Sure! But the dashes, instruments, steering wheels of these early cars represent an era when the possibilities seemed endless, in the field of styling, as well as in more profound matters. The driver's view in a 1953 is seen to the left. The odometer, by the way, has just rolled over to the nine-thousand-mile figure. To the right, the impressive view in a 1960. And above, the same basic style seen in a 1962. These second-generation steering wheels are by far the best looking of the lot.*

Shown in this spread, engines that highlight a spectacular rise to power! On this page (top), the straight six of 1953, with its three Carter carburetors and 150 bhp. On the opposite page (far left), the 283 bhp of 1957, a V-8, fuel injected for the first time. Next, the 360 bhp of 1963, still fuel injected. The 1967 435 bhp (near left) had given up fuel injection for the triple Holleys. The peak of performance, the 1969 ZL-1 (above), with its aluminum block, unofficially producing 580 bhp!

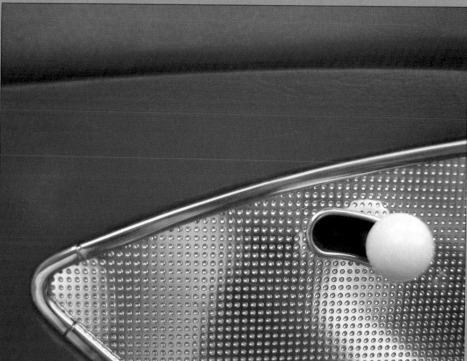

**A** reoccuring theme in fifties styling was a design element that became prominently exemplified in McDonald's "golden arches". In Corvette styling this element can be found, for example, on the side panel of a 1957 (left), or on the door panel of a 1960 (upper right). Soft curves could be found all over, in the wheel cover of a 1962 (above), or in the lower edge of the dash on a 1953 (right). Note that the large dial, the tachometer, has an unusual feature, a revolution accumulator.

**B**ackgrounds can say much about a car. To the left, the most power packed of all Corvettes for the road, the 1969 ZL-1, is mated with the ultimate performance machine, the locomotive. To the right, the larger-than-life plumbing of a waste-recycling plant (no double meaning intended) reinforces the resourceful lines of the 1978 Pace Car. Above, the slick surface of a tile wall emphasizes the clean and purposeful design of the 1984 Corvette.

**O**n historic ground! Corvette designer Jerry Palmer poses with the finished product. A team effort, to be sure, it is still an experience afforded few men, to drive a car that is so much the product of his own creative efforts. The photos were taken in the closed viewing area at General Motors Technical Center, where all Corvettes, except the 1953, have first been shown to corporate dignitaries.

# A Homecoming of Sorts.

Nineteen fifty-three was a year of beginnings as well as endings. It was a significant year. But maybe every year seems that way when you look back and discover that history has already been made. Stalin died. That was the end of something. The fighting in Korea also came to an end. And Truman gave way for Eisenhower. Another ending. Another beginning.

But some things didn't change. In boxing, Rocky Marciano held on to his heavyweight crown. And in baseball, the Yankees won the World Series for the fifth time in a row.

In the movies there's always something new. The craze that year was 3-D. Anyone remember seeing *Kiss Me Kate* through those cardboard-frame glasses?

On the automotive front, the wraparound windshield made its production car debut. And General Motors introduced a new sports car, the Corvette. That, certainly, turned out to be the beginning of something!

I have just finished shooting Corvette number 181. It sits parked on the green grass of a football field. Right on top of the fifty-yard line. Tooth-grinned and spaceship-tailed, it sits there as a symbol of things past.

The round sloping front fenders with their faired-in headlights might have been inspired by the 356 Porsche, first seen in 1949. Jaguar's XK 120 also came in 1949, but there's nothing about the looks of the Corvette that resembles the Jaguar. Unless the headlights, meant to have ple-

*(continued on overleaf)*

The first public viewing of a Corvette took place at the Motorama in New York on January 17, 1953. The event was held in the Grand Ballroom of the Waldorf-Astoria. Pictured to the left, Number One surrounded by an admiring crowd. Notice that the spear on the side panel has its fin pointing down; on the production model it was changed to point up. On this page, two dream cars for the 1954 Motorama. Above, the fastback Corvair (all Chevrolet models had to begin with a "C" in those days). Right, a Corvette with a removable hardtop. The hardtop became an option in 1956. The Corvair never made it to production.

Of the three hundred Corvettes created in 1953, one fourth are still missing. The discovery of a lost one sends ripples of excitement through the Corvette fraternity. Especially when it has as little as nine thousand original miles on the odometer, and still rolls on its original set of tires!

Chip Miller, of York, Pennsylvania, owns this Survivor, chassis number E53F001181. The first owner drove it on vacation to Colorado, but didn't like it, so he sent it home on the train. Sentenced to life in an unheated garage, it did not emerge until 1972.

xiglass covers, were influenced by the C-type, Jaguar's 1951 Le Mans winner. The grille looks somewhat like that of the 1952 Mercedes 300 SL. But the Mercedes didn't arrive until after the shape of the Corvette was already set. Maybe that grille could be traced back to Pinin Farina's 1947 Cisitalia? Be that as it may, the Corvette still is an original. An American original.

It's homecoming week. And time for the game to begin. Players come running in on the field. All of them too young to remember. But they're curious. Even in the midst of their excitement they must stop to admire the object that tells the story of another time, happily simple, optimistically limitless, innocently wild.

The referees are old enough to remember. But they tell us to move the car. Now!

I'm behind the wheel. What a wheel! Big. Beautiful. I'm sitting close to it with my arms doubled-up. The feel is that of an old car. But the sensation that stands out comes from the Powerglide, that smooth, even motion, accompanied by that smooth, even exhaust note. Nothing sporty about that sound! The Powerglide makes the straight-six sound like a boat. Not a speed boat. Just a plain old motor boat.

The odometer turns over to 9061. I feel nervous about putting miles on it. The owner, Chip Miller, one of the most knowledgeable, genuine, and amicable Corvette enthusiasts you'll ever meet, and partner in The Flea Marketeers (which organizes the big twice-annual swap-meet events in Carlisle, Pennsylvania,) sits in the passenger seat. As we roll slowly down the main street of York (the top is down), I stay aware of the surrounding traffic like never before; this car isn't only worth a lot of money, it's also a piece of history. It can't be replaced!

"One of my friends heard the car was for sale. They all knew I was crazy about Corvettes, so he told me. The owner of a radio station in Niagara Falls had bought it new. It came out of the estate after his death and was never advertised. Those early cars were only sold to celebrities, so I guess owning a radio station must have qualified him. He didn't drive it much. But he did take it twice all

There is a curious case of missing files in the archives at GM Design. The reference catalog shows subjects and numbers. But all early negatives pertaining to the Corvette are missing from its cabinet—destroyed, lost, stolen—who knows? The picture above, the only in the file, dated November 29, 1952, shows the prototype top mechanism just a month and a half before introduction. It may be the earliest photograph still in existence. Left and right, dated August 26, 1953, the Motorama car in the lobby of the GM Building. Above, right, dash of the production version.

the way to Colorado. The second time he must have become fed up with the primitive weather protection or something, because he shipped it back on the train and put it away in his garage. When I got the car in 1972 it had 8,788 miles and a 1962 sticker.

"I went to see the car. It was sitting by itself in a small garage. It was terribly filthy. I could hardly tell it was white. I wiped off an area on the fender and saw that the paint was fine, but very yellow. The top was up. I checked it, too. It was like new under the dirt. Not a stitch was torn. And I checked the serial number to be sure it was a 1953. At first I could hardly believe the low mileage. But the more dirt I wiped off the more I saw of the condition of the car, and I began to think it was possible. I also looked at that engine revolution counter on the tach. It checked out. The mileage was original!

"I gave them my bid. It was high. It was high, back in 1972! It doesn't sound like much today. But I wanted that car badly!

"Every time the phone rang I was a nervous wreck! For a long time, long for me, I didn't hear from them, so I finally called. A policeman had offered 2500 dollars. But that wasn't anywhere close to my bid. So the car was mine!

"I can remember it was in the middle of the winter. And it had been snowing. And I had an open trailer. The car did run, although a muffler was shot and the fuel pump was leaking, but I didn't want to put any miles on it, so I trailered it in spite of the bad weather.

"It took me a couple of months to clean it up. I used soap and water. It hasn't been restored, except for some minor details. But that's the way I want it. Let others discuss what an original 53 should look like. Mine is still the way it was when it came from the factory!

"How about the radio?" I ask. We're out on the open road now. The boat is plowing through the fresh autumn air, that monotonous exhaust note coming smooth and even.

"Original, too!" Chip says. "In fact, if you push this button, it will play How Much Is That Doggie in the Window?"!

57

# Rock'n'Roll Rocket.

It's 1957. Khrushchev consolidates his power in Moscow. Castro marches on Havana. And Great Britain becomes the third nation to explode a hydrogen bomb. At home, Eisenhower wins another term. Communist-hunter McCarthy dies in May. And there are race riots in Little Rock.

In sports, Floyd Patterson is boxing's new heavyweight champion. And the Milwaukee Braves beat the New York Yankees for the World Series title.

At the movies, Doris Day and Rock Hudson are the big box-office attractions. The Oscar goes to *The Bridge on the River Kwai*.

Radios and juke boxes across the nation glow red hot with Pat Boone's *Love Letters in the Sand* and Elvis Presley's *Jailhouse Rock*.

And in October, Moscow's Sputnik, the first earth satellite, awakens Americans to the dawn of the space age.

Somewhat enigmatically, with the arrival of a new age, the new Corvette had lost its rocket ship taillights. But then, they were always more of a Buck Rogers fantasy than a Wernher von Braun reality.

The new Corvette style had come in 1956. From the front, the grille was unchanged, but the headlights were now conventional, set high in the more drawn-out fender pontoons.

On the hood, two parallel bulges, like on the Mercedes 300SL, had been added. The new headlight arrangement could also be traced to the 300SL. (Photographs taken in early 1955

At least two full-size models showing the suggested restyling for 1956 were posed for viewing and photography on February 1, 1955. The sequence on the opposite page shows that one of the models featured scooped-out coves behind both the front and the rear wheels. Notice also the exhaust pipe protruding through the fender, behind the rear wheel. At this stage the rims around the headlights were still painted, the wheel covers in preliminary form and the hood emblem small and accented by a chevron. Left and above, the various components of the fiberglass body as they were shown in GM's viewing complex.

show that GM indeed had a Gullwing on hand for inspiration and comparison.)

Seen in profile, the most obvious new element was the cove in the side panel, flaring back from the front wheel like a stylized cloud of fire and smoke. Similar designs had been seen before, on, for instance, the 1955 La Salle II Motorama show car and, even earlier, on Bertone's 1953 Arnolt Bristol coupe. But, as applied to the new Corvette, that cove became something of a trademark. Photographs, found in the GM files, show full-scale mock-ups featuring shorter coves behind the front as well as the rear wheel. Obviously, the single, long cove won.

From the rear, the elimination of the old rocket ship taillights created a smooth look with the new lights recessed in attractive, scoop-shaped bezels that did not interrupt the flowing line.

The overall form was clean and homogenous, and, especially from the front, aggressive looking. The three-quarter front view, with the somewhat overweight rear obscured, was an especially flattering angle. While criticizing the heaviness of the rear, one must at the same time complain about the small, nonfunctional air scoops on top of the fenders, just ahead of the windshield. It was the beginning of an unfortunate trend of make-believe embellishments that would escalate on future models. On the other hand, visually and historically, those details are a part of what makes this era so memorable. If the scoops had only been real! They were first seen on the original 1953 Motorama Corvette, but had vanished on the production model. The scoops weren't there on the 1956 preproduction mock-up either. Then, at the last minute, they showed up again. The chrome strip outlining the shape of the cove on the side panel was another last-minute addition.

I squeeze in behind the wheel of collector Waldo Adams' all-restored, show-condition 1957. The interior looks the same as in the old model, but the seats are now covered with the waffle-pattern vinyl. The light-beige interior

(continued on overleaf)

**N**ot only one of the best looking Corvettes ever, the 1957 was also one of the best performing. The reason was fuel injection. The Cascade Green Survivor featured in these photographs, chassis number E57S102924, owned by Waldo Adams of Laguna Hills, California, has the most unusual and desirable option combination, fuel-injected 283 bhp and four-speed transmission.

contrasts nicelywith the Cascade Green exterior. The steering wheel is still big, but it has been redesigned, looking very racy with its three drilled-out spokes. The driving position still adheres to the close-to-the-wheel attitude.

I start it up. It comes to life with a deep, rumbling, big-engine sound. I reach for the stick. One is up to the left. Two is down. Three is up to the right. And four is down. Yes, four! Waldo's is one of the few 1957s with the combination of four-speed and fuel injection. I press the gas pedal, lightly, and let go of the clutch, slowly, carefully.

"Pop it! Step on it!" Waldo calls out from the seat beside me, obviously willing to let me experience what his pride and joy is all about.

I do as he says. I step on it. And I pop it. Off it goes! No more motor boat like the 1953! No, sir! This one sounds as good as it goes. First there is that loud hissing from the fuel injection. It comes like the sound from when you open up the nozzle of a hose on a fire engine. Then there's the roar. And the vibration. And the smell of aromatic gases; odors from gasoline and exhaust, with some burning rubber mixed in, flow through the cockpit. I shift to second. Off it goes again. Bouncing. Leaping. Sliding. It feels like it wants to get away: like it's wrestling itself out of the grip of my hands. Beast! It's that famous, or infamous, wildness of these early Corvettes!

"It takes getting used to." Waldo shouts over the roar. "But once you do, it's a fun car to drive! Pop the clutch in third. But be careful. It can fishtail!"

I decide not to exercise that option. In fact there isn't enough road. Nor is there enough road for fourth. I brake and come to a standstill at the wayside. The 283 rumbles calmly, as if nothing had happened. Of course, I know that the juices still flow fast inside that chunk of iron, just as the blood flows fast inside my veins.

"Now I know why they didn't need those rocket ship taillights anymore," I say.

"How is that?" Waldo wonders.

"Instead of looking like a rocket, it goes like a rocket!"

A prototype fitted with a Duntov-modified engine and new 1956 body panels was brought to Daytona Beach in early January. Above, John Fitch distorts the image on the film as he speeds by. Driven by Zora Arkus-Duntov, the car reached 150 mph. But Duntov had something much more exciting up his sleeve: the SS racer. It made its debut at Sebring in the spring of 1957. Left, Juan Fangio tests the "mule." Lower right, cockpit and engine of actual SS. Upper right, Piero Taruffi at the wheel during the race, which, for the SS, ended after 23 laps.

**60**

# Double-Lights, Double-Good...

In 1960, players of The Big Game make significant moves to improve their positions and realize their goals.

Elvis Presley returns from his Army exile in Europe. His new release, *Are You Lonesome Tonight?*, shoots to the top of the charts. Cassius Clay wins an Olympic gold medal in Rome. Soon afterward he turns professional.

De Gaulle has become president. Castro has overthrown Batista. Khrushchev is firmly in power. And Kennedy wins the presidential election with a narrow margin.

At General Motors, William L. Mitchell is now head of styling. For several years he has been toying with ideas for a new Corvette. One such experiment is the 1957 Q-Corvette. Although its time has not yet come, it nevertheless turns out to be the embryo of a future Corvette. The same styling ideas are further refined in a new sports racer, first seen in 1959. Because of an agreement between the automakers not to engage in racing, Mitchell develops and enters this car on his own. It can't display the Corvette badge. It's instead named Sting Ray. The first year reveals serious shortcomings, but as these are corrected, the 1960 season sees the sleek silver machine capturing the SCCA championship.

Another personality at GM is also making a steady advance. He is Zora Arkus-Duntov, an engineer with a uniquely made-to-order background. His energy, for the first few years applied to improving the existing models, is then focused on the Q-Corvette, but as it becomes

Even before the 1956 model arrived in the showrooms, the styling staff had been busy at work to prepare for the changes that would be implemented in 1958. Left, the double lights and triple grilles as they looked on January 17, 1956. Notice that the chrome strip around the cove continues almost all the way to the headlights. Also notice the different bumper alternatives. Above, the wide chrome bands on the trunk lid are tried out. Upper right, the front is getting closer to its final form but still has a mesh grille. Both pictures are dated January 30. Lower right, the final look, dated August 7.

DAYTON
1-30-56

12911

clear that this effort is premature, he returns to the existing Corvette, specifically the 1960 model. His labors result in increased performance and improved handling.

In spite of the ban on racing, the enthusiasts at GM, with Duntov in the lead, find ways to keep the Corvette competitive. The secret lies in the option packages. With the fuel injected 283, the positraction axle, the four-speed transmisson, the heavy duty brakes and suspension, and the twentyfour-gallon fuel tank, the Corvette is ready for almost anything!

In addition to the succes of the Sting Ray, Corvettes capture first in class in the Twelve Hours of Sebring, eighth overall at Le Mans, as well as another SCCA championship.

In Middleburg, Virginia, another player of The Big Game is quietly laying the foundation for a future career in the automotive field. In 1960, William Gray is ten years old. Already as a two-year-old he amazes people by being able to distinguish between the various makes that pass on the street in front of his parents' home. As a ten-year-old, none of the facts and feats of the Corvette elude him.

In 1958, the Corvette receives its share of the superficial embellishments showered on automobiles at this time. In addition to the already fake scoops on the fenders, it also gets fake louvers on the hood and fake vents in the side panels as well as twin headlights, triple grilles, and double chrome strips on the rear deck lid. Thanks to Mitchell the act is cleaned up quite a bit for 1960 and, together with the improvements resulting from Duntov's work, it is now a most impressive machine.

This 1960 Corvette proves too much of a temptation to a man in La Jolla; he becomes an owner, in spite of the almost five-thousand-dollar price tag. He pays 16 dollars extra to get the cove painted Ermine White. He opts for the fuel-injected 275 hp, 283 ci engine, costing 485 dollars, the four-speed transmission, 188 dollars, and the whitewall tires, costing an ad-

*(continued on overleaf)*

Some say it was over-decorated. But it is easy to see why, in spite of, or thanks to, the dual lights and triple grilles, the 1960 Corvette made every head turn! Owner William Gray of La Jolla, California, bought this beauty, chassis number 00867S103004, from its first owner. A nine-thousand-dollar paint-job, part of a cost-no-object restoration, makes this Survivor sparkle in front of a not-so-still Pacific.

ditional 32 dollars.

He keeps his prize possession in perfect condition. But not like a show car. After all, he drives it. As the years go by, and new models come out, he still likes the good old 1960. He never falls for the temptation to change things, add things, not even to paint it.

When William Gray turns fifteen he buys his first car, a 1948 Buick Sedanette. At seventeen, he buys his first new car, a 1963 Chevrolet Impala Super Sport. Both cars are bought with money he has earned himself. During the following years, spent studying business administration and marketing, cars remain a central part of his life, but only as a hobby. In 1975, after having made his money in real estate, he decides to devote himself full time to cars, opening a showroom in San Diego, featuring classic and special-interest cars.

The same year, he also becomes aware of that certain 1960 Corvette rolling on the streets of nearby La Jolla. He locates the owner and befriends him.

It takes five years until the man is ready to sell. He realizes that he will never be able to restore the car the way William Gray will.

William Gray has never before owned a Corvette. But he remembers the year of 1960. He wants this one for himself. To keep. And he wants to do it right, in every detail.

"I don't think I should advertize how much I spent on restoring this car," Gray says. "But I can tell you that the paint job alone cost nine thousand dollars!"

"Can you really justify investing that much in a Corvette?" I wonder.

"Yes. To me, the satisfaction lays in seeing a car brought back to its original condition without having to compromise. Besides, based on my experience in the business, I feel the Corvette is still one of the biggest sleepers around."

He says it with a conviction that makes me feel that he knows what he is talking about. And he most likely does. For William Gray has a record of doing things right, as well as doing the right thing.

TRENT 12-9-55

These never-before-published photographs provide a fascinating glimpse of what goes on behind the curtains of secrecy. On this page, interior shots from one of the design studios, dated December 9, 1955. The unfinished mockup is an Oldsmobile dream car, the Golden Rocket. Its headlights and grille provided the ideas for the 1958 Corvette. Opposite page, these photos, dated December 29, were taken in the new viewing complex. The mockup is ready to be seen by the brass. Notice the split rear window and the roof panels that opened with the door. Present was also the new Corvette and a sampling of competitors.

# The Right Stuff.

Nineteen-sixty-two was a year of milestones. John Glenn became the first American to orbit the earth. The Telstar communications satellite was launched and began relaying transatlantic broadcasts. The Missile Crisis brought the world to the brink of nuclear war.

Marilyn Monroe died. John Steinbeck won the Nobel Prize. And James Meredith was admitted to the University of Mississippi.

In the world of Corvette, one more year would pass before a milestone appeared. Although, to a lesser degree, the last year of each generation should also be considered milestones; the 1962 was indeed a last.

The basic body style had not been altered, but an important change had been made the year before, when the tail section had received a new look. It took its inspiration from the 1957 Q-Corvette with its hip-level crease, running all around the car. This look was further refined on the 1959 Sting Ray racer. And, as we know, it would ultimately end up on the new Corvette. In fact, in retrospect, it looks like a carefully orchestrated plan to educate the public; first came the Q-Corvette, then the Sting Ray sports racer, then the XP-700, then the 1961 redesign, then the Shark and finally, the culmination: the production-version Sting Ray.

But the 1961 face lift, or should we say bottom lift, incorporated this treatment only at the rear. A positive result was that the heaviness of the old tail section was eliminated. A negative effect was that the front and rear no longer harmonized. Nevertheless, the new look allowed the

*Man of many coats! Zora Arkus-Duntov was the name most significantly linked with the continuous progress of the Corvette. He brought to GM an expertise in both racing and engineering; knowledge gained in Europe. Above, Zora is keeping warm while waiting for his turn behind the wheel of the Porsche he brought to a class win at Le Mans in 1954. Left, at Sebring in 1961. Right, showing off the ZL-1 to reporters at a Phoenix drag strip in 1969. Far right, a different coat was donned during sessions at GM, where he was often called upon to argue the case for all of America's true sports car enthusiasts.*

basic style to stay in production.

While Mitchell had instigated these alterations to the body, Arkus-Duntov had not been neglecting the mechanics, although both men and their staffs by now were seriously occupied with a successor. In fact, as is true in most cases, the longer a basic model runs, the more it tends to be improved. At least, this seems to be true when it comes to the mechanics; the 1962 model is no exception. For this continued progress, one must credit a man who, through his determination, became one of the most forceful movers behind the Corvette: Zora Arkus-Duntov.

Looking back, tracing the events that led Duntov to GM, it seems more like a coincidence than a plan that this man, possessing the perfect credentials for the job, would in fact end up being hired by Research and Development.

Zora Arkus-Duntov was born in Belgium while his Russian parents completed their schooling in that country. The year was 1910. In the post-revolution years we find the family in Leningrad. But life in Russia must not have been what it promised; they moved to Germany.

As is often the case with creative minds, school does not seem to agree with them. This was the case with young Zora. Not until he began studying engineering, first in Leningrad, then in Berlin, did he seem to find his purpose. His final work was in the field of supercharging.

During the prewar years Zora launched a career in engineering, cultivating contacts in Belgium, France and Germany, working on projects as diverse as motorcycles and locomotives. The outbreak of war put a halt to these activities. The early capitulation of France found him in that country's air force. An American visa unexpectedly brought him to New York, where he was enrolled in the war effort, designing aircraft engines. After the war, Zora started a company that specialized in speed equipment. His Ardun overhead valve conversion became a popular item. In the early fifties we find Duntov tied to Allard in England as a consultant. In 1952 and 1953, he drove Allards at Le Mans.

*(continued on overleaf)*

**N**o teeth in the grille. Four round rear lights. These are some of the changes introduced in 1961. In 1962, the side vents were redesigned, as can be seen in the photograph above, featuring Pat Connells' of Costa Mesa, California, fuel-injected 327. This Survivor, chassis number 20867S112637, represents the last of the body style; a style etched into the eye of every American car enthusiast; an image as American as that of a baseball batting cage.

It was during that time a friend encouraged him to make contact with GM. A letter from Ed Cole, the chief engineer, and later a visit to Detroit, ultimately led to his hiring. Earlier in 1953, before he began at GM, Duntov had seen the first Corvette at the New York premier showing. He seems to have been impressed by its looks more than its performance. This impression was confirmed later when he had a chance to test-drive it. Although he was not involved in the Corvette program at that time, through his background and inclination, he was inevitably drawn to it. Covertly he began to suggest changes which resulted in improved steering and suspension.

In 1957, Duntov became the chief engineer of the Corvette project and could devote himself wholeheartedly to the work his previous experiences had groomed him for, gradually upgrading the production models, but also creating a most exciting sports racing car, the SS. Unfortunately, the SS saw action only once. Its potential was obvious. Both Juan Fangio and Stirling Moss tested the car and were impressed. But there were shortcomings. Regrettably, before these could be corrected, the ban on racing put a halt to all further activities. One of the planned assignments for the SS had been an all-out attack on Le Mans.

It is obvious that Duntov had in mind to establish a reputation for the Corvette that, if he had been allowed to follow through, could have given even more glory to the marque. It would have been a picture to savor for the future, to have seen the Corvette SS cross the finish line at Le Mans in 1957 as the winner!

Fortunately, Duntov was successful in persuading management to let him continue to develop those exciting options for the road cars. For 1962, this took the form of an enlarged engine, the 327, with the highest power output yet, 360 hp.

Just as John Glenn had what it took to make that first flight a success, Zora Arkus-Duntov had what it took to turn the Corvette into a real sports car. The right stuff.

The touch of Duntov began to make itself felt on the racing circuits in 1956. Opposite page, upper right, hard-charging Dick Thompson and Paul O'Shea duel at Sebring, with the Corvette the winner. On this page, left, Bob Bondurant entering turn six at Riverside in 1960. John Fitch and Bob Grossman drove to an honorable eighth overall at Le Mans in 1960. Above, the same year, Lilley and Gamble crossed the finish line in tenth place, but had not covered minimum distance. Opposite page, center, the start at Sebring in 1961. Bottom, Elkhart Lake 1961. Yenko and Lother, number 11, won

63

# Of Sting Rays and Flying Saucers...

It makes a lot of difference where and when you see a car. Crowded parking lots and busy downtown streets certainly don't work to a car's advantage. Even showrooms, often cramped and badly lighted, seldom provide the proper setting for viewing.

The open road is a good place to see a car. Especially if you stand at the wayside for the sole purpose of taking in the image of the car as it passes, as I have done on many occasions.

One of the most memorable of such events took place in Northern Italy. It was a narrow road that curved its way up a hillside. From where I stood I could only see a short straightaway and the sharp, slanting curve that led into it. The car was a 1929 Alfa Romeo 1750 with a beautiful sound that echoed between the hills as it worked its way up the incline, decelerating, shifting, accelerating. When the red Alfa finally appeared, sliding through the curve, there was no other time or place when and where it could have looked better.

The time is early morning. The place is a gravel pit in York, Pennsylvania. Three individuals inhabit the otherwise deserted location: a 1963 Sting Ray, its owner George Wagman, and myself, camera equipped as always

George got "the bug" in 1976 when he visited a friend who still owned a 1956 Corvette he had bought new. A new Corvette did not provide the nostalgia he had originally sought; a 1966 coupe became the first in a long string of older ones. Best from a show point of view, was a red-on-red

*William L. Mitchell, for two decades vice president in charge of General Motors Styling, loved cars with a passion. To the left, he is seen in one of the studios. On the table are scale models of GM experimentals, Firebird I, II and III. In the background the full-size clay model of the Firebird IV receives careful attention. This page, top, Mitchell is seen with the 1959 Sting Ray racer and a production version 1963 Sting Ray. Above, the 1961 Shark, together with the racer, heralding the new Corvette look. Right, "The Flying Dentist," Dick Thompson, in the Sting Ray racer.*

1963. That coupe, on one occasion, brought him Best Paint, Best in Class and Best of Show! The bug had bit him to a degree that he finally owned ten Corvettes. By then he realized that it was too much. He couldn't enjoy them all. He decided to sell. The one to keep, curiously enough, but typical of a true enthusiast, was the dark blue coupe now standing at the bottom of the gravel pit, not the restored red one, but the all-original one, the one that could be driven without worry.

The sun is barely up, and it's not going to reach the bottom plane of the pit for several hours yet. That's the way we want it. But we do need stronger illumination from above, from the sky. As soon as the car has been placed in the right spot in relation to the anticipated light and the sloping mountains of gravel, looking through the camera, I know this is another of those perfect settings. The dark blue coupe is complemented by the cool blueness of the still unlit gravel.

William L. Mitchell was born in Cleveland, Ohio. The year was 1912. His parents soon moved to Greenville, Pennsylvania, where his father became a Buick dealer. It was not unexpected then that young Billy quickly became a certified car enthusiast. During the summers of his high school years he worked as an office boy in a large New York advertising agency. This awakened his interest in commercial art. This period also refined his interest in automobiles as he spent many of his off-hours visiting the elegant showrooms of the best of the European classics of the day. Upon graduation he joined the firm full time.

The sons of the firm's owner happened to be consummate sports car enthusiasts. Bill often joined them in their road racing adventures. He did not only drive the cars, he also recorded the action in sketches. Some of these were seen by a friend of Harley Earl, in charge of styling at GM. Bill was encouraged to send his work to Earl, and in the fall of 1935 he was hired.

He must have shown an unusual amount of flair for his job; at the age of twenty-four he was

(continued on overleaf)

**C**orvette's finest hour? Many connoisseurs feel the split-window coupe of 1963 is just that! As it turned out, it was just a one-year feature, making it especially unique. With its fuel-injected 327, four-speed transmission, side-mount exhaust, this Daytona Blue Survivor, chassis number 30837S110222, owned by George Wagman of York, Pennsylvania, represents the best of the best!

promoted to head the Cadillac program. He proceeded to create many outstanding designs, among them the 1938 Sixty Special, and the 1941, introducing the "egg-crate" grille.

When Earl retired in 1958, Bill Mitchell was chosen to succeed him. A long row of superb designs were created under his reign, starting with the Riviera, and continuing with such milestones as the Toronado, the Eldorado, the Camaro and Firebird.

But his special pet was always the Corvette. This could be expected from a true sports car enthusiast, one of the few to inhabit the vast organization. Through many battles with the "bean counters," as Mitchell called them, he and the few faithful managed to keep the Corvette alive and exciting.

George and I still wait for that perfect light. In the meantime, the shape of that Sting Ray becomes the focusing point. As I try, in my mind, to relate the basic look to other designs, for almost nothing is entirely new under the sun, I recall the 1952 Alfa Romeo Disco Volante, by Touring. It had that same hip-level crease running all around the body. The object was to create a smooth, flat shape, as low as possible, like a saucer turned upside down (Disco Volante means Flying Saucer), and then place protrusions for the wheels in the four corners. Mitchell might very well have been inspired by this design when he drew his 1959 sports racer. Although, he made the lines sharper, crisper, and the crease more pronounced, giving the Sting Ray a look all its own. Mitchell's ingenious solution for the headlights of the production Sting Ray added further to that quality.

When the right light comes, it comes suddenly, and it never lasts long. In the rush of searching for the right camera angles I have the opportunity to discover the many beautiful and exciting facets of the Sting Ray style. I find that Bill Mitchell indeed lived up to his own philosophy. He felt that a car must have enough areas of interest so that every time you look at it you will see something new.

*Much of the work that goes on inside the design studios never reaches production. Naturally, the final look is not arrived upon without trials and errors, illustrated by the unique series of photos reproduced on these pages. Opposite page, upper row, a possible replacement for the 1961 model. The date is February 4, 1959. Only the tail section made it. Lower row, a couple of suggestions for treatment of the lights, dated April 26, 1961. Fortunately, they did not make it. Above, one of the full-size clay models after having served its purpose. Left, a suggested design for the air-conditioning outlet.*

**65**

# Reflections From the Cockpit.

Of all Corvettes, which is the most rare? The most beautiful? The most desirable?

Questions like these are asked whenever Corvette enthusiasts get together. Ferrari, Porsche and Mercedes people all have the same questions. (Cobra enthusiasts have it easy.)

To come up with answers that satisfy everyone is impossible. Sure, there are certain basic facts. But facts can be interpreted differently. Just like two religious organizations can have opposite views of the same text, the Corvette faith also leaves room for individual opinions. Some, for instance, may think of the dual headlights as being beautiful, while others may think of them as being horrible. Who's to say what's right? (Of course, there's something, called "educated taste.")

Here are my personal reflections (for what they're worth).

The award for Most Unique Corvette must go to the 53. Obviously, with only 300 built, that category is simple. The number of cars made is just right. Not too few, which would have made the model too obscure. Not too many, which would have made it too easy to obtain. A 55 with the first V-8 is also unique, but it certainly can't top a 53. After all, the 53 represents the beginning of it all. You can't beat that!

With its lowly six-cylinder engine and its unsporty Powerglide transmission, the 53 wasn't outstanding mechanically. On the other hand, it was very good looking, but would certainly not qualify as the best looking of all Corvettes. It seemed overweight. Too wide. And then there

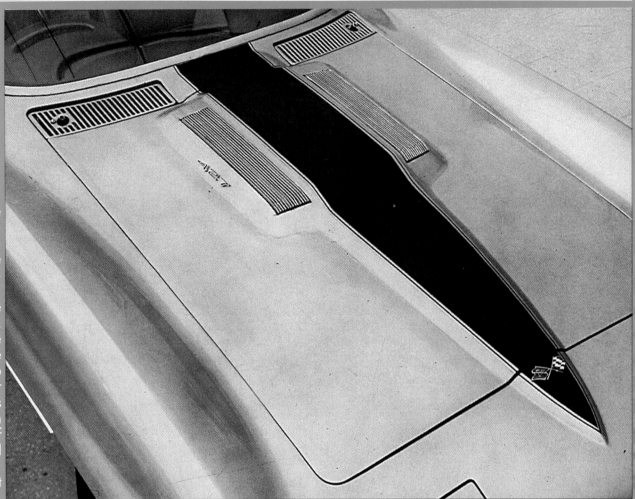

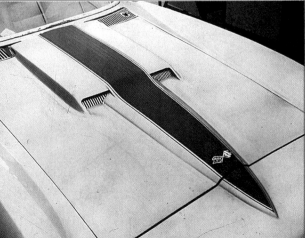

With the introduction of the new Mark IV engine in 1965, a larger hood bulge was required. As can be seen in the photos on this page, various designs were considered. The alternative chosen is barely visible in the photo on the opposite page, top. This car is fitted with the 1967 type knock-off aluminum wheels with its wingless nuts. The 1967 shown in the photo to the right is fitted with wheels of a new design introduced that year. Curiously enough, at this point, the wheels are still sporting three-winged nuts that later had to be removed, due to new safety regulations.

were the rocket ship taillights. Embellishments unbecoming a sports car.

Deciding which model is worthy of the award for Most Beautiful Corvette isn't easy. Using the method of elimination might help.

The first generation is already out of contention, as indicated above.

How about the second generation? Well, toward the end, 61 and 62, there was the unfortunate combination of two different styling philosophies (when the Sting Ray type tail was introduced). In the middle, 58 to 60, the cars looked like Christmas trees, with all their louvers, lights and vents. The early years, 56 and 57, were very good looking, but the rear was too heavy, too prominent. Try to visualize the stinger section of a bee. That's the look. (To some this may be just what they like!) The curves were just a little too round back there. Also, the stylists had not bothered to taper the fenders (looking at them from above now), like they did on, for instance, the Jaguar XK 120.

The fourth generation, 68 to 82, was characterized by a continous change of shapes. Although the basic design was always exciting looking, the surfaces undulated too much. There was a feeling of exaggeration in the lines. The coke-bottle effect, caused by the shape of the rocker panels, didn't help matters. To me, there was also something unpleasant about that sugar-scoop design behind the rear window. The design looked better as a fastback, as seen in the Mako Shark and the Manta Ray. With the introduction of the integrated front and rear bumpers, the overhangs became too great. With the arrival of the fastback, things looked better, but by then it had all been around too long.

The 1984 Corvette may very well turn out to be the most beautiful. I wouldn't be surprised. But it's really too early to tell. There needs to be a period of time for the design to mature.

That leaves only the third generation. The original Sting Ray. But what year to choose? The first year, 63, had the split window. Certainly a unique element. But it also had the fake louvers

*(continued on overleaf)*

**S**ting Rays also looked good in convertible form. Actually, coupes were outsold two to one in 1965. This Silver Pearl copy, chassis number 19467S100230, selected from the inventory of Southern California Classics in La Jolla, shows off its simple, clean shape. If anyone doubted that the Sting Ray meant business, all he had to do was to look at the badges, by now representing real racing victories.

and vents. The last year, 67, had none of these. Even the superfluous badges had been removed. Now it's finally as clean and pure as it should have been in the first place. So, coupe or roadster? The roadster is certainly superbly balanced. There's a perfect harmony between front and rear. But it lacks the character of the coupe. The coupe has that tapering fastback.

So, by using the unscientific method of subjective evaluation combined with the scientific method of elimination, the Most Beautiful Corvette has been selected: The winner is the 1967 Sting Ray coupe.

How about Most Desirable Corvette?

To the east I have the San Diego Bay. In the corner of my eye, I can see the gray silhouettes of the warships anchored over by the Naval Station. To the west, immediately beside me, I have the sands of Coronado Beach and the waves of the Pacific. Straight ahead, my eyes catch the tower-and-turret outline of the old Del Coronado Hotel. Off to the right is the concrete-and-steel rainbow of the Bay Bridge, and beyond it, the San Diego skyline. Surrounding me, I have a sleek silver roadster, its body shivering from the strain of acceleration, a lovely, deafeningly loud sound of rapid-fire explosions rising from the off-road exhaust pipes, mounted just below the doors. The engine is finnicky, like a race horse; only when I keep the revs high does want to run right, the fuel injection coming on in a hissing rush then. And, topping it off is that wind shooting by, warm, soothing, bringing with it that salty, intoxicating smell of ocean.

So, how about the Most Desirable Corvette?
Well, here's where anyone can have a say. This is the individual's choice.

My choice? A 1965 Sting Ray (for independent suspension and disc brakes) with the biggest, fuel injected engine and close-ratio box (for acceleration and shifting pleasure).

Oh, yes, it has to be a roadster. Naturally, for open-air motoring and well-balanced, simple lines!

In 1962 Duntov was pushing yet another racing venture. It was the ill-fated Grand Sport. One hundred units were to have been built, allowing GT homologation. With five cars completed, management axed the project; the cars were sold to privateers. During the 1963 Nassau Speed Week three Grand Sports gave a show of what could have been; by 1965 it was no longer competitive—to the right, Delmo Johnson finished far back in the field at Sebring. Left, Dick Thompson in a Z06 Corvette at Marlboro in January 1963. Above, a design study shown at the 1964 Auto Show in New York.

67

# The Quest for the Best.

Providence, Rhode Island.
October 22. Afternoon.
Raining all day. Saw the Corvette this morning. Best I've ever seen. Met the owner, Anthony Pate. Has service station. Father had it before him. Anthony added nice new building. Sells Corvettes and other special-interest cars out of it. Used to work for his father at the station. That's when he first got interested in Corvettes. Used to service a 53 for years. Got to know it pretty well. Owned a 65 at that time. Bought new. But didn't appreciate it then. Was into motorcycles. Competed in motocross for ten years. Ran races all over New England. Corvette appreciation came later. In 1974. Began looking through *Hemmings.* Checked ads locally. Looked at many cars. But couldn't find one that was good enough. Kept searching. Saw ad one day: 1967 Corvette, 400 hp, tri-carb, four-speed, air, redline tires, bolt-on wheels. Sounded just like the kind of car he had been wanting. But when he went to check it: junk! Couldn't find a car that was good enough. Not until Brainerd. At the Corvette show. Now he knew the good cars existed. Met Chip Miller there.

Midnight.
Went with Anthony to Italian restaurant for dinner. Had ravioli. Talked motocross. Haven't done that for years. Turned out Anthony knew all the names I knew. Who was World Champion that year? Who was the best BSA driver? Fun game. Small world. Talked location for shooting the Corvette too. Said he would go anywhere. Has brand new, covered trailer. Distance

The 1967 marked the high point of the Sting Ray series. Superfluous ornamentation had been removed and there were also various other improvements of a subtle nature. Even though the coupe must be considered the foremost example of the Sting Ray style, the roadster had a superbly balanced look, especially with the optional hardtop fitted, as seen in these photographs. This roadster has the standard wheels. Rim width had been increased to six inches, improving both looks and handling. The interior had received new seats and the handbrake had been relocated to a more logical location between them.

doesn't matter. But said he wouldn't take it out in the rain. That's understandable.

October 23. Noon.
Still raining. Have been looking for location in spite of. Having hard time finding what I want. Want something special. Something worthy of that black beauty.

Evening.
Think I found a good spot. Boat yard. Saw several America's Cup entrants. Ted Turner's *Tenacious* also. Some of world's best boats. One of world's best Corvettes. Could be good. Also looked closely at the car this afternoon. Incredible restoration. Chip Miller owned it before Anthony. Bought it from original owner. Tuxedo Black with black vinyl interior and red hood stripe. Has all the right options. The 435 hp 427 ci engine, transistor ignition, positraction rear axle, four-speed close ratio transmission, special front and rear suspension, side mount exhaust, tinted glass, special cast aluminum bolt-on wheels, redline tires, AM-FM radio. Owner pampered it. Paint was great. Everything was great. Didn't need restoration. Just one thing wrong: Main cross-member had been butchered to make room for four-inch pipes. Chip took it to Ken Heckert to get that taken care of. Body had to be pulled off. Once body was off, one thing led to another. In the end Chip had a full-fledged show car. Anthony saw it both before and after. When it was done, he knew he had finally found what he had been looking for.

Midnight.
Had dinner with Anthony. Cannelloni. He showed snap shots of restoration. Frame looks so clean you could have displayed it in an operating room. Painted exactly the way they did it at the factory. Even has the original markings restenciled on the frame and elsewhere. Talked motocross too. That Swede, what's his name, he was good! Bill Nilsson! Right. Did you ever see him? Yes, saw him in Sweden. Strange thing about him, he never looked fast. He was so smooth. It's still raining. Raindrops play the

*(continued on overleaf)*

**B**lack on black. Tuxedo Black, no less. And a little touch of red, like the rose in the lapel. How subtle! Because this is not the one to take to the theater. This is the real brute, the last and the fastest of the Sting Rays. Of course, if you are a bit late, five seconds to sixty can make a difference. This 1967, chassis number 194377S111704, owned by Anthony Pate of Providence, Rhode Island, is so perfect, it must be one of the finest around.

drums on the motel room window. Melancholic motel music. On the news they say it's going to clear up tomorrow. Let's hope so.

October 24. Morning.
Not raining. But doesn't look safe. Able to talk Anthony into going shooting anyway.
Afternoon.
Was wrong about the boat yard. No good. Too busy looking. Difficult to place car right in relation to boats. Also, owner of yard complained about noise from the Corvette. Sound is terrific. Terrificallly beautiful. That guy is no enthusiast. I guess sails and motors don't mix! Got one good shot only. Was working on another when it started to sprinkle. Barely got the Corvette inside the trailer when it began pouring down. Offered to help Anthony wipe off a few drops. But he wanted to do it himself.
Midnight.
Had dinner with Anthony. Veal marinara. Talked motocross. It's raining. On the news they say its going to be overcast tomorrow, but no rain. Phoned Anthony about emergency location. Have to move on tomorrow. Can't wait any longer. Have to be in Detroit. Meeting with Jerry Palmer at GM already set up far in advance. Need a location badly. Don't want to take just anything. No golf course. Not in front of fancy house. Not that conventional stuff. Something typically American! How about Coca-Cola trucks? Anthony says. I have a friend over at the bottling plant. I'm sure he'll let us do it there. I'll call him, Anthony says. Anthony calls back. Friend on vacation. Decide to try it anyway.

October 25. Midnight.
Coca-Cola location worked fine. Did all shooting in half an hour because it started to rain. Turned out fine though. Things go better with Coke! But didn't get to drive it. Close ratio box! Over four hundred horses! Would have loved it! My bad luck. Anthony's good luck. Should have left earlier but wife Susan served spaghetti with homemade meat sauce in front of TV while Anthony and I watched motocross.

For a long time it was the common opinion that the price level of the Sting Rays did not warrant too thorough a restoration of these cars. But sometimes a market has to be tested before a breakthrough will take place. Some of the foremost experts and enthusiasts on the East Coast were involved in the project captured in snapshots on these pages. (The car is also the feature of this section's color photos). Chip Miller was the owner, Ken Heckert the restorer, both of York, Pennsylvania, and Anthony Pate of Providence, Rhode Island, purchased the completed car. The three proved that "a quest for the best" always pays off.

Virginia
ZL1 ● 69
1776 ● Independence Bicentennial ● 1976
82

# Wildest of the Wild.

It's the kind of idea that pops into my mind, uninvited, unwanted, but intriguing.

In the July 1969 issue of the now-defunct *Car Life* magazine, the editors reported on the "Wildest Corvette Test Yet." It took place on the dragstrip and road-racing course of Mel Larson's Sportsland, outside Phoenix, Arizona. There were two stars present. One, a pre-production ZL-1. The other, its creator, Zora Arkus-Duntov. He recorded a quarter-mile time of 12.1 seconds, driving leisurely.

Now, as I stand here on the tarmack of Richmond Racetrack, Virginia, site of the annual Richmond 400, talking with Wayne Walker, admiring his yellow ZL-1, the idea knocks on my brain again: Should we try to beat that time?

It wouldn't be quite scientific, of course. All I have is my wristwatch chronometer. At Phoenix they had the dragstrip timing setup. Another problem: The straightaway here is probably just barely quarter of a mile long, which would force us to enter the turn at about 120 mph.

Also a problem: We only have permission to take pictures. No racing. But I figure we would be able to squeeze in a couple of fast laps without anyone noticing. However, I decide not to mention the idea to Wayne yet.

Duntov's ZL-1 started out as a stock L-88. Its engine was replaced by the ZL-1 unit; its aluminum block weighed 100 pounds less. Otherwise it was, basically, identical to the L-88, using the same aluminum heads and intake manifolds. The car was actually prepared for racing, with everything unnecessary removed: headlights,

The Mako Shark II, opposite page, was very much the expression of Bill Mitchell's taste. He was fascinated with the shark them and carried it through to the extreme with such things as a paint job that copied the graduated tones of that prowler of the deep. The same basic theme is evident in the full-scale mockup pictured to the right. The photos were taken on December 2, 1964. In my own opinion, this is how the new Corvette should have looked! Lack of rearwo visibility probably killed it. Left, a photo of more recent date, sometime in 19 shows an alternative approvach to the racing striping that was to adorn the ZL-1.

bumpers, upholstery, spare tire, heater and so on. Weight was down to 2,900 pounds.

Wayne's ZL-1 is what Duntov made available to the customer, in 1969, as part of the option list. For some reason, only two were assembled. Wayne's ZL-1 is quite a bit heavier than the one driven by Duntov at Phoenix; it has all the standard features of a street Corvette, albeit minus radio, fan shroud and a few other things. But Duntov's car had the 3.70 gearing. Wayne's has the 4.11. That, plus some aggressive clutching and shifting, I figure, might give us the edge, should we decide to try to beat Zora's time. There's that blasted idea again!

Wayne's ZL-1 must be one of the most rare Corvettes in existence. Not only as it stands completed today, the only one known to exist, but also the way it got here.

It was originally ordered as a company car by an engineer at the St. Louis Corvette plant. The sticker was $10,771. When the engineer moved on, the ZL-1 was left for his successor, who arranged for it to be sold. It ended up on the lot of a Chevrolet dealership in Richmond, sitting there for quite a while. Finally, a friend of Wayne bought it. On the first night out he blew the engine. Next day he took it back to the dealer to have it replaced under warranty. When the new engine arrived, the friend decided to use it in his drag boat instead. At some point, the blown engine disappeared from the dealership. And was lost.

The yellow Corvette, with the distinctive black racing stripe on the hood, sat with a for-sale sign at the friend's gas station for a couple of years. Nobody would want to pay $3,000 for a Corvette without an engine, Wayne remembers thinking. A 454 was put into it. The car then went back to the original dealer. After sitting there for a while, it was finally sold. And lost, too.

The years passed. One day in 1976, Wayne read an article that mentioned the rarity of the L-88 and ZL-1 options, and he had a sudden flashback to the ZL-1 his friend had once owned. He looked him up and it turned out that the car

(continued on overleaf)

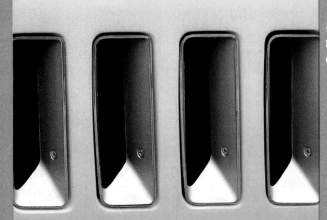

**S**ure, the black stripe on the hood doesn't mean much, unless you know what it stands for. What does it stand for? The ultimate!

Simply, the most unique, the most powerful, the most fascinating Corvette ever offered to the public, the ultimate beast: the ZL-1. Wayne Walker (driving the locomotive, for a change) of Mechanicsville, Virginia, owns this 1969, chassis number 194379S729219, one of two built, and the only one left.

was still in the area. Actually, just two blocks from where Wayne worked. After some convincing, he managed to buy it.

The task was now, as Wayne saw it, to find the right kind of engine. He finally managed to locate one in Pittsburg.

But, unexpectedly, out of the blue, Wayne got a call from a drag racer who had heard that Wayne was restoring the ZL-1. He said he had the original engine.

Now, having had the spectacular luck of finding the original engine, Wayne became serious about restoring the car. As soon as the ZL-1 was fitted, he took it out on the back roads, only to blow the engine. But, his enthusiasm was awakened. He decided to go back to square one, doing a total restoration of engine, frame and body. At that time, however, he had just started a new company, Zip Products, specializing in Corvette parts, and the ZL-1 again had to be placed on the back burner. A couple of years later, with the company off the ground and running smoothly, the project was tackled again. When completed, it captured a Gold at the 1981 Bloomington Corvette Corral.

The shooting is done now. Well, almost. We just need a few shots of the ZL-1 doing a dragstrip take-off. Vrooom! There's that ear-shattering, spine-tingling roar. The wheels are spinning. There's a cloud of blue smoke. The car is fishtailing. But Wayne has it under control. Off he goes, shooting on through turn one. As I stand there, absent-mindedly winding the film, looking at the ZL-1 accelerating down the straightaway, that stubborn idea crops up again. I decide to break it to him when he comes around.

He's coming out of turn four. Looking good. Sounding good. But, suddenly, I see smoke! Wayne slows down and comes to a stop. No, it's not smoke. It's steam. It's boiling!

So much for my idea. I don't seem to be able to lay my itching hands on a high-power Corvette. First, Anthony Pate's L-71, rained-out. Now, Wayne Walker's ZL-1, boiled-over. Someone out there doesn't want me to have any fun.

It's probably my Guardian Angel.

*The most powerful option ever to be offered on the Corvette, the ZL-1, was shown to the editors of Car Life magazine early in 1969. Duntov himself took time out from his busy schedule to attend the event which took place at a drag strip in Phoenix. Bill Motta, Road & Track's art director, ably covered the occasion with his camera: Left, the ZL-1 at speed. Above, Duntov at the wheel. Right, Duntov in one of his many coats. Far right, top, shooting the breeze, flanked by the ZL-1 and gear. Bottom, a pack of Corvettes crowd the corner in one phase of the test, labeled "Wildest Corvette Test Yet!"*

75

# The Last Convertible.

The day has been clear and crisp, but windy. Now dusk has arrived and Marty and I turn to the horizon as a small plane comes in for landing, just in time to beat that last long light. The plane comes floating slightly sideways. A few rudder corrections compensate for the wind, and it lands on the short grassy field, bouncing as it touches the ground. This must be the only plane stationed here on this seemingly abandoned field a few miles south of East Berlin.

No, this is not the prologue of a spy novel. And we are not in East Berlin, Germany. We are in East Berlin, Pennsylvania. Marty is not an escaping Communist dignitary with the secret locations of missile bases on a microfilm hidden in his leather cap. He is the owner of a Flame Orange 1975 Corvette convertible, now parked in front of the hangar. And I am not the CIA station manager. I am the omnipresent photographer, here because of Marty and his car, one of the best of the last of the convertibles.

Why here? Well, when searching for a suitable background in a countryside dominated by barns, trees and fields, a lone hangar, its corrugated walls covered with black and white checkered squares — like the flag in the Corvette emblem — was too obvious to ignore.

In 1975, with the disappearance of the convertible Corvette, a tradition disappeared with it. For 23 years there had always been an open Corvette. In fact, for the first three years, it was the only choice. Then, with the introduction of the 1956, a hardtop became available.

The new Corvette offered a variety of choices for the wind-in-the-hair enthusiast. The convertible top, above, was easy to operate and stowed neatly under its lid. The coupe had an unorthodox solution to blue-sky access; it was possible to remove not only two roof panels, right, top, but also the rear window, bottom, allowing almost unobstructed flow of air. The removable rear window was no longer available in 1973. Left, the one-piece roof panel of the 1965 Mako Shark was also planned for the 1968 production Corvette, but a last-minute change, delaying production, was required because of lack of rigidity.

When the third-generation Corvette was introduced, in 1963, the star of the show was the new coupe, the fastback Sting Ray.

In Europe, the fastback had been around for a long time. The mainstay of Porsche's production was the coupe. Aston Martin's DB2 was also mainly sold as a coupe. But the Italians, with their Ferraris, Lancias and Maseratis, were the innovators; they introduced the "berlinetta," which, more or less loosely translated, means "small coupe." The emergence of the Mercedes 300SL, in 1955, gave this closed body style a significant shot in the arm. First available only as a coupe, it was restyled as a roadster in 1957. Jaguar's E-type, introduced in 1961, came in both coupe and roadster versions.

So did the Sting Ray. The first year's figures show that sales were divided equally between the two; about ten thousand were made of each. The following year the trend had swung in favor of the convertible. This trend continued for the entire Sting Ray run; in 1967 there were almost twice as many convertibles sold, 8,500 and 14,500, respectively.

For the first year of the fourth generation, 1968, the roadster still outsold the coupe two to one. But the following year a dramatic turnabout took place; there were now 22,000 coupes made, as opposed to 16,500 convertibles.

Was the turnabout attributable to the looks of the coupe? Or was it a matter of domestication? Did the makeup of the Corvette buyer change slowly? Did it swing toward a concern for safety and comfort? By 1971 the coupe outsold the convertible two to one. By the end of the convertible era, in 1975, the coupe dominated totally, outselling the open car seven to one.

Marty Scholand was always ready for a Corvette. All it took was for an old high school buddy, a salesman at a Chevrolet dealership in Rochester, New York, to wave to him as he passed in his Dodge Charger. On the lot sat a brand-new, last year model 1968 convertible. Less a result of the friend's salesmanship than of Marty's ripe condition, the Charger was traded
*(continued on overleaf)*

**O**ver the years, demand for convertibles has varied. After the introduction of the new bodystyle in 1968, sales of roadsters dropped steadily, until in 1975 GM called it quits. Less than five thousand were made that last year. Marty Scholand, East Berlin, Pennsylvania, owns this pristine Orange Flame copy, chassis number 1Z67J5S413884. In fact, with just over two thousand miles on the odometer, this decade-old Survivor is still brand new!

in. That was the beginning. After having owned a string of various Corvettes, he now has a well-rounded collection consisting of a 1953 (in need of restoration), a 1963 Sting Ray coupe (won Best of Show at the 1973 NCCC Convention in Indianapolis), the 1975 convertible (has gone just over 2,000 miles), and a 1978 Pace Car.

Marty is lucky to be able to own the cars he dreamed about as a boy, but even more lucky to be able to share his avocation with his wife, Connie. (In fact, she owns the 1975.) Together they are active in the local York County Corvette Club, counting close to 50 members. A now-legendary annual event, the Fourth of July Rally is hosted by Connie and Marty. They have also attended several events on the national level. Illustrating that Connie is not just a tagalong is the fact that she won the Ladies Class at the 1980 regional NCCC drag meet. Her time was 14.20. Marty also competed (although, not in the ladies event). They both drove the same machine, the Pace Car. Fortunately, for the preservation of peace and harmony in the family, Marty beat her time, but by only one tenth of a second.

Marty's (Connie's) convertible was originally delivered to a dealer in Philadelphia, who in turn was to present it to Bobby Clarke, Most Valuable Player of the NHL that year and a member of the Philadelphia Flyers hockey team. Due to a last-minute disagreement, the car instead went to a doctor in Dover, Delaware. He bought it for his wife, but she was not comfortable with the four-speed, so the car went on to Downington, Pennsylvania, where it was stored for over a year, until Marty got it in 1977.

The plane is taxiing toward the hangar, its motor revving, its propellor whizzing, its rudders flapping. We better move. Quickly. Marty tells me to drive, and as we make our getaway (Marty still in possession of the microfilm), accelerating down the narrow road, open fields surrounding us on both sides, the drowning sun coloring the horizon red, the cool wind pinching the skin, I am again reminded of the true spirit of the classic sports car.

What a shame that era had to end.

*This collection of never-before-published photographs show some of the various stages the fourth-generation Corvette went through on its way to final product in 1968. A close-up study of each photograph would surely reveal a multitude of abandoned details and concepts, too complex to expand on here. But, touching on just a few in brief: opposite page, bottom, the row of three photos show a rear window similar to the one on the Sting Ray. Top, far right, shows a much more attractive rear end design, with the tails of the scoop longer and straighter. This page, closing in on the final look.*

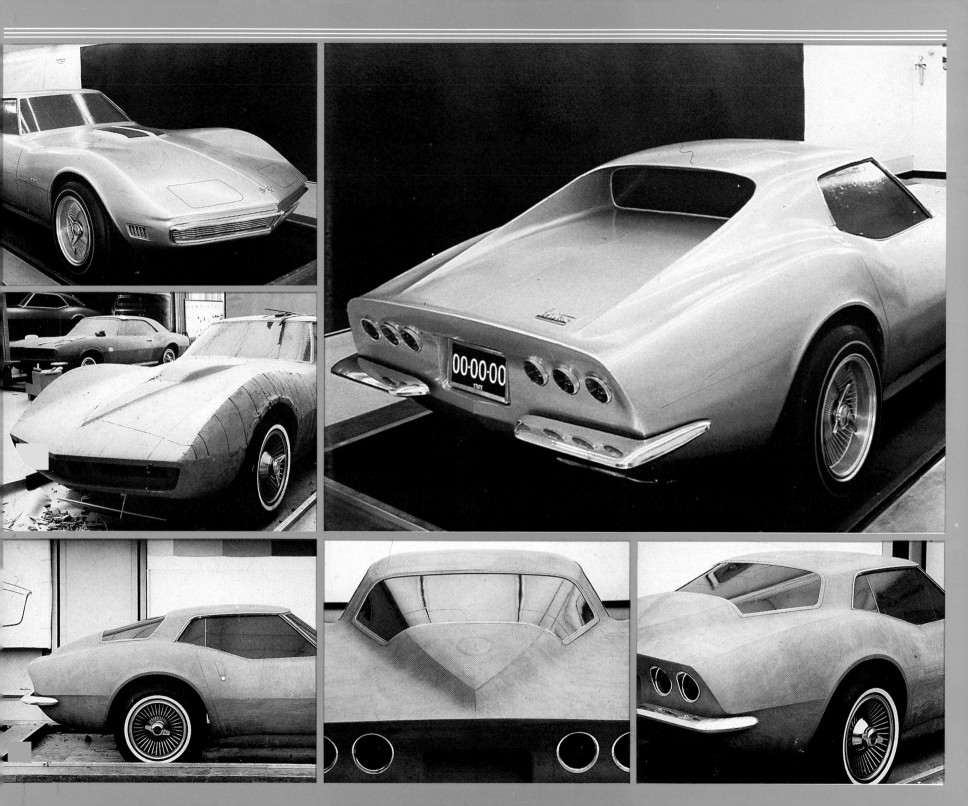

# Commemorative Commodity.

In 1978 the Corvette had been around for 25 years. To the enthusiasts who had followed its growth from the first stumbling steps in 1953, through the gradual rise to eminence, both in the marketplace as well as on the racetrack, and to the engineers and designers and marketing men who had constructed and created and promoted, who had fought the battles to keep it alive, there was cause for celebration.

Looking at world events, the path leading through those 25 years was full of unforseen turmoil. The latter half alone had seen both the assassination as well as the impeachment of a US President, the abundance of energy as well as the apparent lack of it, war as well as its painful ending, recessions as well as periods of expansion. There had been the American bicentennial celebration. There had been the hippies. There had been the Beatles. And there had been the disco craze. The Corvette had survived it all.

In 1978 the biggest problem facing the auto industry was inflation. The annual rate was close to ten percent. It took $200 of 1978 money to buy the goods you paid $100 for in 1967. For example, the base price for a Corvette coupe was $4,388 in 1967; $9,351 in 1978.

Jimmy Carter was President. The Camp David Accord was signed. Muhammed Ali lost his crown, but won it back later in the year, becoming the first to twice recapture the title. The New York Yankees beat the Los Angeles Dodgers to win the World Series for the second time in a row. Bjorn Borg won at Wimbledon for the third time in a row. Woody Allen's *Annie Hall* got the Oscar for best film. Dolly Parton was named

*Pictured here is a variety of nose jobs. On this page, the two photographs above show what the designers came up with, trying to meet the impact regulations in 1973. The photograph to the left shows the stylists experimenting with the shape of the turn signals. On the opposite page, the finished products: top, the 1968 and 1969 nose. In 1970 the grille received the "egg-crate" grille and square turn signals. Center, the 1973 urethane bumper. In 1975, although reengineered beneath the skin, the only external difference was small rubber pads. Bottom, the 1980 redesign lasted to the end of the fourth generation.*

entertainer of the year by the Country Music Association. And Mario Andretti became the second American to capture the World Championship title in Formula One.

In 1961 the auto industry had seen a low point of 5.4 million cars manufactured. In 1973 it had reached a high point, 9.9. Things were bad again in 1975; down to 6.4. In 1978 the figures were back up again, to 8.9. The sales of Corvettes, however, did not follow these trends. In 1961, production reached a new high; the 20,000 barrier was broken. In 1973 the 30,000 barrier met with the same destiny. In 1975 the sales figures nibbled at the 40,000 mark. And in 1978 total output came close to 50,000 units. The Corvette had shown remarkable progress and adaptability, thanks to the skill of the people whose job it was to sense the market. When styling gimmicks were in fashion, the Corvette got its share. When there was a cry for horsepower, the Corvette became even more muscular. When there was talk of smaller displacement and energy conservation, the Corvette met those demands as well.

The 1978 Indianapolis 500 was hot and fast, with 350,000 fans ensuring high temperatures in the bleachers, and a scorching sun guaranteeing a track reading of 120 degrees. Danny Ongais, in a Parnelli/Cosworth snatched the lead from pole-sitter Tom Sneva, driving a Penske/Cosworth. Ongais held on to the lead until lap 70, when Al Unser, also Cosworth powered in Jim Hall's Lola, managed to pass. The two dueled for much of the race, with Unser continuously in the lead. On lap 145 Ongais had to give up the chase due to a burned-out rotor on his turbocharger. On lap 179, with Sneva now 28 seconds behind in second place, Unser was held up when he overshot his pit and caused some damage to the car. This was the last pit stop, and when both contenders were back circling the track again, it was evident how close the race had become. During these last exciting laps Unser managed to hold on to the lead, finally crossing the finish line as the winner, eight seconds

*(continued on overleaf)*

**N**ew for 1978 was the fastback styling, reminiscent of the old Sting Ray. While reminiscing, GM decided to make something special to commemorate the 25th Anniversary of the Corvette. Featured here is the Limited Edition replica of the Indianapolis Pace Car. Just over six thousand were minted. California enthusiast Sy Baylos of La Palma, owns this beauty, chassis number 1Z87L8S904021.

ahead of Sneva. It was Unser's third win and the second closest ever.

This was the atmosphere in which Chevrolet had chosen to celebrate the 25th anniversary of their sports car; pacing these horsepower giants was a special Corvette, distinctively dressed up for the occasion.

The original plan called for a limited edition of 1,000 replicas of the Indianapolis Pace Car. Various color combinations were tested; black on the upper body and silver on the lower was the alternative finally settled on. In addition to the fastback styling, new for that year, the Pace Car also sported prominent front and rear spoilers. Completing the exterior dress-up was a set of decals for the doors and rear side panels. The application of these was left up to the owner. Most thought they were too much and left them in their wrappers. The interior also received special treatment; the seats featured a design similar to the ones to be introduced the following year. Silver was the only interior color, but there was a choice of all-leather or leather and vinyl combined. The sticker price of the Pace Car was 13,653 dollars. This included most of the available comfort options. The decision on engine and transmission was up to the customer.

As word of the limited edition spread, so did demand. Instead of only 1,000, it was decided to produce one for each dealer, or roughly 6,500 units. Demand had its way with the price as well. Many reportedly went for double the amount on the sticker.

The anniversary would have been the perfect occasion to introduce an all-new Corvette. But the Pace Car was not this long-overdue machine. It was not even representative of a high point in Corvette styling and performance. Nevertheless, it was the machine Corvette chose to bring out in commemoration of its anniversary. And, as such, it will always be special.

At the point of this writing, six years later, the Pace Car has lost some of its original sparkle and value. But, it will make a come back. Rest assured. All it takes is time.

*In 1978 the Corvette celebrated its 25th anniversary. To mark the occasion the Limited Edition Indy Pace Car was issued. An exact replica of the pace car used in that year's Indianapolis 500, the limited edition immediately became a popular collectors item. The pictures above, show the Pace Car in full regalia. To the left, a photograph showing a prototype for testing the effect of various paint schemes. Opposite page, the search for new shapes never stops. Some ideas make it, others don't. This series of never-before-published photographs from the the GM files show some that didn't.*

# Encounter With Space Ship Corvette.

Like people and animals, cars, too, send signals. It has to do with looks. We do not expect a corpulent man to be quick and agile. But we do expect a deer to possess those qualities.

The sleekness of the E-type Jaguar made it look light and fast. The similarly styled D-type, however, even though it was faster, did not look as fast; it looked more powerful, thanks to its rounder, more massive body. One of the fastest sedans ever, the Mercedes 300SEL 6.3, certainly did not look like it could outrun, by two to one, Michelotti's sleek little Triumph Spitfire. The Mercedes, of course, was not intended to look fast; it had what it took without showing it. The Triumph, on the other hand, could afford only the look, not the goods.

These observations, subjective, and certainly kept on a most primitive level, do lead to a question: What kind of signals do the various Corvette models send?

The 1953, in spite of its toothy grin, did not look particularly fast or ferocious. The most effective speed-evoking element was the windshield. True, the body was low, but it was also too massive looking, somewhat pudgy. And there was a submissive look to those headlights, in the way they peered up at you.

The 1956 restyling improved matters a lot. The headlights now had a more purposeful expression. The downward motion of the rear made it look like it was ready to leap, like it had its hind legs firmly and capably planted on the ground.

Four basic tail end designs characterized the fourth-generation Corvette. Above, the original design stayed unchanged until 1974 when the new regulations forced the introduction of the urethane bumpers, opposite page, bottom. For 1974 it was a two-piece design, with a seam running vertically down the middle. In 1975 it was a one-piece design. Guards with a rubber pad had also been added. Above, a fastback window came in 1978. And in 1982, opposite page, top, it could finally be opened. There was also a spoiler, part of the bumper assembly rather than an add-on, as on the Pace Car.

Adding the cove to the side panel was a dramatic gesture; its presence certainly sent a signal of power and speed.

The 1958 addition of headlights and grilles did make the Corvette more mean looking, although not more beautiful, nor more refined.

The 1963 was a much more honest effort. Although it had certain dishonest features, such as fake vents, the basic styling relied purely on design. It sent out signals of power and speed in every direction. There were no headlights at all, no eyes, to communicate the message; their absence emphasized the purpose of the machine. The domes above the wheels, with their tapering tails, as well as the tapering tail of the fastback roof, all spelled speed. Where William Lyons was influenced by the sleek, ready-to-leap cat in his design of the XK120, William Mitchell took his inspiration from the smooth, flowing lines of a shark on the prowl.

While the 1963 Sting Ray was at home in the deep, the 1968 Stingray seemed to belong on the surface; there's one wave after another, and behind them, a vacuum, a wake, and a little spout from the propellor. Well, cars were not animals anymore; they began to look like paper planes, wedges, arrows. In 1970 Pininfarina finally sent the sports car into space with his Ferrari Modulo dream car.

These scattered thoughts come drizzling into my mind as I stand at the bottom of a gravel pit outside Pontiac, Michigan, shivering from the early morning chill, looking at Bob Larivee's 1980 Corvette. This is the closest a Corvette ever came to space! As I stand there the sun rises above the edge of the gravel mountain, sending long slices of light that greedily reach for the awesome looking, all-black machine, like the rays from the guns of the Martians I fully expect to show up next, silhouetted against the sky up there on the ridge. That's the sort of signals this Corvette sends. With its flat, massive, chromeless look, its spoiler fins, its nostrils, its curved glass surfaces, its mirrored roof panels, the Corvette

*(continued on overleaf)*

**M**artians are invading, and they are flying black Corvettes! Remarkably enough, after twelve years, the old body style could still excite. Of course, it had been updated from time to time. For 1980, the smoothly integrated spoilers did their thing, visually, and aerodynamically. The captured intruder chassis number 1Z878AS432749, belongs to Bob Larivee of Pontiac, Michigan.

looks like the amalgamation of a Star Wars monster and a Darth Vader helmet.

Bob Larivee is a car enthusiast whose sphere of interest is uncommonly broad; his collection consists of not only a 57 Chevy (original, low mileage), but also a Ferrari Lusso, a 31 Cadillac V-16 Dual Cowl Phaeton (People's Choice at Black Hawk and Third in Class at Pebble Beach), and a 32 Ford Phaeton hot rod, just to mention a few. But, confesses Bob, he is, above all, a Trans Am man; he has quite a variety of those. And, of course, he has a selection of Corvettes; there are at least four of them stored in various places. A Sting Ray (his favorite), an all-red 62, a 78 Pace Car with only 20 miles on the odometer, are some of them. The last two are on loan to Harrah's in Reno. The 1980 is the driver. He keeps it near at hand behind his office.

Bob was born in Detroit. His first significant involvement with cars occurred when he entered the Soap Box Derby. He was 15 then. At 21, he started racing real cars. That career lasted until 1977. In the beginning he raced Ford flatheads. Later he switched to Chevrolet power, racing both small-blocks as well as big-blocks, Chevys as well as Camaros.

Bob's business, Group Promotions, naturally revolves around cars. For more than a quarter of a century now, it has produced custom car shows all over the US and Canada. In fact, it is now the largest car show organization in the world, running a packed schedule, totaling approximately one hundred events per year.

The shooting is over. The sun is up. But the new day is still cold. Fortunately, I can start it off with a drive in Corvette's hot space ship. Lighter now than before, thanks to lower-density roof panels, reduced gauge in hood and doors, thinner glass, reduced gauge in the frame, and new aluminum differential housing as well as cross member, the signals sent by that awesome-looking body are not empty threats.

Oh yes, I discovered that the speedometer now stops at 85 mph. That's very convenient: You don't have to worry about the degree of bad conscience anymore!

*During the seventies the Corvette continued to be a force to reckon with in racing. Lack of space allows only a limited sampling: Allan Barker, opposite page, top, was the SCCA B-Production Champion more than once. Corvettes did well in endurance events: Daytona, Sebring and Le Mans. To the right, Dave Heinz and Bob Johnson took fourth overall at Sebring in 1972, best ever for a Corvette. Far right, Jerry Hansen was the 1980 B-Production Champion. Here he is seen winning at Road Atlanta. This page, Le Mans in 1976; John Greenwood had one of the best times during practice but was not able to finish.*

**84**

# Dedicated to Design.

There is that seen-in-so-many-pictures courtyard, its floor covered with that dark-brown, hexagonal-shaped tile. It is completely secluded from the outside world, surrounded by a twice-man-size wall. Immediately inside that wall, a tight row of long-limbed, neatly trimmed trees form a second line of defense.

And there is that landmark dome, with its series of always-curtained, green-tinted windows running all around the base, and, above it, its silvery roof, arching to infinity.

This is the viewing complex at General Motors' Design Center in Warren, Michigan. It is holy ground. It is to the man involved with automotive design what the White House lawn is to the man following presidential politics. Since the mid-fifties, every design to emerge from GM, be it sports car, family sedan or utility van, have all had a meeting with destiny here.

Today, a sunny afternoon in the fall of 1983, the courtyard is occupied by a red Corvette. It is the personal car of its chief designer, Jerry Palmer. He and I, plus the man in charge of moving it, plus the man in charge of detailing it — this is union territory — stand around, admiring the slick, shining beauty.

"The Coke-bottle waist is gone. The exaggerated fender domes are gone. All the excesses are gone. But it's still a Corvette!" I say, my arm sweeping the length of the smooth body.

"Yes, that was one of the basic goals for the new design," Jerry says. He seems to be energized by a genuine enthusiasm.

The process of designing a new car is a long one, the path littered with spent ideas and efforts. By the end of 1979, the Corvette designers had arrived at the final shape. On the opposite page, top, the full-size clay mockup is getting a last touch-up before the paint-simulating coating is applied. Pictured to the right and far right, front ends featuring headlight designs that were later abandoned. Above and to the left, for the new Corvette, the designers didn't concern themselves just with the exterior: engine compartment, and especially induction housing, received a lot of attention.

1985 CORVETTE

"The new design had to carry on the Corvette heritage," he continues. "The design is really very straightforward. The surface development is based on what's underneath. And underneath is a machine. In other words, designers and engineers worked hand in hand. The main hurdle was the location of the engine. Once that was decided the project took off."

"You were involved in the mid-engine Aero-Vette project. What was behind the decision to go with the front-engine instead?"

"Well, first of all we had the Corvette tradition to consider. Then we had the introduction of Porsche's 928. If a manufacturer who had built its reputation on rear-engined cars now saw fit to go with the engine up front, then, certainly, we knew the climate was changing. But more than that, our own engineers were sure they could keep the front-engine position and still achieve ideal weight distribution.

"Another hurdle was passed when engineers and designers together came up with a solution that lowered the H-point of the car." Jerry goes on. "We created a larger central tunnel that made room for the exhaust system and allowed for an almost horizontal driveline. This was crucial. It meant that the base of the windshield could be lowered, which in turn enabled us to lower the entire car."

Jerry Palmer is a product of Detroit. Not only was he born in the automotive capital of the world — the year was 1942 — but he also received his education there. His father was a car salesman. What else? And young Jerry was already early-on sketching cars, in fact, anything connected with transportation, trains, boats, planes. In 1962 he enrolled in the Art School for the Society of Arts and Crafts. In 1964 he was accepted for a summer program at GM Styling. The following year he was hired full-time. His early involvements were with the boattail Buick Riviera and the Chevrolet Vega.

To have been so completely educated in the "School of Detroit" may seem like a handicap, (continued on overleaf)

**W**orth the wait? Unequivocally, yes! A more worthy, a more fitting, a more valid replacement would be difficult to imagine. From its shape to its handling it displays the thoughtful thoroughness of its creators. It is in one stroke both advanced, and, something the Corvette often lacked, refined. In these photographs, the personal car of Corvette designer Jerry Palmer, chassis number 1G1AY0782E5118028, is captured at its birthplace, General Motors Technical Center in Warren, Michigan.

maybe not from the viewpoint of learning how to work within the system, but from the viewpoint of individual growth. However, Jerry's accomplishments — his design group was responsible for the 1982 Camaro as well — certainly do not support these fears. When confronted with the question, Jerry credits the special freedom that exists at GM Design. All the chiefs, Harley Earl, Bill Mitchell, and presently Irv Rybicki — with Chuck Jordan immediately responsible for the Corvette project — have always given their designers freedom to explore and experiment.

In 1972 Jerry, Chuck Jordan and Henry Haga, were involved in the Aero-Vette program. In 1974, when Haga left for Opel, Jerry took over as chief of Chevrolet Exterior 3.

The 1984 Corvette is Jerry's eighth. He also owns a Ferrari 308 GTB. From a styling viewpoint, some of his favorites are Ferrari's 330P4 and 512S, Porsche's 917 and the Lola T70.

"So, how do you feel about it now, seeing it all finished?" I ask Jerry.

"Well, one of the things we wanted was a wheel-oriented look. We accomplished that. We also wanted to shorten the distance between front axle and dash. We accomplished that, too. In fact, looking at it now, it came out remarkably close to one of the first sketches I made back in 1976!" Jerry says.

It is time to take pictures. The man in charge of moving the Corvette is set in motion: the angle of the car in relation to the dome must be just right. A lot of back-and-forth adjusting follows. Then the services of the man in charge of detailing is called upon: the tires are a little too shiny.

Everything looks all right now. I have the car and its creator framed in the camera. I ask him to say something, anything, just to give his face expression. He could have said cheese. Instead, subconsciously, his mind comes up with another word, a word that embodies the relentless search for the perfect shape in every little detail, the sum of which is the new Corvette. He says it with that energized enthusiasm.

"This car is designed... designed... designed..."

*The fourth-generation Corvette lasted an unprecedented fifteen seasons. During all those years the designers had, of course, been working on various ideas for a replacement. Most efforts revolved around a mid-engine concept. The first fairly firm ideas for the new front-engine Corvette took shape in 1976. Chief designer Jerry Palmer's sketch from that year shows how close the final product came to the initial concept. The first full-scale mockup was completed in 1978. The series of photographs on these pages show some of the intermediate steps that led to the final shape.*

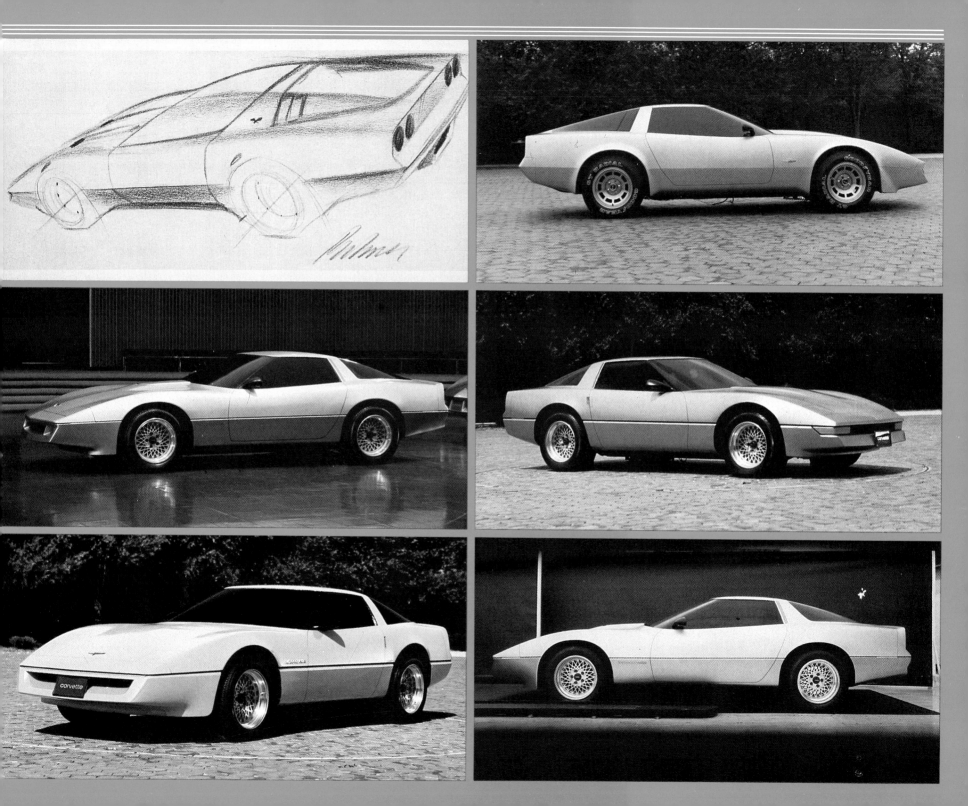

"Corvettes for the Road," ninth in The Survivors Series, was photographed, designed and written by Henry Rasmussen. Assistant designer was Walt Woesner. Copy editor, Barbara Harold. Tintype Graphic Arts of San Luis Obispo, California, supplied the typesetting. The color separations, as well as the printing and binding, were produced by South China Printing Company in Hong Kong. Liaison with the printer was Peter Lawrence.

The black and white pictures were mainly obtained from two sources: the photo archives of General Motors Design, where Charles Jordan cleared the way, and Dominic Villari and Floyd Joliet helped with the research; and the library at Road & Track, under direction of Otis Meyer.

Special acknowledgements go to Chip Miller of York, Pennsylvania, for sharing both his wealth of knowledge as well as his connections in the Corvette world; to Bill Kosfeld of Motorbooks International for his pleasant handling of day-to-day matters connected with publishing; to Tom Warth, of Motorbooks International, whose continued support made yet another title in this series possible.

The author also wishes to thank these contributors: Deryl Cherry, William Clark, Art Fisher, Thomas Kreid, Raymond Pannone, Billy Sawyer, and Paul Sawyer.

# Ferraris For The Road

# By Henry Rasmussen

# FERRARIS
# FOR THE ROAD

First published in 1980 as
*Ferraris For The Road*

By 1957 several years had passed since Ferrari had built his last dual-purpose roadster, the famous Barchetta. Richie Ginther, who was racing for California Ferrari dealer John von Neumann, suggested he promote the production of another. The idea was passed on to Modena through the U.S. importer, Luigi Chinetti, and in December of 1957 the first Spyder California was delivered. It was essentially the very successful 2600 mm wheelbase 250 GT berlinetta without a roof. The three-liter V-12 was tuned for 260 hp at 7000 rpm using three large Weber carburetors. It could push the 2,700-pound roadster from 0-60 in only 7.2 seconds. The reliable Ferrari four-speed fully synchronized gearbox carried the torque to a live rear axle with the standard lightweight center section. It was positioned by semi-elliptic leaf springs and tubular torque control arms. As development continued on the racing berlinettas, the refinements found their way into the Californias. No fewer than five different three-liter engines, of the Colombo type, were used between 1959 and 1963. Seven rear-axle ratios offered top speeds from 126 to 167 mph. When the berlinetta had its wheelbase shortened by 200 mm, the California was redesigned for that chassis and began another era of very effective club racing. Both long and short wheelbase versions were used in international endurance racing with success, but Bob Grossman's fifth overall at Le Mans in 1959 must be the high point. Scaglietti built fifty each of the two Farina-designed models and each was available for $12,000.

Ferrari's road cars have epitomized the term Grand Touring since he put roofs on his racing machines, and they had been available for a decade when the 250 GT was introduced. Not since Bugatti, had an individual automobile so captured the imagination of the motor sports world. After three years of dominating the GT category in international racing, a major revision was made. To make the cars lighter and more responsive, 200 mm were removed from the 2600 mm wheelbase, giving rise to the name Short Wheelbase or Berlinetta SWB. If you had 14,000 of the 1960 dollars you could have a virtual duplicate of the championship-winning car. Like it, your car would have Ferrari's robust, forged A-arms and coil springs for front suspension. The simple live rear axle with its leaf springs and torque control arms would carry your choice of axle ratios for dazzling acceleration or incredible top speed. With a 4:1 ratio, 0-60 took 6.5 seconds and allowed a maximum speed of 145 mph. A big, four-speed gearbox filled by powerful, non-silent gears with Porsche-patent synchromesh transmitted the 280 hp at 7000 rpm from the three-liter V-12 ahead of it. Like all road Ferraris, it carried three double-throat Weber carburetors. Disc brakes were now standard, too. The SWB was actually built in two versions, with the body in either aluminum or steel. Scaglietti built two hundred Farina-designed cars, of which seventy-seven 2,380-pound competition examples and seventy-five 2,700-pound road examples are accounted for in 1980.

# 250 GT California 1957-1963

# 250 GT SWB 1959-1962

A literal translation of "berlinetta" is "little sedan," but in the contemporary jargon of the Ferrari cult it describes a high performance, two-place coupe. "Lusso" in Italian means "luxury." There you have it. It just might be the loveliest form ever put on a Ferrari chassis. Though designed by Pininfarina, all 350 Lussos were built by Scaglietti. The chassis was very similar to the famous 250 SWB, with the 2400 mm wheelbase, but with concessions for comfortable touring. Touring here must be qualified. One suitcase would fit behind the seats. The trunk could hold a couple of sweaters and the fat 184x15 spare tire, so rather short tours would be in order. But however long the trip, it would be accompanied by the melodies of that marvelous three-liter V-12. It was all there, the three Weber carburetors, the singing, triplex timing chain for the single-overhead-cams, and 250 prancing cavalini at 7500 rpm. The precise four-speed gearbox allowed 0-60 in 8 seconds, a 150-mph top speed, and 14-17 mpg could still be obtained from the 2,995-pound car. The front suspension included a substantial sway bar which allowed relatively soft springing with little body roll in cornering and predictable understeer. The rear suspension remained effectively firm. The semi-elliptic springs and tubular torque control arms had to steady the tail with thirty gallons of 50¢ premium fuel suspended behind the live rear axle. Still one of the most sought-after Ferraris, it originally sold for $13,375. A reliable and economical Ferrari for daily use.

"Click! Key on. Click! Fuel pump—tick—tick—tick—tick—tick—tick—tick. Starter—rowrowrow, WHOOM! The first time you start a Ferrari in the morning is always just like the first time ever," said *Car and Driver* in their rapturous road test of Ferrari's new 3.3-liter spyder in 1965. The nineteen-year-old Colombo V-12 had been stretched again. It still carried the SOHC heads and the standard, triple Weber carburetors. The dual-purpose, 3.3-liter GTB had been introduced with 280 hp. The GTS was detuned to 260 hp at 7000 rpm in deference to its more luxurious character. That does not imply the absence of the typical Ferrari's function. With the newly-enlarged engine came even more radical departures from traditional Ferrari road car practice. The five-speed, all indirect gearbox, first used in the racing cars, was fitted in unit with the differential. Four-wheel, independent suspension with fabricated, parallel wishbones was also introduced on the series, all within the well-proven 2400 mm wheelbase. Magnesium alloy wheels were standard, but more romantic fourteen-inch wire wheels were optional on both cars and they mounted fat, 205-sized tires. Top speed for the spyder was 144 mph, with 0-60 times of six seconds available in the rather heavy 3,318-pound machine. It still managed a respectable 15 mpg on the highway. Pininfarina designed and built two hundred examples of the new generation spyder. They were available for $14,500 in 1965. Not inexpensive until you consider their present value is twice that.

# 250 GT Lusso 1962-1964

# 275 GTS 1964-1966

Jerry Titus was a musician, engineer, technical editor of *Sports Car Graphic*, and a respected race driver. In his test of the "sober," luxurious air-conditioned 330 GTC, he described the cornering power thus: "The curve-warning speeds in Nevada are pretty realistic and generally can only be exceeded by 20 mph or so in a good vehicle. We stopped the speedo-reading when the Ferrari went through a '35-mph' corner at 95 and still wasn't very hung out!" Based on the chassis of the 275 GTB (front engine, rear gearbox), but with a four-liter, SOHC V-12 and 300 hp, the GTC was meant for *fast* touring. It retained the five-speed gearbox with the shift gate, the three big Weber carburetors, full independent suspension, four giant disc brakes and Ferrari's established 2400 mm wheelbase. The road performance was not far removed from the dual-purpose berlinetta, but at 3,100 pounds its destiny was unmistakable. Most of the examples imported to the West Coast even included air conditioning. As the car became available to road testers the phrase "finest all-round road Ferrari ever" became the standard description of the chunky coupe. It lived up to its reputation. At $14,900 it was also the most expensive production Ferrari ever (the super-expensive Superamericas were not for "production"). The factory claimed 165 mph for the GTC and contemporary tests put 0-60 times at a bit over seven seconds. Still a well-respected car among the cognocenti, its strong performance and ageless Pininfarina shape are maintaining its value in spite of its 10 to 15 mpg fuel consumption. Six hundred examples were produced by Pininfarina before the Daytona became "The Ferrari."

A curious anomaly exists in hand-formed cars. They are all imperfect. Not just a little. Not like Detroit's misaligned doors, but doors of two different sizes. The ends are not horizontal, they are frequently not even parallel. They are exquisitely inaccurate. The 275 GTBs are thus. They were $14,680, 166 mph, 0-60 in 6.2 seconds, GTO-inspired sculptures. The 3.3-liter V-12 was given four overhead cams. Six Weber carburetors, once reserved for racing, were present in their awesome glory. It all produced 300 hp at 8000 rpm. The race-bred, indirect, five-speed gearbox was hung in the rear. All racing car stuff, but that wasn't all. Fully independent suspension for each of the four wheels with parallel wishbones was also used. Fat 205x14 tires enhanced the fantasy. The voluptuous form was stretched over the customary 2400 mm wheelbase and it all weighed 2,663 pounds ready to do battle on Woodward Avenue. Scaglietti produced 280 GTB/4s after building 460 original two-cam GTBs to Pininfarina's design. A few GTBs found their way onto race tracks, but the 275 GTB/C was the factory race version and the GTB/4 had optional air conditioning just to establish its real purpose. Here was the consummate sensual machine. They even left out just enough insulation to let in the bite of the cacophony that is a Ferrari. It cannot be driven casually. It demands the attention of all your senses. Quick, agile, responsive, animal-like in its attachment to the root of your spine, it is the quintessential sports car.

# 330 GTC 1966-1968

# 275 GTB 4 1967-1968

Gloria Steinem notwithstanding, this is a man's car. Big, muscular, graceful in the manner of Nureyev, and brutally fast. It was introduced to the European market at the Paris Salon of 1968. Not until March of 1971 would the American Ferraristi be able to purchase a reinforced and detoxed example. While other exotic car manufacturers were extolling the virtues of mid-engined, racecar-like machines, Ferrari put his mighty 4.4-liter four-cam, six-carburetor, 352 hp V-12 in the front of his new 174-mph cafe racer. He did put the massive five-speed gearbox in the rear for balance, but the visual effect was an ancient concept in a modern shape. Though dubious at the outset, after a day with the car *Road & Track's* testers called it simply, "the best sports car in the world". It equalled the mid-engined exotics in almost every way, but was much more forgiving to the skilled amateur driver. The well-proven 2400 mm wheelbase now carried 3,600 pounds but 0-60 could still be done in 5.9 seconds. The parallel-wishbone, fully-independent suspension had been strengthened and refined. So effective was the combination that several enthusiastic owners began competing in the touring car category of the long distance races with some success. The factory eventually built fourteen racing cars called the 365 GTB/4A. Scaglietti built 1,300 Daytonas to Pininfarina's timeless design before the Boxer took its place. It originally sold for $19,500 in 1971. Most included air conditioning and, with detoxification, delivered 13 to 14 mpg. Nevertheless, it remains one of the most desirable Ferraris.

When a prototype alfresco Daytona was shown on the Pininfarina stand at the Paris Salon in 1969, phones began to ring at the factory in Modena. Production was simply not in Ferrari's plans. However, demand was high and Scaglietti seemed to be building more Daytonas than Ferrari could produce chassis. It was determined that they could slow Scaglietti and satisfy the demand by having the top cut off every fourth coupe until fifteen spyders were built. Five would go to Europe and five each would be sent to America's east and west coasts. These first cars were basically topless Daytona coupes. The 4.4-liter, DOHC, 352 hp V-12 still carried that marvelous row of six Weber carburetors. The rear-mounted, five-speed gearbox separated the independent rear suspension. The wheelbase and weight remained the same. The Daytona Spyder finally did go into a per-order production of about 125 cars, each selling for $25,500 in America. While the top speed remained 174 mph, for some reason the road test showed a 0-60 time of 6.7 seconds—0.8 seconds slower than the coupe. Scaglietti produced all the spyders, but a phenomenon occurred in the late seventies. The Daytona Spyder cult pushed the price up near $100,000 and a replica business exploded on the scene. You could buy a coupe for $30,000 and for an additional $15,000 you could have a car that looked exactly like the $90,000-plus real thing. By mid-1980 approximately fifty pseudo-spyders had been made around the world.

# 365 GTB 4 Daytona 1969-1974

# 365 GTS 4 Spyder 1971-1974

"A Ferrari for the mature enthusiast," said *Road & Track* in their July 1972 test. To establish the character of this luxurious car, one of their primary complaints was an ill-fitted bit of weather stripping which allowed wind noise to intrude on the passengers. In a Ferrari?! There was a time when *gear noise* drowned out wind noise in an *open* Ferrari. The GTC4 was introduced in Geneva in March of 1971 as the replacement for the 365 GTC and it took that gracious concept to new heights of refinement. To complement the luxurious new interior, the car had a very modern flat nose, a low hood, and the greenhouse was drawn in a graceful arc above the unadorned sweep of the side panels. The 4.4-liter V-12 was used, but there was a difference. A new series of heads had been cast with the intake ports between the intake and exhaust cams. Six side-draft Weber carburetors were suspended out over the fender wells to permit the extremely low hood. Though exotic looking indeed, the new configuration produced only 320 hp at 6200 rpm. At 3,800 pounds its only purpose was very comfortable, high-speed touring. It still managed 0-60 in 7.3 seconds and 152 mph. A smaller, front-mounted gearbox left room for small rear seats and the self-leveling, fully independent rear suspension maintained the ride. The handsome tourer was given a 2500 mm wheelbase to add space. At $27,500 it was the most costly Ferrari road car ever, but it did include air conditioning and a stereo/tape player. Pininfarina built five hundred GTC4s in three years.

Accolades flowed from the motoring press when the "little Ferrari" was introduced in 1967. It had a 2300 mm wheelbase, an all-aluminum body, an aluminum, two-liter, four-cam V-6 engine with 180 hp mounted transversely amidships, and a shape as exciting as an Italian mistress. It was named for Ferrari's son, who is credited with suggesting Ferrari build a V-6 engine. Two years passed before the new Dino was "federalized" for America. When it arrived it had gained 40 mm in wheelbase, a steel body, a cast-iron engine block, 400 cc of displacement, 15 hp, and about three hundred pounds. At 2,700 pounds its 0-60 acceleration was 7.9 seconds and fuel consumption had climbed to the 13 mpg range. However, it was still the most exciting shape available for road use. The engine had a legitimate claim to a couple of Ferrari world championships and that marvelous form bore a definite resemblance to recent Ferrari racing cars. Two additional years passed before the very popular spyder appeared. The steeply raked steering wheel, the joyously firm and positive five-speed gear change with its position gate, its busy, metallic drone that crept through the firewall all combined to prove its heredity. With fully independent suspension and enormous, ventilated disc brakes, the Dino was meant to be driven. It was stable at its highest attainable speed (about 144 mph) and its cornering power was highly praised in the contemporary press. By 1974 Scaglietti had produced 2,732 Dino GTs and 1,180 Spyders. In America they sold from $12,000 for a GT in 1970 to over $18,000 for a GTS in 1974.

# 365 GTC 4 1971-1974

# 246 GTS Dino 1972-1974

It seems incredible that in these homogenized, detoxified autumn years of the twentieth century you can purchase an automobile which can travel at greater speed than the fastest racing cars of only fifteen years ago. A Ferrari Boxer can not only consume three and a half miles in one minute, but you can converse in a normal voice and enjoy Verdi in air-conditioned opulence while doing so. The Boxer prototype was introduced at the Turin Show in 1971. It went into production in 1973 as the 365 GT/BB. The refined BB512 appeared late in 1976 with its 12-cylinder opposed (boxer) engine increased to a full five liters. The horsepower was actually reduced from 380 at 7500 rpm for the type 365 (the factory admits some exaggeration there) to a realistic 360 for the BB/512. Using current Ferrari race car technology, the Boxer has a large flat-twelve engine mounted amidships, but it is above its five-speed gearbox. The DOHC heads support four, three-throat, down-draft Weber carburetors. The 3,084 pound curb weight includes air conditioning, electric windows and stereo radio/tape deck. Interior space is quite generous, but the 2500 mm wheelbase and 4400 mm overall length allow little or no room for luggage. The performance figures of the two cars are identical, with 0-60 in six seconds and a top speed of 188 mph, but the mid-range power of the BB/512 makes it a much more pleasant car for daily use. Boxers are built by Scaglietti to a Pininfarina design and are available in Europe for the equivalent of $85,000. American conversions are an additional $30,000.

The first four-cam V-8 Ferrari, née Dino, was received with a great deal of skepticism. A Ferrari engine was a V-12. Even a V-6 was a Ferrari engine, but a V-8, even with four Webers, smacked of Fords and Chevys and — Fiats. Beyond the engine, the Bertone-styled 308 looked like an overweight Lamborghini, not a lithe, muscular classical Ferrari, but when the Pininfarina 308 GTB finally arrived it was joyously welcomed as the return of Ferrari and the salvation of the eighties. The four-cam V-8 was still there, transversely amidships, over its gearbox; but the car now looked like a Ferrari. In fact, it was all Ferrari. The new three-liter engine pumped out 225 hp at 7000 rpm — more than the old 250 V-12 did in its normal street tune. The wheelbase was 2300 mm, the same as the 246 Dino. Actually the American 308 equaled the 246 Dino in performance. It was more powerful, but 300 pounds heavier at 3,000 pounds. Early in 1978 the GTS was introduced. It was received with even more enthusiasm and has been an even greater sales success. With air conditioning and the ubiquitous stereo radio/tape deck standard, it sold for $34,195 on the East Coast and $36,411 in the West. By mid-1980 the price of the 3,300-pound spyder has escalated to $45,000 and still sales are active. A top speed of 151 mph and 0-60 time of 8.2 seconds are enjoyed in conversation if not in actual use. Fuel consumption in the 15-16 mpg range doesn't seem to deter the megadollar buyer. As of June 1980, 2,437 308 GTSs and 2,701 GTBs have been built.

# BB 512 Boxer 1977-

# 308 GTS 1978-

# What's in a Name?

The Ferrari name is shrouded in glory, surrounded by mystique, and mentioned with respect. Ferrari enthusiasts all have different reasons for their loyalty to the marque. One can look back on having seen the first Ferrari win at Silverstone in 1950. Another still remembers the sound of the legendary vee-twelves as they came screaming by the pits at Le Mans in 1957.

I was never that lucky. For me it began with a picture in a Swedish newspaper. I believe the year was 1956. Ingrid Bergman had been selected to receive that year's film prize at a gala ceremony in Stockholm. The picture showed the actress and her director-husband Roberto Rosselini arriving in the Swedish capital after a non-stop drive from Rome.

The elapsed time quoted in the caption translated into an incredible average speed. I could visualize the Ferrari negotiating curvy mountain roads in Northern Italy, hear the echo as the car roared through the long tunnels into Switzerland, and imagine it almost airborne as it traversed Germany on arrow-straight autobahns.

From then on the name Ferrari meant something special to me, and I could always recall the feeling by conjuring up the image of the satisfied look on Rosselini's face as he peeled off his perforated driving gloves with their cut-off fingers and grinned into the flashing cameras.

It would take more than two decades before I was able to increase my knowledge of Ferraris, before I had time to research the different models, and before I had the opportunity to drive them. Often, when you remove the nostalgia to uncover the naked truth, you find yourself disappointed. Not so with Ferraris — the more you know about them, the better they become.

The incredible performance of these machines, the beauty of their sculptured bodies, the glory of the victories — all is encapsuled in the name Ferrari. And these are the things I have attempted to recreate on the pages of this book — for my own enjoyment and yours.

Open spaces, free speed, no limits. It's all between the car, the road, and your own skill as a driver; and that's the way you want it to be when you are behind the wheel of a Ferrari. To the left, surrounded by golden California hills, Mike Cotsworth steers his Spyder California straight into the setting sun. Above, Bart McGrath guides his Spyder Dino through the sharp curve of a winding mountain road high above the Pacific Coast. To the right, John Dekker's brand new Boxer, precariously placed were it not for the unobstructed view across the endless Colorado prairie, tries its wings for the first time in freedom.

Ferrari

Presented to Enzo Ferrari by the parents of a World War One flying ace who was slain in the line of duty, the Prancing Horse was destined to reach worldwide recognition as a symbol of the ultimate sports car. Ferrari first used it for his racing stable, La Scuderia Ferrari; he placed the black stallion on a yellow shield, yellow being the official city color of his native Modena. In these photographs the Prancing Horse decorates, from left to right, a Daytona Coupe, a 275 Spyder, a 365 GTC4, and a 308 Spyder. The characteristic Ferrari script in the picture above right is found on the rear deck of the Boxer.

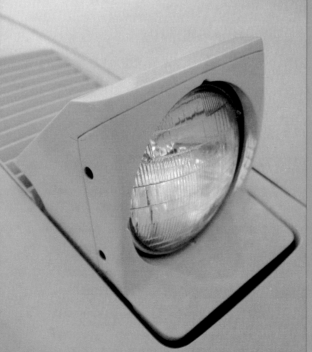

**G**lowing eyes in the twilight – eyes of an animal called the car. The eyes of a cat or a horse are vital to its function – but decorative as well. This is also the case with the headlights of a car. It was especially true when automotive design took its inspiration from the voluptuous, sensuous, streamlined forms of animals – remember the smooth shark noses, the toothy grins, and the aggressive nostrils? But even now, when computers have a hand in designing cars, the animal theme is visible – one can recognize a frog, a lizard . . . . Pictured from left to right are a 275 GTS, a 330 GTC, a 365 GTC4, a 275 GTB, and a 308 GTS.

S umptuous elegance already characterized Ferrari's interiors in the early
production models, as attested to by
the above photograph of a 1960 Spyder
California. The steering wheel, with
its decorative horn button and engraved
spokes, remained unchanged in the 275 GTB,
right, and in the Lusso, farther right. The large photograph on the opposite page shows the interior of
the 1971 365 GTC4, today still rivaling the 400 GT as
the most civilized Ferrari. The new steering wheel
is small and leather-covered. Below this picture, the top
has been removed to show the intimate two-seater
arrangement of the 308 Spyder.

**B**orrani wire wheels were standard on the early production cars, and available as an option on later models. Wires were used in racing as well, but with increased torque came the demand for stronger wheels. An alloy wheel was developed for racing and then introduced on the 1965 line of production models. A 1966 show car sported star-shaped wheels. This design was used on the race cars during the following year and then appeared on the Daytona when it was introduced in 1968. The same design is used on the Boxer, pictured on the left, as well as on the 365 GTC4. This model, however, still looks good with wires, as can be seen in the picture above. The Dino received its own design, pictured on the far left on this page.

**H**eart of a Ferrari – the engine. To the far right, the massive under-hood view of a 365 GTC4. A low profile required side-draft mounting of the six carburetors. Below it, the Ferrari script on the valve cover of a restored 250 engine. In its original form, it was not polished. Shown beside it, a Lusso engine with standard air cleaner. The decorative row of velocity stacks is the center of attention in the picture to the near right, featuring a Spyder California. The stacks were only used for racing, but their impressive look, as seen above on a SWB Berlinetta, makes them an irresistible option to the enthusiastic restorer.

**O**wner's pride takes on a humorous twist when furniture manufacturer Jim Hull puts on his Yellow Cab hat. Not that he needs any additional help in attracting passengers – his yellow 275 Spyder does it alone. To the right, Steve Gilman, behind the wheel of his Daytona, enjoys the reward of a successful entrepreneur. He wears a driving jacket of his own design, produced by his own automotive fashion organization – the Style Auto Company. The large photograph on the opposite page captures long-time Hollywood Ferrari dealer Chic Vandagriff. The early morning sun is showing above the edge of a Palm Springs mountain chain as he takes a pleasure drive in his 308 Spyder. Pictured below is Denver nightclub owner John Dekker warming up his brand new 512 Boxer for its maiden voyage.

# A Chronology of Production

Enzo Ferrari has devoted his entire life to motor racing. That and his son have been his two great loves. Had his racing programs not required the additional revenue that production would bring, it is doubtful there would ever have been any Ferraris for the road.

The influences that trigger and direct genius are legion. For Ferrari they began with the "anvil chorus" from his father's metal fabricating shop below the room he shared with his brother. In lieu of engineering school he spent several years of apprenticeship with Fiat and Alfa Romeo, mastering the science of automobiles. During those formative years he made contact with the leaders in racing car design. He was given the opportunity to work with the innovative designer Vittorio Jano and his protegé Giocchino Colombo and the development wizard Luigi Bazzi. In the future, each would play a vital role in the saga of the Ferrari.

Early in 1930, when he was thirty-two, Ferrari formed a partnership in the northern Italian village of Modena for the purpose of selling and racing Alfa Romeo cars. It was called "La Scuderia Ferrari" (The Ferrari Stable). The young entrepreneur took a great stride into history when Alfa Romeo decided to end factory participation in racing and gave the entire team and its equipment to his fledgling firm.

Under Ferrari's leadership the team was nearly invincible in the mid-thirties. When the might of the Third Reich entered the scene, Scuderia Ferrari alone tried to compete. To assist in the struggle, Alfa sent Colombo to Modena to develop new twelve- and sixteen-cylinder machines in the scuderia's own shop.

In the summer of 1938, Alfa recalled the entire team to Milan, including its disgruntled leader. Ferrari, "the great agitator" and high priest of spontaneity,.and Gobbato, director of Alfa Romeo and meticulous planner, shared only intolerance for one another. The inevitable clash

brought an end to Ferrari's twenty-year affiliation with Alfa.

The sales and service partnership of the scuderia was liquidated. With that capital Ferrari established a small manufacturing operaion in the scuderia building, which he owned. Wartime expansion and the government's recommendation of dispersement of industry caused him to construct a larger factory on a piece of land he owned near the village of Maranello. It was there he would create the racing car that would bear his name.

In 1946 Colombo was commissioned to draw up the engine for the new machine. He could not work quickly enough to suit Ferrari, so the services of a young draftsman named Aurelio Lampredi were secured. Many sound technical reasons supported the decision to build a V-12, not the least of which was Colombo's prewar experience with Alfa.

As Colombo spent less and less time in Maranello, Lampredi took on more and more responsibility. While the concepts of the all-alloy (single overhead-cam) V-12 are Colombo's, Lampredi and Development Chief Bazzi must be given credit for its refinement and ultimate success.

Until 1953 Ferrari's output of road cars was divided among small batches of V-12 types 166, 195, 212, 250, 340, 342 and 375. The "type" numbers represent the displacement of one cylinder in cubic centimeters. The under-three-liter V-12s were based on the original Colombo block dimensions. The three-liter and larger displacement engines were based on a new "long engine" designed by Lampredi. It was similar in concept and in many details to the earlier style SOHC V-12.

During its years of automobile construction, the foundry and machine shop of Ferrari have manufactured all the casting or forgings required for the engine blocks, heads, transmissions, differentials, suspension components, etc. Like most manufacturers, electrical parts, shock absorbers and such were purchased from the best firms available. Chassis frames have always been produced by small firms near the factory. In the early days, complete, driveable chassis were shipped to carrozzerias (coach building shops) to be clothed in the latest fashions. Later the chassis/body combinations were assembled and trimmed then sent to the factory for the installation of the drive train.

Several different small carrozzerias built the bodies, but the most representative examples of "the look" were from Pinin Farina, whose firm became the exclusive designer of Ferrari road cars about 1953. Heavily involved in mass production for Alfa Romeo, Fiat and Lancia, Pinin Farina opted to design and produce only

*Enzo Ferrari, to the right, on a rare occasion photographed behind the wheel of one of his creations. The picture dates back to the early fifties (Interfoto, courtesy Road & Track). The photograph above captures the massive strength of Mr. Ferrari as, stripped down to shirt sleeves and suspenders, he prepares for action (Gunther Molter, courtesy Road & Track). Photographer Henry Wolf recalls having to wait most of the day before permitted five minutes of Mr. Ferrari's time. Mr. Wolf asked him to think about his new racing engine, and "Il Commendatore" took this now-famous pose. The portrait is from the mid-sixties.*

the prototypes until the sales volume was sufficient to use the production line. Generally, the very limited production was left to the small shops of Mario Boano, who produced road cars, and Franco Scaglietti, who became associated with Ferrari through race car construction.

The **250 Europa**, introduced in 1954, was the first luxury production Ferrari. Twenty were built on a 2800 mm wheelbase with the long-block engines. Another thirty-five, produced during 1956 with a 2600 mm wheelbase, were designated the **Europa GT** and used a new 250 engine based on the Colombo block. This engine was destined to become the basis for much of Ferrari's competition success, as well as all production engines during the next decade.

The Europa GT was followed in 1955 by the **250 GT**, which was singularly responsible for making Ferrari a household word. At least eleven body styles were built on two different wheelbases. They were all called 250 GT but the Ferrari cult has attached its own nicknames in order to distinguish one from the other.

The first series had a 2600 mm wheelbase and the early models were thinly-disguised racing cars. Only a few were built. Two production coupes were introduced at Geneva in 1956, a berlinetta (a dual-purpose coupe used for touring or racing) and a luxury touring car with only fast, comfortable touring as its purpose. Scaglietti built seventy-three examples of the berlinetta during the next four years. They would bring Ferrari the World Championship for GT cars. It would come to be know as the **250 GT Tour de France** after its first overall win in that famous event. Boano built over 120 copies of the luxury model to a handsome Pinin Farina design. It is now known as the **250 GT Boano**.

In the midst of the 250 GT production, Ferrari introduced a new series at the Brussels Show in 1956. Conceived as exclusive transportation for the very rich, it was known as the **410 SA** (for Superamerica). Only sixteen were built by Pinin Farina to special order over the next four years.

A new and elegant line was developing at Pinin Farina. Its first offspring was a luxurious and rakish roadster, introduced at Geneva in 1957. It enjoyed a brief success as the **250 GT Pinin Farina Spyder**. Only forty-seven were built.

Ferrari production was beginning to develop rapidly by the close of the decade. Racing success was bringing production success.

The summer of 1958 saw the introduction of two important new Ferrari models. The first was an open version of the successful berlinetta. At the suggestion of Richie Ginther and West Coast dealer John von

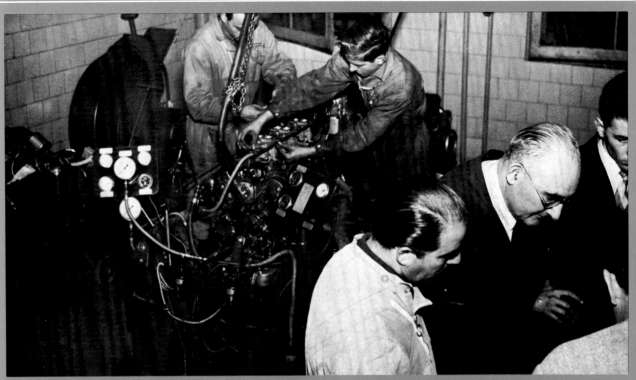

**U**nique interior photographs from the Ferrari factory, dated 1952. The view above shows an engine testing room with its center piece, the dynamometer. Luigi Bazzi, the long-time friend and collaborator of Enzo Ferrari and the man responsible for engine development, is seen surrounded by associates. Notice the single-carburetor engine resting on a stand along the wall. In the photograph to the left, a brake drum is being manufactured. The picture above right shows the assembly area for frame and suspension. Note the more complete chassis in the background and the gas tank to the left (Publifoto, courtesy **Road & Track**). The photograph to the right was taken in the factory courtyard at approximately the same time as the interiors. The rolling chassis, in this picture probably a 375 Mille Miglia, was tested this way and then driven to the coach builder for completion (courtesy Hilary Raab).

Neumann, American distributor Luigi Chinetti proposed the construciton of a dual-purpose roadster. It was called the **250 California** and Scaglietti made fifty on the 2600 mm wheelbase. The other was a very luxurious coupe, quite understated and formal in its styling. Though a very effective road car, it remains underrated by the serious Ferraristi. It has become known as the **250 GT Pininfarina Coupe**. Pininfarina (the new name in 1958) made over 350 of these lovely cars.

The fall of 1958 was spent testing and developing a successor to the remarkable Tour de France Berlinetta. The Paris Salon of 1959 hosted the introduction of the new berlinetta as well as an all-new car. To distinguish the California from the Pininfarina Spyder, a new **250 GT Cabriolet** based on the more sober lines of the Pininfarina Coupe went into production. By 1962 two hundred had been produced. The big news was the berlinetta. It was made more effective by shortening the wheelbase by 200 mm, at once making the 250 GT both lighter and more agile. The dual-purpose coupe became a legend as the **250 SWB** or **Short Wheelbase Berlinetta**. Scaglietti produced 166 bodies to Pininfarina's design. An additional fifty Californias were made on the new short wheelbase and renamed the **250 Granturismo Spyder California**.

At Le Mans in 1960, Ferrari unveiled its new family sedan. The **250 GT 2+2** or **GTE** was built on the 2600 mm wheelbase chassis with the engine moved forward by having new motor mounts cast into the block. Pininfarina made one thousand units, the last fifty of which had the bores increased to bring the capacity up to four liters. These few cars were called **330 Americas**.

Using a shortened **410 SA** chassis, Pininfarina began to experiment with automotive aerodynamics and aesthetics in 1956. The **Superfast I** was the result. Pininfarina had **Superfast II** built on a still shorter chassis in 1960 for his own use. It carried the concept into a new, modern direction. The introduction of the **400 Superamerica** at the 1960 Geneva Show put the Superfast shape into limited production. Pininfarina produced forty-eight examples. Further development produced a vast expanse of glass on the **400 Superamerica Superfast III** in 1962. The final statement in the series, **Superfast IV**, had four exposed headlights and was the least successful. The culmination of these studies was the **500 Superfast** of 1964. It combined the best of all the previous studies in a large, handsome form. Pininfarina built thirty-six of them.

The Paris Salon of 1962 was Pininfarina's choice for the introduction of his most elegant production shape. Combining the results of aerodynamic studies and tradi-

tionally conservative taste, Pininfarina excelled in the beautiful **250 GT Berlinetta Lusso**, built on the short wheelbase chassis. Scaglietti produced 350 during two years.

An interesting change occurred at this time. Prior to the Lusso, all Scaglietti bodies were hand-hammered, in either aluminum or steel, to line of sight. It wasn't until midway throught the Lusso production that a wooden buck was used to assure a consistent form for the bodies.

Concurrent with the Lusso was a new, larger 2+2. It would now seat four adults in comfort. In order to maintain Ferrari's reputation for the fastest road cars, a further increase in the capacity of the 1.5-liter Colombo V-12 took it to four liters. The new car was known as the **330 GT**. Its four-headlight nose did not set well with the customers, so a revised two-headlight arrangement was introduced along with a full five-speed gearbox to replace the four-speed-plus-overdrive of the first version. Power steering and air conditioning were offered as options for the first time on the renamed **330 GT 2+2**. A total of 1,085 were built by Pininfarina.

The 250 GT had run its course. Market pressure forced innovation. A five-speed gearbox and fully independent suspension were now *de rigeur* in a modern exotic car. The venerable, parallel-tube frame was redesigned to locate the big, race-proven, five-speed gearbox in unit with the differential. Fully independent rear suspension was included in the transformation, and a new era Ferrari was born. The incredible Colombo V-12 had its bores changed again, bringing the individual cylinder capacity to 275 cc and making the engine displacement 3.3 liters. Pininfarina created a form both modern and traditional that said Ferrari without question. The introduction was made at Paris' popular Salon in October of 1964 as the **275 GTB**. Scaglietti made 460 examples.

Sharing the debut of the GTB was the more conservatively drawn spyder, known as the **275 GTS**. Only two hundred of these handsome cars came from Pininfarina.

Inherent high-speed instability demanded a redesign in the GTB. A longer, lower nose was added in 1966, along with a worm and sector steering box which replaced the overly sensitive rack and pinion. The driveshaft was enclosed in a tube for the revised model. The open driveshaft with a center bearing had proved unreliable in the berlinetta but was retained in the spyder.

Approximately six months after the introduction of the 275 GTS, Ferrari offered another variation on the same

*ictured here are limited-production Ferraris and one-offs showing the styling development leading up to the first full-scale production models offered for 1959. Viewed clockwise: the 1953 250 Europa, the one-off 1955 375 America Cabriolet for ex-king Leopold, the 1956 Europa GT, the 1956 250 GT, directly influencing the limited-production 1957 Boano, the almost identical 1958 Ellena, the 1957 410 Super America, the one-off 1957 250 GT Spyder for race driver Peter Collins, and the 1958 410 Super America. (Photographs by Pininfarina, Rob de la Rive Box, Publifoto, Bernard Cahier, courtesy Hilary Raab and Road & Track).*

theme. Using the 275 chassis, he installed the big four-liter engine and Pininfarina drew up a very conservative, luxury coupe. The **330 GTC** was a powerful and popular road car. A convertible model, the **330 GTS**, based on the body of the GTC, soon followed. Pininfarina built six hundred of the coupes and one hundred of the spyders.

As a replacement for the 500 Superfast, Pininfarina built fourteen enormous convertibles on the 330 GT 2+2 chassis and installed 4.4-liter engines. They were the **365 Californias**.

With the production touring cars now at four liters and 300 hp, an improved, dual-purpose berlinetta was needed. The **275 GTB/4** made its debut at the Paris Salon in the fall of 1966. It was the first production Ferrari with four overhead-cams and six carburetors. Its power output now matched the four-liter touring cars and, with the marvelous 275 GTB body it still carried, it weighed only 2,663 pounds. Scaglietti's craftsmen hand-formed 280 copies. Another request from Luigi Chinetti for an open car resulted in the construction of ten **275 GTS/4 NART Spyders**.

The enormous success of the new cars forced the doubling of the production facility at Maranello. Though the stresses of manufacturing continued to dissipate his energy, racing remained Ferrari's primary interest. The 1965 Formula Two rules, requiring engines built in minimum quantities of five hundred, had brought a veteran engine back to life. Franco Rocchi, who had joined Ferrari under Lampredi in 1949, redesigned the four-cam Dino V-6 so it could be mass produced by Fiat. In 1967, after the Fiat Dinos were well into production, the Ferrari design staff developed a Dino of its own. It used the same Fiat-produced, two-liter V-6, but mounted it transversely amidships, ahead of a new five-speed gearbox. Only 150 aluminum-bodied **Dino 206 GTs** were produced. Scaglietti built the bodies to a Pininfarina design.

By 1968 Ferrari found himself in a pitched battle with his old customer Lamborghini for the world's fastest road car. Though having successfully built mid-engined racing cars for some time, Ferrari was not yet willing to give up the forgiving handling of the front-engine, rear-gearbox design developed in the 275/330 series. Rocchi's staff designed twin-overhead-cam heads for the big, 4.4-liter engine originally developed for customer racing cars only three years before. Six twin-choke Weber carburetors were mounted and an output of 352 hp was the result. The sweeping shape which Pininfarina designed was again produced in the shops of Scaglietti. It was called the "Daytona" by the European press in honor of Ferrari's win at that race in

January of 1967. There were 1,300 **365 GTB/4 Daytonas** built between 1968 and 1973. From 1972 to 1973 125 **Daytona Spyders** were built as well, but only on a special-order basis.

A new, even larger 2+2 was introduced in 1968 which used the big 4.4-liter engine but with single-overhead-cams and three Weber carburetors. It also incorporated the front-mounted gearbox of the 330 GT 2+2. Pininfarina built 801 examples of the **365 GT 2+2** during its three years of production.

The 4.4-liter engine was used again in the 330 series coupe and spyder. The resulting models were called the **365 GTC** (150 were built) and the **365 GTS** (only twenty were built).

The ever-increasing demands of the production side of his company caused Ferrari to take a closer look at his affiliation with Fiat. An agreement was reached in 1969 which gave Fiat control of all Ferrari production, but left Enzo Ferrari with final approval on any new product and control of all racing. Guiseppe Dondo and Francesco Bellicardi moved to Maranello from Torino, and another era began. In order to isolate themselves from the increased activity at the factory, Franco Rocchi, Angelo Bellei, and Giorgio Salvarani, all twenty-year veterans of Ferrari design, moved their technical staff of twenty men to Modena and a sparkling new facility.

The first product of the new arrangement was a revised Dino. The four-cam V-6 was redesigned with a cast-iron block and increased to 2400 cc. The wheelbase was up two inches and Scaglietti now made the bodies of steel. The **246 GT** was duplicated 2,732 times between 1970 and 1974. An alfresco model called the **246 GTS** was introduced in 1972 and 1,180 were produced in the next two years.

The 365 GTC, the body of which dated back to 1965, was beginning to look a bit long of tooth. It was replaced by an even more luxurious tourer called the **365 GTC4**. More than a simple revision, it was a totally new car. Its most innovative departure from traditional Ferrari practice was the new head design. In order to permit a lower hood line, the intake ports were placed between the camshafts and six Weber side-draft carburetors were placed horizontally away from the engine center line. A new, smaller five-speed gearbox was mounted immediately behind the flywheel/clutch assembly and the self-leveling, fully independent rear suspension of 365 GT 2+2 was used. A very rakish new body was designed and built by Pininfarina. It survived for only two years and a production run of five hundred.

In 1972 a totally new 2+2 was introduced. It included most of the mechanical innovation of the GTC4, but had

Pinin, Ferrari's first four-door, was introduced by Pininfarina in the spring of 1980. The classic rounded forms conceal the powerful Boxer engine mounted up front. To the left, the rear end treatment of the Pinin, and to the right, its elegant lines from a three-quarter angle. The frontal styling returns to the upright grill of early Ferraris. At the point of writing, eventual production plans have not been disclosed. The remaining photographs show the Mondial – a two-door four-seater, introduced in Europe in 1979, but not available in the United States until the summer of 1981. Pininfarina's styling shows the heritage of both the 308 GTB and the Boxer (Pininfarina, courtesy Giancarlo Perini).

an extended wheelbase to accommodate four adults in its leather-lined interior. Pininfarina built 524 of the **365 GT4s** before the engine was increased to five liters and a GM automatic transmission was added to create the **400 Automatic**. By the summer of 1980 550 have been produced; of those about thirty percent have had the optional five-speed manual transmission.

The Dino prospered during the fuel-conscious seventies, but production costs continued to drive the retail price up as America's emission laws drove the performance down. An all-new three-liter V-8 was designed by Rocchi's team to power Ferrari's new export car. It was first available as the **308 GT4**, a popular and practical, four-place car designed by Bertone and introduced at the Paris Salon in October 1973. In 1977 a two-liter V-8 version was introduced as the **208 GT4**. Now out of production, Bertone manufactured 2,850 three-liters and 700 two-liters by 1980.

In 1974 the eagerly-awaited two-place coupe was available for tests. The **308 GTB** was delightful. Bob Bondurant called it "the best sports car I've ever driven." Both the GTB and the **308 GTS** that followed were designed by Pininfarina and built at Scaglietti. They are the first Scaglietti-built bodies formed by electric-power hammers rather than human-power hammers. As this is written, there have been 2,701 GTBs, 1,100 of which were in fiberglass, and 2,437 GTSs manufactured.

The *pièce de résistance* of the Fiat-controlled production was certainly the device first shown to the public at the 1971 Paris Salon. Though an enormous visual success, it was not approved for production until late in 1973. The *Reparto Industrial*, the official name of the production arm of Ferrari, took on a truly monumental task: a flat (boxer) twelve with 380 enthusiastic cavalini mounted amidships over its five-speed gearbox. A delicious new and modern form to surround all the machinery and two fortunate humans. It was called the **365 GT/BB**. It might have been the Ferrari magic carried to its ultimate conclusion, but for one thing. It was replaced after Scaglietti had built only 387 by an even more awesome machine. The **BB512** was the same car more finely tuned. Scaglietti has built about 550 of the improved car by 1980.

As this is written the next generation 308, the four seater **Mondial,** has just been introduced and Ferrari's first four-door has been seen at selected auto shows. Named **Pinin,** it is a tribute to the maestro whose name it bears. It is elegant in an aggressive way. The great boxer twelve resides under its expansive hood and an opulent, electronic, leather-lined compartment invites human occupation. It may be the last of the great twelves.

# 250 GT CALIFORNIA

# Of Cops and Canvas Ripping

I have always known that some facts are more intriguing than others. I mean facts like these.

During the summer of 1959, a certain Bill Helburn decided to purchase a new Ferrari 250 GT Spyder California. He placed his order with the Chinetti dealership in New York, who in turn passed it on to the Ferrari factory in Modena.

The California was completed during the early part of 1960. Onto the identification plate on the fire wall was stamped: 508 D/1641 GT. Onto the engine block, on the flywheel housing: 1641 GT. And onto one of the timing chain covers: 168.

What intrigued me was that now, twenty years later, after the California had spent its first decade in relative obscurity, and its second in total obscurity — symbolically hidden under a tree — it was still possible to place the car in its historical space just by researching some letters and numerals. It was not just a beautiful sculpture of cast iron and aluminum with an anonymous past. No, it had roots, and they could be traced!

The number 508, for instance, referred to the type of chassis used and meant that the car was built on the 2600 mm long-wheelbase frame. The letter D indicated that the chassis was in its last stage of development, just before it was changed to the short-wheelbase configuration, type 536. 1641 was the individual chassis number, and a closer look at the factory records revealed that it was the fifth from the end of the long-wheelbase production run.

So far so good! The numbers made sense, except for the number found on the timing chain cover — 168. It

*The two pictures on the right-hand page show a Pinin Farina Spyder, chassis number 0789. A forerunner to the Spyder California, it is often mistaken for the latter. A noticeable difference is the crease along the side of the body; another is the high location of the taillights. At the top of this page, the dashboard and engine of the Pinin Farina Spyder. Above, a photograph from the Ferrari factory, labeled "chassis of the new California." To the left, a short-wheelbase, open-headlight Spyder California. (All photos by de la Rive Box, courtesy the Hilary Raab Collection, except the Factory shot by Bernard Cahier, courtesy Road & Track.)*

was confusing, since long-wheelbase Californias were normally fitted with type 128 engines. Type 168 seemed wrong for the car. But engine and chassis numbers corresponded, which indicated that the car still had its original engine. Something unusual had happened here!

That is what I mean. Some facts are more intriguing than others.

When Mike Cotsworth first found out about 1641, he had been searching for an open Ferrari for some time. He had looked at the Pininfarina Cabriolet, but had realized it was unsuitable for racing, and he wanted a car he could race. He knew about the California, and how few had been made, but he had never seen one. And if by chance one would have come up for sale, he knew he would never have been able to afford it!

In 1978, while attending the Historic Races in Monterey, to his surprise he discovered a California parked in the paddock. While he was taking a closer look, a man dressed like a cowboy walked up next to him.

"I have a car like this, but mine is aluminum," the man said.

They talked about it for awhile. The man said he had not driven his car for the past seven years. He also seemed willing to sell it if the price was right.

A few days later, Mike and his wife, Vicki, went to see the car. A four-hour drive south along the Pacific Coast brought them to its hiding place. As soon as Mike saw it sitting under the tree, he knew he wanted no part of it!

The car was covered with straw and dust and wrapped in cobwebs. The seats were torn and rotting. The wood-rimmed steering wheel was faded and cracked. The plexiglas headlight covers were broken and had been hidden in the trunk. To top it off, there were dark spots on the paint from the acidic berries that had fallen from the tree over the past seven summers.

The car was cleaned off with a broom and started. It was a wonder that it ran. The timing was off, and when they took it for a test drive it sounded more like a lawn mower than a sports car!

Afterward, Mike took Vicki by the arm and told the owner they were going for a short walk. As soon as they were beyond hearing range, Vicki started talking, with excitement written all over her face.

"Mike! Do you see what it can look like? All it needs is a real clean-up! Well, the seats have to be redone. But we can fix the steering wheel ourselves. And I know you can do the engine. It might not need much work at all. Did you see that it had gone only 40,000 miles? Aren't

*(continued on overleaf)*

Spyder Californias were dual-purpose cars. You could drive them to the track, race them with success, then drive them back home again. But only a few Californias, such as the example photographed here, were actually built by the Factory specifically for racing. Under the skin of original paint, the body is all aluminum; the quick-release filler cap leads to an oversized gas tank; the engine is hot, delivering considerably more power than the normal Californias. This car is the fifth from the end of the Long Wheelbase production run. The chassis number is 1641, and it was completed in January of 1960. In spite of the fragile body, present owner Mike Cotsworth drives his California to the limit in vintage racing events. Before ending up in Mike's hands, the car had been sitting idle under a tree for seven years, losing all traces of its previous history. It's about time the car sees some action, reasons Mike. After all, that is what it was built for!

you pleased?"

Mike was startled. He had been sure Vicki felt the same way he did. Now he stopped abruptly . . . looked at her . . . then at the California. And suddenly he too saw it! They walked back to the owner.

"Well. We have a deal!" Mike said and reached for his checkbook. He still knew he could not afford it.

"Swell!" The owner looked relieved. "The Ferrari was too much for me. Always liked my Corvette better!"

The next day, Vicki got a loan from her Credit Union.

The red Ferrari sat quiet on the dark pavement of Zinfandel Lane. The day was coming to an end, and the budding green of the vineyards slowly turned orange as the sun set over Napa Valley.

I opened the door and let my body slide down along the back of the seat. As I sank down in the leather, my eyes eagerly recorded the view of the classic Ferrari steering wheel, the two large dials behind it, the black crackle-finish dash; beyond the windshield was the vast red surface of the long hood with its protruding air scoop in the center and the two sweeping fenders on each side.

"You race it at vintage events, I know, but did the first owner race it too?" I asked Mike as he sat down in the passenger seat.

"I believe he must have," said Mike, "because the car is definitely set up for racing. It has an all-aluminum body, a Tipo 168 engine, the 130 cam shafts with a 10 mm lift, and very wild timing. It has the ribbed, light-weight gearbox; it has an oversized gas tank with an external filler cap, and four-wheel disc brakes! It was all done at the factory. I have a copy of the factory assembly sheet showing it."

I turned the ignition key. The ticking sound of the fuel pump reached me from behind. After a few seconds its rhythm slowed down, indicating that the carburetors were filled. I pushed the key. And there it was — the legendary canvas-ripping roar of the Ferrari vee-twelve at my command!

I lowered my hand to the gear-shift lever and pushed it forward. There was some resistance at first. I applied more pressure; it was immediately pulled into place. I soon realized there was not much need for first gear. Quickly into second! Now I really felt the acceleration. Into third! The end of Zinfandel Lane came up on me abruptly. I turned right on Highway 29 and accelerated again. There was too much traffic on 29, so I turned left at Oakville and cut over to Silverado Trail, crossed it, and went up Howell Mountain Road. The next few miles were filled with beautiful curves as we climbed higher

and higher up the steep hill.

The ride was stiff but not uncomfortable. There was some play in the steering wheel: I had a hard time getting used to it. I felt a slight understeer as well. The car had a tendency to roll a little in the corners, and the back end jumped a few times. But my overall impression was one of surprise at how easily the car could be controlled. Everything was lighter than expected — the steering, the shifting, the clutching. Everything but the brakes. Mike warned me repeatedly about them as we turned and went down the hill, returning to St. Helena.

We crossed Silverado Trail again and were safely down in the valley. I practiced shifting on the short straightaway back to the highway.

Leaving the stop sign and turning left in front of Christian Brothers Winery, I noticed a black-and-white. The policeman stared longingly at the Ferrari as he passed in front of us. I knew what he wanted, so I gave it all I had, accelerating up between the long rows of century-old moss-covered trees. I passed the cop right in front of Beringer Winery, doing over ninety. I caught a glimpse of him as he flung himself back against the seat, counteracting his kick on the gas pedal. But nothing helped — he was standing still! I watched in the rear-view mirror as the black-and-white was reduced to a dark spot in the distance.

Of course, it was all in my imagination. But I felt good just fantasizing about it. I kept my thirty miles per hour, patiently trailing the police car until I reached Zinfandel Lane again. I turned left on it, continued up to the end of the road and switched off the engine. The sun was now completely obscured behind the hills to the west. I knew this was the quiet time of the day — except in my ears, where the lovely canvas-ripping sound remained. I listened to it for awhile.

Mike finally turned to me. "I don't think I told you this before," he said. "There is an interesting diagram in the factory assembly sheet. It shows the results of the dynamometer testing of the engine. During the first session, they recorded a power output of 256 hp; this was done at 7000 rpm. Then — and this is the significant thing — they made another test, this time at 7500 rpm. Now they recorded 272 hp!

"Well, that definitely proves that it had the 168 engine all along. The standard engine could never have performed that well!

"It also means that my California is one of the few competition versions left with the original engine still in it!"

Like I said, some facts are just more intriguing than others.

*Pictured on the left-hand page, the Pininfarina Cabriolet in three different appearances: top up, top down, and with optional hardtop. The pictures on this page feature the classic lines of the Pininfarina Coupe. Both of these models were too conservatively styled to be well-received at the time. Today, they are experiencing a well-deserved re-evaluation. Above, a Pininfarina styling-rendering, which, if produced, would have given the Coupe a sportier look. Notice the low greenhouse and the hood scoop. To the right, the elegant interior of the Coupe. (All photos by Pininfarina, courtesy the Hilary Raab Collection.)*

# 250 GT SWB

# Dual Purpose Dilemma

The weather was still beautiful when an announcement suddenly came crackling over the speaker. A hailstorm was on its way.

I looked around and saw expressions of surprise and disappointment. There were over 100 Ferraris at the Road America race course. It was the annual gathering for members of the Ferrari Club of America. I could imagine what hail would do to those polished surfaces.

I looked to the west. There was a mass of dark clouds hanging on the horizon. I looked up. The sky was still blue here over Elkhart Lake.

Suddenly, as if on command, all heads turned in the direction of a savage sound like that of thunder. But it had nothing to do with the approaching storm. In fact, the hail was forgotten while all eyes concentrated on the swarm of Ferraris accelerating up the straightaway toward the pit area.

First in view was a 312 T3 Formula One car. With its 12,000-rpm capability, its high-pitched scream almost shattered my ear drums. The 312 was chased by a 512 Le Mans Boxer, equally inconsiderate, except that now the damage was done by a deep, metallic roar.

Then came the sound I had been waiting for — that of the classic vee-twelve engine eagerly working itself up to top revs, increasing in ferocity as it approached, nostalgically melodious as it passed. It was hard-charging Chuck Reid in his 1961 Short Wheelbase Berlinetta. He shifted to fourth just in front of the pit. The nose of the car dipped for a moment as Chuck let up on the accelerator, then it changed angle again, the rear squatting deep, the

*Photographed before its participation in the 1959 Le Mans race, the Interim Berlinetta prototype stands ready for action. (Photo by Pininfarina.) Below it, a 1960 competition SWB Berlinetta. Note the sliding plexiglas windows with ventilation holes. The row of interior pictures shows the variation in dashboard layouts. From left to right: an Interim Berlinetta, a competition version, and a 1962 steel-bodied car. (Photos by de la Rive Box, except far right by Dean Bachelor.) Pictured on the upper right, Stirling Moss at speed in the 1961 Nassau Tourist Trophy Race. (Photo by Action Ltd., courtesy Road & Track.)*

nose pointing high, as he opened up the throttle and let the 265 wild horses dig in with full power.

Chuck's mechanic, Windy Foreman, was standing beside me. We both followed the dark blue Berlinetta intently with our eyes until it disappeared over the top of the hill, shooting down toward Turn One. There was a faint trail of blue smoke behind the right pair of exhaust pipes.

"Do you think it means trouble?" I shouted to Windy, trying to make myself heard over the noise of a passing Testa Rossa.

"Probably not. But you never know!"

In the good old days of sports car racing, most cars were of dual-purpose character. This meant that you could drive the car to the track, compete successfully with it after a minimum of changes and afterward, with passenger, luggage and trophy in place, drive it back home again. The fastest production sports cars of today are too much on the road but not enough on the track. The Short Wheelbase Berlinetta was the ultimate dual-purpose car; it was nimble and flexible in traffic, yet fiercely competitive as a race car.

The SWB was based on the successful competition berlinetta of the mid- and late fifties. A new berlinetta, still built on the long-wheelbase chassis but clearly showing the new styling, made its debut at Le Mans in 1959. It is referred to as the Interim Berlinetta. In the Tour de France, the interim version took first overall. Only seven cars were made before the Short Wheelbase prototype was unveiled at the Paris Salon in the fall.

The SWB captured the four first places in the GT class at the 1960 Le Mans, and the three first overall positions in the Tour de France that year. The following year it took the four first overall places in the same event, and it again won the GT class at Le Mans. These were only some of the more prominent wins. In addition, there were innumerable victories in international, national and local events the world over. All this was accomplished with about 100 actively-raced cars out of 200 that were built.

Chuck Reid's SWB was still smoking as it came by on the next lap, although it seemed to be running beautifully. But on the third lap, as he rounded Turn Fourteen, instead of accelerating he raised his arm out the window, signaling that he was coming into the pit.

"What's wrong?"

Windy was immediately at the window, asking the question even before Chuck had pulled off his helmet.

*(continued on overleaf)*

**E**arly Ferrari production models were thinly-disguised race cars, but never was it more evident than with the Short Wheelbase Berlinetta. If you had the money, you could buy a car like the one that won at Le Mans in 1960 and 1961. There were differences between them, notably in weight and tuning, but the car you drove on your Sunday morning excursions would for all practical purposes be identical to the famous Le Mans winner. Chuck Reid, owner of the 1961 chassis number 3087, photographed here by the Elkhart Lake race track, also owns another SWB. He keeps one in California for vintage racing, and another at his home in Texas. Can't live without them Berlinettas!

"Nothing serious! It just feels like the engine is running out of gas when I'm doing top revs in third. Could I be low on gas already?"

"Not a chance! You should have plenty left!"

"What about the fuel pump?"

Windy took Chuck's place in the driver's seat. He flicked on the switch operating the manual pump, but the clicking sound was not heard.

"It's not working!" he exclaimed.

Windy came out from behind the wheel and quickly squeezed under the car. Chuck was relaxed; easing up on the neckband of his driving suit, he turned to me.

"Why don't you put on a suit and a helmet? I've checked with the starter and you can go along as a passenger for two laps. This problem shouldn't take long; it's probably only a faulty connection."

I looked around. Dyke Ridgley happened to walk by just then; he seemed to be about my size. I must not have concealed my excitement very well, because I only had to say a few words before he began to strip. The suit was tight, but I managed to zip it up and press the helmet over my head without peeling off my ears. I was in my seat just as Windy gave us the go-ahead signal. We accelerated onto the track and reached Turn One just ahead of a Daytona.

Chuck kept it in third through Turn One, then accelerated, leaving it in third on the short straightaway up to Turn Three, where he prepared for the sharp curve by braking strongly and downshifting to second. He accelerated out of the turn, the car leaning low, and licked the marker on the left side of the track; he ran it up to 7400, shifted into third, ran it up to 7400 again, and shifted into fouth. We now had a long straightaway ahead of us, and I ventured a question.

"Do you always double-clutch?"

"Yes! You bet!" he replied emphatically. "You want to be as easy as you can on the clutch and the gearbox. I also listen to the sound of the engine to know when to shift, but it's best to look at the tachometer!"

"Next is a blind corner," he said, as we passed a bridge. We were coming up on Turn Six.

"You want to be in second before you reach the bridge. Then you want to tap the brake, like this. You want to tilt the balance of the car over to the right; that's very important!"

The corner went ninety degrees to the left, but I had no idea of that until we were already in it. Chuck shifted into third as we entered the Carousel. This was a long sweeping curve.

"You want to stay in the middle of the road here, giving the car more throttle as you advance, keeping the nose

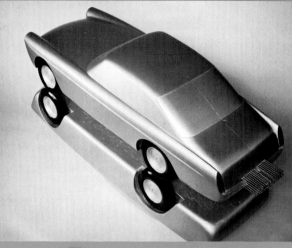

*The 1963 400 Superamerica, pictured at the left, is one of very few examples produced of this top-of-the-line 2+2 model. The smooth frontal area and the luxurious interior were distinctive features. At the other end of the spectrum was the 250 2+2, or GTE. Pininfarina's prototype is pictured at the top of this page. The dash was attractive and well-organized, above. Featured to the right is the rear quarter of the production version. Compare this view with the rare photograph, top left, of Pininfarina's scale model, specially-crafted for aerodynamic studies. (All photographs are by Pininfarina, courtesy the Hilary Raab Collection.)*

pointing to the right, until almost to the end of the curve when you ease it over to the right, clipping the markers, and then you let it drift out to the left. Marvelous corner, isn't it! It's fantastic!"

He smiled as we came out of the curve with screaming tires. I didn't smile but I did agree with him. We were approaching Turn Eleven.

"I enjoy this one too! It separates the men from the boys. If you keep the correct line through it you don't have to let up at all!"

We swept around the last few curves and accelerated up the start-and-finish straightaway, completing one lap. For the first time I had a chance to look at the speedometer. We were doing 130.

After letting me off on the next pass, Chuck went out again. He wanted to put in as much driving time as possible. We saw him come by two more times, the car still running like a clock. The third time, he should have appeared between two Daytonas, but he did not show at all. Had he spun? Was he hurt?

Twenty minutes later the tow truck arrived with the SWB dangling lifelessly behind it.

"What happened?" Windy asked.

"There was a metallic sound in the engine coming out of the Carousel," Chuck said. "I pulled off immediately and killed it. I couldn't run it one more second. It sounds serious, I know that!"

Chuck was still behind the wheel. I sat down in the passenger seat. The sky was very dark now.

"That's all for today," he said with a sigh, and wiped off his forehead with the back of his hand.

"Depressing, isn't it?" I said. "The car breaks down and now we're getting a hailstorm too!"

"Yeah; it's depressing. I don't mind the storm, but now I can't drive the car back home to Houston. That bothers me!"

Chuck was quiet for a moment, then he said:

"Marvelous car though, isn't it? A true dual-purpose car. So flexible. So strong. Great car!"

We sat in silence for a long time, then Chuck broke the silence abruptly.

"Well, what the heck! Let's have a cigar!"

He reached across to the glove compartment, pulled out a box, opened the lid and invited me to take the first one. They were Joya de Nicaraguas.

"Contraband from Nicaragua," he smiled.

"Do you have a match?" I wondered.

"What do you need a match for? We'll use the cigarette lighter in the car. Here! I told you it was a true dual-purpose car!"

# 250 GT LUSSO

# The Beauty and the Giant

Life is full of disappointments. One that many a Ferrari enthusiast is all too familiar with is the disappointment of not being able to afford what he wants. But it could be worse!

Imagine that you have picked out the Ferrari of your dreams. You have the money. You just want to try it out before you make the deal. But when you squeeze your body behind the wheel, you find that you don't fit. You are too tall!

Mister X, a Ferrari enthusiast from Saratoga, California, who prefers to remain anonymous, knows all about that kind of disappointment. He is six-foot-six!

Mister X had wanted a Ferrari ever since he first heard the sound of one at a race in Pebble Beach. The first model he tried out was a Pininfarina Coupe. He didn't fit. Then he tried an SWB. Again, he didn't fit. The one that finally gave him enough room was a 250 GTE 2 + 2, so he bought it. The car was white with a black leather interior, and he drove it to and from work every day.

Although he was quite satisfied with the 2 + 2, Mister X never felt it provided everything he expected from his dream car. He wanted something sportier! And he wanted a machine he knew to be the ultimate, one he could keep forever and always be satisfied with — mechanically, esthetically and historically.

The styling of the Lusso was already being praised when the prototype was first shown in the 1962 Paris Salon. The passing of time has confirmed it as one of Pininfarina's most outstanding Ferrari efforts. The rare photographs printed on these pages, showing interiors from Pininfarina's styling studio and Scaglietti's assembly line, have never before been published. On the clay model, above left, notice the lack of an air inlet on the hood. At this point it still only has a blister, much like that on the GTO, but more specifically rounded at the beginning. The picture to the right shows the crude state of the model, as if the final smoothing touches have not yet been added. The unique combination of blinker and bumper guard is already there, but the driving lights have not yet been removed from the grille. (Photographs courtesy the Hilary Raab Collection.) The other two pictures show the unpainted Lusso steel body, without and with running gear. The hood, doors and trunk lid were of aluminum. (Photographs courtesy of John Hajduk, Motorkraft, Bensenville, Illinois.)

Late in 1964, a certain gentleman from San Francisco took delivery of a Lusso at the Factory. The car had chassis number 5955, and was the last to roll off the production line — a fact no one seems to have taken special notice of at that time. He drove the Lusso in Italy for a while, on one occasion even showing it in a Concours d'Elegance at Montecatini. A picture of him with the car appears in the Ferrari Yearbook of 1964.

Later, he shipped the Lusso to San Francisco, where he drove it a total of about 5,000 miles. Then he left it with the local Ferrari dealer on Geary Street, who was also a Buick dealer, and stored it there for a long time. But one day it was gone.

At the time, no one knew why he had accepted the dealer's offer of a new Riviera and a new Skylark in an even trade for a Ferrari.

Meanwhile, Mister X had been promoted, and his travels occasionally took him to Italy. As expected, at first opportunity he visited the Ferrari factory. He was honored when the plant manager himself conducted the tour. At the conclusion of the tour, which happened to coincide with the end of the workday at the factory, they found themselves at the main gate. They were exchanging final niceties when suddenly, without warning, a door opened in the terra-cotta-colored building.

A group of men emerged, all very formal in dark business suits. They created a curiously comical picture as they filed out in the hot afternoon brightness. The unreal mood of the moment was amplified by the loud and relaxed conversation of the workers on their way home. It was a surprise when the last man to come out appeared without a jacket, his white shirt and suspenders creating a startling visual contrast to the dark suits. The tall and massive figure exuded unusual strength and self-confidence. It was "Il Commendatore" himself!

The plant manager excused himself and sprinted after Ferrari, who, during a brief exchange of words with the manager, glanced over his shoulder in the direction of the visitor. He then went back to the building reappearing a few moments later wearing a jacket. Adjusting his tie, and with the plant manager in tow, Ferrari smilingly approached Mister X, stretched out his arm and greeted the customer with a firm handshake.

"Mamma mia, cacaldo!" he exclaimed

"Very hot!" the plant manager translated.

"It's always a pleasure to talk with a customer. What do you own?" Ferrari continued.

"I have a 1961 2+2. I like it very much, although, I wish I had a Berlinetta. But all the models are very exotic

(continued on overleaf)

Graceful, elegant, refined – a few of the many superlatives used to describe the styling of the Lusso. In one word, it is referred to as the most beautiful of the Ferraris. Certainly Pininfarina's design, drawing inspiration from both the SWB Berlinetta and the LMB, is very seductive. From the aggressively-protruding front and the swelling fenders – stopping just short of becoming fat – to the smoothly-sinking curve of the roof, ending unexpectedly in the cut-off rear, it all translates into a powerful yet graceful sculpture of motion. The 1965 Lusso decorating these pages was photographed in the wooded hills above Saratoga, California. The chassis number is 5955 – the last of the Lussos!

and beautiful machines."

"Thank you. I build road cars so I can continue racing. Others race so they can sell the cars they build!" Ferrari said, and examined Mister X's six-foot-six frame.

"I have difficulty fitting behind the wheel, as you can see," Mister X explained.

"Perhaps we can build a car especially for you," Ferrari said with a smile, and then indicated with another handshake that the brief audience was over. He returned with energetic steps to the still-open door, and was again consumed by his own creation.

Mister X would always remember the occasion.

The Lusso that once belonged to the gentleman from San Francisco had been in the hands of Mister X for almost fifteen years when I met him. I arrived at his home in Saratoga around seven-thirty in the morning; we had agreed on meeting early so we could drive the Lusso up into the hills and photograph it there just as the morning fog disappeared.

"The sun will begin to burn it off in about an hour, I would say," Mister X told me as he came out in front of the house, where I was looking up at the hills. There was a heavy blanket of fog seeming to reach all the way up to San Francisco, totally enveloping the mountain chain.

"Well, let's look at the Lusso in the meantime." I suggested, as I caught a glimpse of its swelling fender forms in the darkness of the garage.

"It looks even better than when it was new!" I said. "I can see that it hasn't been restored. When a car is well-kept, over the years it acquires a patina. It becomes better than new!"

"Thank you! I'm happy that you, too, are of that opinion," replied Mister X. "Not everyone would agree with you, you know."

"When a car has been maintained like this, there's no question about it."

"Thanks! I have to tell you the story of how I got it. I went to a dealer one day, looking for parts for my 2 + 2. Just by chance, I became intrigued by some unfamiliar forms under a cover. When it was rolled back, revealing the Lusso, I really liked what I saw. When I sat in it and found that I fit, I knew it had to become mine. I felt like Enzo had fulfilled his promise and built a car for me!

"I told the dealer I had to have this car," Mister X continued. "He said it belonged to a customer, and that it wasn't for sale. But, I returned often and bugged him about it. Finally he said he would see what he could do. It's thanks to my persistence and his negotiating skill that I own it today!"

I sat down behind the wheel and was overcome with a

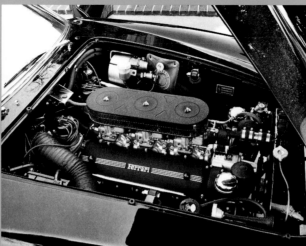

*The Lusso was a magnet wherever it appeared. In the picture top left, possibly at the Frankfurt Show, it has just been uncrated. To the left, captured in an unknown location, it sports a for-sale sign as an encouragement to prospective buyers. The picture above shows the good-looking racing-style buckets, but the most intriguing features of the interior were the large tachometer and speedometer gauges. The center location was obviously a concession to styling – it was hardly practical. But then, driving a Ferrari, you don't want to know how fast you are going anyway! The engine compartment picture shows a well-restored example. (Photographs courtesy Road & Track.)*

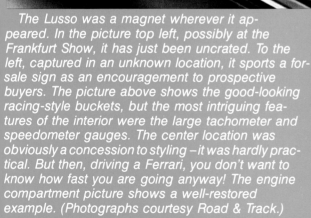

strong feeling of pleasure. This sensation was the result of three things: the spaciousness created by all the glass, especially by the large quarter windows; the rich elegance of that blue-gray leather, covering the seats as well as the entire luggage area behind them; and the enormous tachometer and speedometer, conspicuously placed in the center of the dashboard. The odometer showed 23,000 miles.

I stepped out and looked at "the most beautiful of the Ferraris" from all angles. I happened to notice that the knock-off wings were totally undamaged.

"How did you manage to keep them that way?" I asked Mister X.

He strode over to his workbench and returned with a curious-looking hammer.

"I make my own hammers," he explained. "I use soft lead. Melt it myself on the stove and pour it into a small orange juice can. I had the model shop at work make this special handle for me."

"What about the hammer in the tool kit?" I asked.

"Are you kidding? I'm keeping everything in that tool kit like new. It hadn't been used when I bought the car, and I plan to keep it that way!

"I do all maintenance myself," said Mister X. "Wouldn't let anyone else near it. I don't even like to show it. I showed it once at Pebble Beach and got second place, but I really don't like it. It's not for me: I'd rather drive it than wrap it in cellophane!"

"When did you find out that it was the last one off the line?" I asked.

"Well, I knew from the beginning that it was a late car: I noticed the dates on the Borrarni wheels. And a few years ago, a Ferrari historian saw it at the Historic Races at Laguna Seca, and he told me it might be the last one. But I wasn't convinced until I saw the complete list of numbers in the Miska Lusso book. It gives my car the historical prominence I wanted."

"By the way," I asked, "have you found any more Ferraris that you can fit into? Any other Ferraris you want to own?"

Before he could answer my question, his wife appeared, balancing three cups of coffee on a tray.

"Did you hear that question, Love?" he said.

"No, I didn't hear anything!"

"Do I fit another Ferrari beside the Lusso?"

"Yes, you fit in the Boxer. Why?" she asked, looking innocently at him.

"Oh, nothing." he said, and smiled back.

I got the feeling he was toying with the idea of getting one, but hadn't prepared his wife yet.

Quite a pair — the Lusso and the Boxer!

# 275 GTS

# To Catch Ferrari Fever

There are so many ways to catch Ferrari Fever. So many dangerous sources of infection. They all have different degrees of future effect. Some get a mild case; others get it bad. Jim Hull got a severe case of the worst kind as a result of his first exposure to a Ferrari. It took place in Europe during the summer of 1962, when Jim was nineteen.

He had been going to school in Salzburg. When the term was over, all the other Americans hurried home. All but Jim, who had to make sure his Volkswagen got on a boat in Bremerhaven for eventual transportation to New York. Jim was supposed to follow a few weeks later.

He got to Bremerhaven late in the evening and spent the night in a youth hostel. There he happened to make friends with three other American students who had just come up with a bright idea — they were going to the twenty-four-hour race at Le Mans, and they were going to see it from the inside! They had no idea how this would be accomplished, but one of them lived in Santa Monica, Phil Hill's home town, and he personally knew the Champion of the World. (Or so he said.) Knowing the right people was all it took. That's what they thought!

This was just the thing for Jim. Forget that the car was due on the boat! He saw it as lucky coincidence that

Above, the prototype 275 GTS as photographed on Pininfarina's "turntable" in 1964. For the first-version production run, the front blinkers were changed to a wrap-around type and a side vent was added, of the same style as that used on the 330 GT 2+2. The second production version, pictured on the left, had a different side-vent design and a chrome strip below the door. (Photographs by Pininfarina, courtesy the Hilary Raab Collection.) The 1966 330 GTS, top right, received a longer nose like that of the 330 Coupe. (Photograph by Gordon Chittenden, courtesy Road & Track.) To the lower right, a Pininfarina photograph shows a curious-looking hardtop.

these guys needed transportation, and that he could provide it. The Volkswagen was turned south, now carrying four people.

They arrived in Le Mans several days before the start of the event. None of them spoke French, and the gendarmes spoke no English. But, by using Phil Hill's name frequently, they managed to get through to the paddock area, where they parked the car and put up their small tent.

They now turned their attention to the fascinating surroundings. Jim recorded it on film: the Jaguars, the Ferraris, the Maseratis, the engines, the mechanics, the Rodrigues Brothers — a circus of colors and beautiful forms. They were really on the inside! They had made it! But not quite yet.

On the morning of the race, Jim was brutally awakened at the ungodly hour of three o'clock. Two gendarmes had grabbed his legs, which, for lack of space, were protruding from the tent. The gendarmes shook him violently. Their car had been discovered lacking the obligatory sticker, and they themselves had no passes. They tried to explain, again using Phil Hill, but nothing seemed to convince the gendarmes. Suddenly, without conferring, the four ran off, disappearing in different directions. It was a long time before they dared to come out of their hiding places. They were eventually reunited, but now there was sin in Paradise!

They had to come up with a way to obtain those all-important passes. Maybe they could run errands for one of the drivers? Phil Hill's name came up again. But, being a member of the Ferrari factory team, he wasn't approachable. They turned to another famous American, Briggs Cunningham. He proved to be very polite, but he already had all the help he could use. As a last thought he suggested that they try Hugus and Reed.

Hugus and Reed? Who had ever heard of them? But they proved to be just the right ticket. They had a very informal setup: no mechanics, no timekeepers, no errand boys. They could certainly use the help of a gang of teenagers. The passes were finally secured; they had made it!

Hugus/Reed were to drive the same experimental Ferrari that Tavano/Baghetti had driven the previous year. The car had since been sold to Chinetti, who had campaigned it in the States. Stirling Moss had driven it to a fourth at Daytona. The car was later sold to enthusiasts in Chicago, who had now entered it at Le Mans. Jim never learned what kind of previous experience the drivers had, but he found them to be very happy and easy-going fellows. The car was beautiful

*(continued on overleaf)*

Shown first at the Paris Salon in October 1964, the 275 GTS, together with its companion, the 275 GTB, represented a new generation of Ferraris. The cylinder volume was enlarged, but more importantly, the cars now had independent rear suspension. They also came with a five-speed transmission and rear-mounted gear box. The featured 1965 model belongs to Jim Hull of Brentwood, California, and carries chassis number 07479. The 275 Spyder may not be Pininfarina's most flamboyant styling exercise, intended as it was for discreet grand touring only. But set against the violent formations of red California rock, and painted the vibrant Ferrari yellow, its elegant lines are brought out to their full eye-catching advantage.

and fast, but it was the sound of it that got to Jim. At the time, of course, he could not have known that historians would later consider this car the prototype for the legendary GTO.

The race itself turned out to be somewhat of a monotonous affair for the crew. Their car ran like a clock; they were in ninth place after fourteen hours. The Ferrari kept roaring by, lap after lap, hour after hour, right on schedule.

Jim and his friends were kept busy. Two of them had the job of showing standings to the drivers. Another handled the communications between these two and the pit crew. Jim was chosen to run between the scorekeepers and the timekeepers, making sure the latest information was at hand at all times.

Their Ferrari was in seventh place after eighteen hours of driving. Everything was going smoothly until two hours remained and it was time for the last change of drivers. When they were ready to take off again, the engine didn't want to start. Panic in the pit! The hood was thrown open and many frantic fingers tried to find out what was wrong. Finally a Maserati mechanic was rounded up. Soon the Ferrari sped off again — delayed one hour!

When the final scores were in it became clear that the Americans at Le Mans had fared very well. Phil Hill piloted the winning Ferrari, Cunningham drove the fourth-place Jaguar, Grossman the sixth-position Ferrari, and Hugus/Reed took ninth!

And Jim Hull had played a part in it.

As the years passed, the Ferrari memories were pushed deeper and deeper into Jim's subconscious. They were suppressed by the responsibilities of serious studies, but also by the sense of anti-materialsm that he developed along with so many young people of his generation. The Ferrari Fever recurred temporarily at the end of 1965, when Jim bought the October issue of *Car and Driver.* It had a picture of a yellow 275 Spyder on the cover.

I busied myself behind the wheel of Jim Hull's yellow 275 Spyder, keeping the engine at about 1200 rpm while giving it the proper warm-up. I listened to the sounds coming from under the hood in front of me, as well as the sounds from the two sets of twin exhaust pipes behind me. Jim sat down in the passenger seat, pointed at the oil temperature gauge, and indicated that it was all right to take off. I backed out, accelerated in first gear, and rolled the short distance to Sunset Boulevard — all while I eagerly took in the view. It was luxurious. The seats

*The photographs on this page feature the 1961 GTO prototype, chassis number 2643. The car was driven twice at Le Mans, where Jim Hull's pit-crew experience gave him his first taste of Ferraris. From bottom to top, the car is shown in different disguises: painted red with Italian colors on the hood as raced at Le Mans in 1961; then at an unknown later date in a Pininfarina photograph; and, finally, painted white with a blue stripe as raced at Le Mans in 1962. (Photographs by Pininfarina, courtesy the Hilary Raab Collection.) Pictured on the right-hand page, the 500 Superfast. Very few examples were made between 1964 and 1966, at a $38,000 price tag.*

were wide and upholstered in soft black leather. There was a strip of wood veneer across the length of the dash. The speedometer was on the left, the tachometer on the right. Between them were small gauges showing the oil pressure and oil temperature. Four more gauges were lined up in the center.

The stubby gear-shift lever had a contoured knob and was placed on the left side of the tunnel. It felt very precise, in spite of the rear-mounted gearbox. I liked the visual effect of the gate plate, an item inherited from the race cars. We were flowing slowly along with the traffic on Sunset. I had no trouble keeping it in third at the low speed; the engine was wonderfully flexible.

"I had never seen a 275 GTS until I discovered this one parked on La Cienega," Jim said. "It was for sale. I had always wanted one, and my furniture factory had just begun to return some of my investment."

I crossed the bridge over the San Diego Freeway, turned right on the other side, and circled down the ramp onto the northbound lanes.

"I bought the Ferrari in 1972, and used it every day for the first five years," he continued. "Never had any major trouble. Only had it tuned up once! But finally it started to smoke. It still ran good, but I was embarrassed at the Ferrari speed meets. It looked bad! So I had the engine rebuilt recently."

It was getting too noisy to keep up the conversation, so we sank a little deeper into the seats and enjoyed the sound, the wind, and the attention in silence. I turned off on Highway 14 after about twenty minutes. The traffic thinned out and I dared to run it up to ninety. The Ferrari felt marvelously solid and stable on the road. I could have continued forever, but our destination appeared on the left.

I had chosen Vasquez Rocks, a well-known location among movie makers. I had scouted it earlier; now I only needed to position the car in relation to the sun. The violent forms of the red rock were a stunning contrast to the refined lines of Pininfarina's yellow sculpture.

It was this understated elegance that had me fooled before I drove the 275 GTS. Now I knew that the subtlety was only skin-deep. Jim must have read my thoughts. He took out a magazine from under the seat; the pages were turned to an article about the GTS. He read a sentence aloud.

"For all its concessions to creature comfort, this is a hairy, demanding GT car that will stretch to the skill of the most talented driver."

I reached for the magazine and turned to the cover. It was a *Car and Driver* from 1965.

The photo was of a yellow 275 GTS.

330 GTC

# Music for Mechanics

"I'm probably the only guy in the world who's gone directly from a fifty-seven Chevy to a Ferrari Lusso! Do you know anyone else? It's a big step. It happened in 1966. I was twenty-four, and had owned the Chevy since my high-school days, so it was almost ten years old. I was definitely ready for a change of image. I had seen a metallic-blue Lusso in Estes Zipper's Ferrari showroom on Wilshire Boulevard in Beverly Hills. Every morning when I drove to work in my Chevy, and every time I had an errand during the day, and every evening when I drove home, I went out of my way to catch a glimpse of that gorgeous Lusso. The more I looked at it, the more my want turned to need!"

Larry Bloomer unlatched the hood of his red 330 GTC, and, while raising it, he continued to tell the story of how he acquired his first Ferrari.

"I was a salesman for Xerox at the time, and it had been a very successful year for me, but not quite successful enough to win first prize in our company's national sales contest. The prize was a new Mustang convertible. I knew all along that I had a good chance of getting it, but one guy was better. It must have been fate! The same day I got the bad news about the Mustang, the Lusso was taken out of the showroom window. That gave me such a shock that I made a U-turn in rush-hour traffic and parked illegally to see what had became of "my" Lusso. I was told that a potential buyer was to test the car the following morning, and the car was being readied. That night I couldn't sleep. I woke up early the next day and found myself pacing outside the showroom waiting for Zipper's arrival."

Larry was still holding on to the open hood. His eyes shifted back and forth between me and the many familiar parts of the engine as he spoke.

"They wouldn't let me drive it. They probably thought I was just another car-crazy kid. Otto Zipper himself finally took me on a short ride after I had convinced him I was a serious buyer. I can still remember the look on his face when I told him I wanted to buy it. He was probably even more surprised when I paid with cash."

His eyes traveled to the back of the garage.

"As you can see, I still own the Lusso. I drove it every

*The 330 GTC, top left and right, had pleasing lines from all angles, but especially the profile and the rear quarter treatments, which were excellent. Pininfarina's styling made the car look both sporty and elegant. Elegance also characterized the interior, to the left, with its wide leather seats and veneer-covered dash. The 365 GTC, above, first shown in 1968 and produced until 1970, had only minor styling changes; the side vent was gone, but vents had been added on top of the hood. The engine compartment of the 330 GTC was dominated by the air cleaner, obscuring the view of the three Weber carburetors. (Photographs by de la Rive Box and Pininfarina, courtesy the Hilary Raab Collection.)*

day for ten years — put more than 200,000 miles on it. Went through the engine twice. Completely refurbished it three times. Now it needs another cosmetic overhaul — I just haven't had the time, because I have been working on this one!"

His 330 GTC was pulled half-way into the garage. A beat-up Lusso rested behind it. Beside the Lusso, under a cover, I recognized the form of a Daytona. And back in a corner sat a 1957 Chevrolet.

"I still have the Chevy as well!" Larry said. "Just can't give up my old cars, I guess. Now when I get the garage finished, I'm going to restore the Chevy. I'm going to put all the cars back in their original shape. The Lusso needs a new paint job again, but the interior and the drive-train have already been redone. I'm almost finished with this 330."

Larry's new garage could hold eight cars. He had included an unusual feature for a private garage — a pneumatic hoist, just like the ones found in gas stations. I gathered he was planning to do some serious work here.

His home is located in Cheviot Hills, one of those hidden communities right in the middle of Los Angeles — an oasis in a vast desert of buildings and streets and cars. Here he is only ten minutes away from his office in Beverly Hills, where he is a commercial real estate agent.

"What was wrong with the 330?" I asked.

"It was smoking! What else?"

"Naturally! And you had to change the rings!"

"No! That's a mistake many Ferrari owners make. When the car smokes, they immediately think it's the rings, when that's actually not the problem most of the time. Most Ferraris are driven very little; therefore, the rings don't get that worn. The valve guides and/or seals, on the other hand, have always been a weak point. They get worn and allow oil to seep into the combustion chambers. That's what usually causes that embarrassing smoke!

"But how can you know without opening the engine whether it's the rings or the seals?" I asked.

"There are several ways. If the seals and/or the guides are shot, and the engine sits or idles for awhile, oil in the valve covers will run down along the valve stems and into the combustion chambers. When you fire up the engine, you get that big cloud of smoke."

"Yes, I understand."

"Replacing the valve guide seals is relatively simple and far less expensive than the major overhaul required to replace the piston rings. If you wanted to find out if the

*(continued on overleaf)*

Under the hood – 300 horsepower and handling to match; the 330 GTC could have done well on the race track had it not been for its weight. Well, it was not a coincidence. The 330 GTC was all Ferrari had intended it to be – a fast, reliable, luxurious, elegant-looking touring machine for two. As such, it was extremely successful – probably the most sensible Ferrari for everyday use to date. Owner Larry Bloomer knows what he is talking about – he has been driving Ferraris on a daily basis since 1969. His featured 1968 model, chassis number 10508, has just been totally overhauled by Bloomer. In the pictures, he takes it for the first test drive, choosing the Santa Monica Mountains with their steep grades and sharp curves; the location is just right for the occasion, all beautifully laid out as it is against the backdrop of the blue Pacific Ocean.

rings are bad too, you can run a compression test. You should get a compression reading on all twelve cylinders. The readings should be within plus or minus ten percent of each other. The hours on the engine will determine the actual pounds in the cylinders. If you get a reading outside the ten percent range, you still can't be sure it's the rings. It could be a leaking valve, for instance. Then what you do is squirt some oil into each cylinder so it surrounds the piston and covers the rings. Then take another compression reading. If it improves, you can be sure the rings are bad. The oil, you see, seals the space around the cylinders, preventing air from leaking past the piston. So if your compression is good, but it smokes bad when you fire it up, you can be pretty sure it's the valve guides and/or the seals. That's what was wrong with my 330 GTC. It had factory-installed seals that were worn out."

"And you replaced them yourself?" I asked. Dressed in his pin-striped suit, he somehow didn't look like he was capable of it.

"Sure. It's not that difficult. I did a lot of engine rebuilding during my high-school years. When I bought the Lusso I began spending a lot of time down at Zipper's. I used to watch the mechanics work and I asked them many questions. And I took notes of what I saw and heard. Richard Van DeWater was Otto's chief racing mechanic then. He was always willing to walk me through problems as he solved them. The complexity of the Ferrari engine is really a myth, in my opinion. It's not all that different from working on two six-cylinder Chevrolet engines with a common crank, if you know what I mean."

"I trust you. But I would never try it myself!" I said.

"It's reasonably simple, but quite exacting! First you make sure the car is in neutral. If it's left in gear, and you happen to bump into the car while working on it, you'll move the cylinders and mess up the timing. And that's bad news! Four degrees off and you bend valves. You start by removing the cover plate over the small opening in the bell housing, between the distributors. Through this opening you can see the flywheel. From the many marks on the flywheel, you can determine the cam, ignition, and valve timing. There is a mark for every cylinder's firing position and lots more. When you understand the marks, numbers and letters on the flywheel, it's like being able to interpret another civilization's language. If you follow it perfectly you will never go wrong. But enough of that. You make sure the number-one cylinder is set top dead-center A. The mark is PM 1/6 on the flywheel. Next, remove the carburetors, including their manifolds. Take off the distributor caps, but

The 330 GT 2+2 was a beautifully-balanced design, styled and built by Pininfarina. It was first introduced in 1964, with a four-headlight arrangement. It was rather uncharacteristic for Ferrari, and did add excitement to the front, but the model was not well-received visually. The outside, larger lights were the low beams, and the smaller were the high beams. The conventional Ferrari look returned the following year, and this model was produced until 1966. The interior followed the theme of the period with a wooden dash. (Photographs by de la Rive Box and Pininfarina, courtesy the Hilary Raab Collection.)

before going on, stop and be sure the rotor is firing the number-one cylinder. If not, rotate the engine 360 degrees to PM 1/6 again. The rotor should now be firing number one. Mark the distributor's bases where they bolt onto the engine, and mark on the distributor's housings exactly where the rotors are pointing before any removal. Now you are ready to tackle the valve covers. Then off with the timing-chain covers. You have to remember to insert wires to hold the timing chain so it doesn't fall down into the cam/timing sprockets. First you remove the rocker arms, then the sprockets and the cams. There you are! Ready to attack the valve guide seals. Doesn't sound too difficult, does it?"

"Are you kidding? That's too much for me," I said. "My head is spinning just from listening to you. Let's start it up instead. I've always wanted to know what makes all those noises. Can you tell them apart?"

"Sure. If you exclude the sound of the exhaust, there are three main sources of sound: first there is the noise of the adjusting screws at the tips of the rocker arms hitting the top of the valves. This sounds a little like constant surf washing against pebbles on the beach. The second source of noise are the roller arms. This sounds like a 'scheeeeeee.' The third source is the timing chain; it's a whining noise. It actually varies, depending on the engine rpm and how tight the chain is. The sound becomes more high-pitched the tighter it is. On the other hand, you can sometimes hear the chain hit the timing case housing when it's too loose."

Larry went behind the wheel and started up the 330 GTC engine, then came back with a rubber hose and a long screwdriver.

"Either of these makes a great stethoscope," he said.

He put the rigid hose on different parts of the engine, with the other end to his ear. He smiled and motioned for me to listen also.

"The screwdriver works almost as well. Start in the upper section here on the valve cover. Then place the other end of the hose near your ear, like this. Here, try it! Do you hear? That's the adjusting screws hitting the valves. Then move the hose down to the center part of the valve cover. That's where the roller bearings on the rocker arms and the cam are. Now move it to the timing-chain cover. Hear the difference?"

"Yes. Beautiful," I replied. "It's like an orchestra. Here are the drums. There are the cellos. And over there are the horns!"

Larry went back behind the wheel, revved up the engine, and all the sounds came together in harmonious metallic tune. He leaned out and grinned.

"Some music, isn't it?"

# 275 GTB 4

# Heritage of a Yellow Shark

I have always been attracted to garages. Ever since my early childhood in Norway during World War II, when I was first introduced to the forbidden mystique of my grandfather's garage, I have felt that they played a vital part in my passion for cars. In the cold darkness of this childhood garage was stored a Model A Ford and a big black Buick. Behind the heavy doors, only to be opened during the night, lingered just the right blend of smells from rubber and gasoline. The few times I had been inside, it had always been against the expressed will of my grandfather, who feared that if it became known what he was hiding there, the Occupation forces would immediately confiscate his beloved treasures. He had not driven them since the first day of the Occupation.

Years later I would see more garages than I had ever dreamed of. One of the best was a garage in a sixteenth-century stone house in England. The floor was full of oil spots, all neatly covered with sawdust. There were tools and engine parts on the work benches. On the walls hung number plates from all the famous rallies in Europe. They had not been collected at swap meets — they were "the real thing." The owner had been a participant, sometimes capturing top honors, in both

*The 275 GTB was unquestionably one of the most exciting cars conceived by the Ferrari/Pininfarina team. The 1964 prototype is featured in the three photographs to the left. Notice that one side had a vent window, while the other lacked it. The picture above shows Pininfarina Senior with his beautiful creation. It also shows the original nose treatment, while the small photograph top right shows the frontal aspect of the new long nose introduced in the middle of the production run. With the appearance in 1966 of the four-cam engine, right, the 275 reached its climax. (Photographs by Pininfarina, courtesy the Hilary Raab Collection.)*

the Monte Carlo Rally and the Tour de France, as well as in the Alpine Rally and many others. This car itself, a 1938 BMW 328, had belonged to the owner ever since it was brand new. And it was still the proud centerpiece of the garage.

One of the most charming garages I have seen recently belongs to Bruce Meyer of Beverly Hills, California. His house is located on a palm-lined street only blocks away from where Howard Hughes garaged his Packard Caribbean.

Parked there among all sorts of memorabilia, such as a swordfish caught in Acapulco, a World War II civil defense helmet, a beat-up duck decoy, Bruce's old motorcycle boots, a Champion Spark Plug sign, an old American convention banner, and two antique chests from Rosa Roma's traveling vaudeville act, is a small but well-chosen collection of cars.

All the way in the back rests a brown Mercedes-Benz 300 S Coupe. In the middle row, awaiting its turn at the paint shop, sits a once-silver Mercedes-Benz 300 SL Gullwing; parallel to it is a two-tone green Packard Dual-Cowl Phaeton. Easily-accessible in the front row are the "drivers:" a dark-metallic-green 427 Cobra, and beside it, the car I had come to see and photograph — a fly-yellow Ferrari 275 GTB/4.

Its engine was turning lazily at 900 rpm.

The 275 GTB/4 is one of my personal favorites. It embodies the best of two worlds — the classic and the modern. Its new concepts do not remove it too far from the old Ferraris, and the 275 engine is closely-related to the basic 250 design. Only it is more powerful now, thanks to the enlarged bore and the four-cam setup. It produces a healthy 300 hp at 8000 rpm!

The suspension is finally independent all-around. The design copies the race-proven 250 LM. The weight distribution is also improved, thanks to the rear mounting of the gearbox, which has five speeds. The front-engined Ferrari sports car has reached its ultimate stage of chassis development!

The styling combines the best from the TDF and the GTO. It is a most harmonious and well-balanced translation of these two classic forms. The new style expresses a powerful agressiveness, even bolder than that of the cars that inspired it.

The GTB can be said to be the culmination of Pininfarina's classic themes as they were seen in both his racing cars and his production models. The beautiful plexiglas-covered headlights are there — first used in
*(continued on overleaf)*

ace car-inspired – in fact, looking much like a fattened GTO with an LM nose – the 275 GTB was another in a succession of formidable street Ferraris with close kinship to cars campaigned on the racing circuit. A specially-prepared version won its class at Le Mans in 1965. With the introduction in 1966 of the four-cam engine, the car, in this form designated 275 GTB4, turned an already-powerful machine into pure dynamite. The 1967 model pictured on these pages, belonging to Bruce Meyer of Beverly Hills, carries chassis number 10615. Lacking high-speed driving opportunities suitable for such a car, the owner often finds himself seeking out other excitement – such as the thrill of hearing the sounds of the vee-twelve reverberating between narrow tunnel walls.

the mid-fifties on the Testa Rossa and others, and later decorating many a TDF and the GTO. The berlinetta roofline is there — inspired by the TDF, the SWB and GTO. The vents behind the side window are there — reminiscent of those on the TDF. The air vents in the side panel are there — taken directly from the GTO. The rear spoiler is there — derived from sports racing cars of the early sixties, and forwarded to the GTB via the GTO and the Lusso. And the nose is there — inspiration supplied by both versions of the GTO as well as the LM. Quite a heritage!

The GTB was first introduced with a short nose. This style was probably more in keeping with the intended visual balance between front and rear end. It also facilitated a larger, more classic-looking grille. But the short nose was found to be incapable of holding down the front end of the car. It would "float" and "skate" at high speeds. The new, long nose took care of this problem. It also gave the new 275 GTB that much-appreciated, aggressive shark look.

Bruce backed the 275 GTB out of its space next to the Cobra. I jumped into the passenger seat, armed with camera and note pad. It was not quite like Dennis Jenkinson getting ready for riding in the Mille Miglia with Stirling Moss in his 300 SLR, but it was still exciting.

The cockpit was small and race-car-like. This feeling was amplified by the way the slanted side window came close to my head. The round shape of the hood and fenders in front of me were carried on inside by the curving ends of the dashboard as it followed the bottom contour of the sloping windshield. The dials and their arrangement were inspired by the classic Ferrari style, and the old Nardi steering wheel was still the crowning centerpiece, just as it had been on a long line of great road cars.

Bruce took it very easy to start with, keeping the load on the engine to a minimum as we slowly drove down Beverly Drive. There were a lot of noises coming from the suspension. It sounded like we had a load of logs. I knew they would go away as soon as everything had warmed up. The ride felt stiff and good. We turned left on Sunset, and Bruce let the machine work a little harder. As we turned left on Doheny Drive, I noticed that he was still keeping an eye on the oil temperature gauge.

"The first owner of this car was actually Bill Doheny. His family was one of the original landowners around here. I believe much of Beverly Hills is built on land that once belonged to them. It's very fitting that we give it a test right here on Doheny Drive, isn't it?"

Bruce gave it more throttle as we approached a long

left-hand curve. We swept through it at about 4500 in third gear. I felt the road-hugging qualities of the car as I was pressed against the side of the door. But I knew it would be impossible in surroundings like these to find out what the car was really good for. It was somehow very discouraging when yellow signs reading "Max speed 25 mph" kept flashing by every so often.

"This is Graystone, the old Doheny estate," Bruce told me. "The American Film Institute uses it now. Let's see if they'll let the car through!"

The guard peering out from the gatehouse didn't seem to recognize the yellow monster that suddenly appeared in his field of vision. He shook his head and we had to back out.

"What's the world coming to when an old member of the family isn't welcome anymore?" laughed Bruce.

We turned left on Summit Drive. The road was parallel to a white wall. The wall unexpectedly curved to the right, following the road as it turned. Bruce stepped on the accelerator on a sudden impulse. The curve kept turning sharper and sharper. There was no way of seeing how it would end, because the wall was always there, obscuring the view. Bruce kept going at 6200 in second gear. The roar was terrific as it bounced back from the white wall. The road just kept on turning, but Bruce didn't want to let up. I was pressed up against his shoulder, leaning heavily with the car. I had no way of steadying myself, since my hands were full of cameras and pens. The tires were screaming and the wall kept coming closer; I was sure we would crash into it any moment. As suddenly as he had begun, Bruce let up on the accelerator and stepped on the brake. We came to a halt with smoking tires, just a foot away from the wall.

"Jeees! That was close! Do you know what this wall is?" Bruce looked at me with a wild expression.

"I have no idea!"

"This is Pickfair! It belonged to Mary Pickford, the queen of the silent movies. The most famous landmark around here. Can you imagine ruining the wall of Pickfair? How embarrassing!"

He grinned mischievously, and I suspected he had done it all on purpose.

We went down Coldwater Canyon Drive, crossed Sunset, and returned safely to Bruce's house, where we parked the Ferrari and immediately switched to the Cobra. The day wasn't over yet! I had to compare the stunning kick of Maranello's fullblood with the lethal bite of Detroit's brute.

We went up the hill, surrounded by a deep thundering roar, and crossed Sunset again, but this time we decided to avoid the street with the white wall.

*The Ferrari sports car production has always been dominated by the Berlinetta theme. Consequently, the total output of true roadsters over the years has been quite small. One historian sets the figure at approximately 900. The 275 GTS/4, or NART Spyder, is an extreme example. This stunning beauty came about as a result of pressure from Ferrari's East Coast distributor, Luigi Chinetti. Regrettably, only ten cars were made. In these photographs by Stanley Rosenthal, the NART Spyder is tested for Road & Track by Ron Wakefield. Future editor-in-chief Tony Hogg is the passenger in the picture to the left. (Photographs courtesy Road & Track.)*

# 365 GTB 4 DAYTONA

# A Paperboy With Exotic Taste

It seems like some men are destined to own Ferraris. Is it determination or is it luck? Who knows? But somehow they always manage to keep at least one Ferrari around.

Steve Gilman is such a man.

Although still young, he has had his eyes or hands on more Ferraris these last few years than most fortunate enthusiasts will have in their lifetime.

It began in Florida when Steve was twelve. He can't remember when he first heard about Ferraris, or what occasion first sparked his interest, but he does recall how he fulfilled his dream.

"I woke up at five every morning and folded six hundred papers before I saw the sun. I was a paper boy with the largest territory in the entire Fort Lauderdale area. I made $300 a week. A week! That's a lot of money for a twelve-year-old."

We were sitting in the living room of his house, delicately attached to the steep hillside, high above Bel Air, California. Through the panoramic window, as wide as a cinema screen, I could see the entire San Fernando Valley, or as much of it as the haze permitted. Beyond the valley rose the blue silhouettes of the San Gabriel Mountains. It was an impressive view. But more provocative to me was the sight of Steve's red Daytona, decoratively parked in the driveway, just below the window.

"I put away money every week. I had one goal. I was determined to buy a Ferrari as soon as I could legally own a car. I was fourteen when I got my driver's license.

On my sixteenth birthday, I spent $7,500 on a used 250. It was red."

A naughty-boy smile lit up his face.

"The euphoria lasted a week. The Ferrari was too much of a temptation. This happened on one of the first evenings. I was showing off, I guess, going pretty fast. Too fast! Soon there were flashing red lights in my mirror. Instead of stopping I stepped on the gas. The combination of the Ferrari acceleration and my knowledge of the back-streets didn't leave the cops a chance. Remember, I was a paper boy, and this was my territory!"

The smile was replaced with a look of thoughtful disappointment as he continued.

"There weren't many fancy red sports cars in that part of town. Not with the kind of sound my Ferrari had. So it didn't take long before the police found out where I lived. My father sold it the next day . . . and he lost money on it too!

We were doing sixty on the Ventura Freeway. Steve was driving the Daytona. We were on our way to his company headquarters in Tarzana. He was just going to check on his messages before we continued north. We were going back into the mountains, where I had already found a location for photographing the Daytona.

I asked how he had come up with the idea for Style Auto, his line of automotive fashion products.

"My wife and I were relaxing in our room at the Plaza San Marco in Bergamo. It was late at night. Bergamo is an old resort in Northern Italy. It's a charming place that I'd like to go back to anytime. It's between Brescia and Milano — a good two hours from Ferrari.

"I was spending the day at Fiorano, Ferrari's test track in Maranello, watching the drivers set up the cars for a race. I forget which one. All I remember is that it was freezing cold all day. Then, late at night, the idea came to me like a flash! Why not make Ferrari sweaters! I got out a pen and paper and made some sketches, showed them to my wife and she liked them. Next day we went to a knitwear factory in Milano.

"We made the sweater green, the prancing horse red, and the Ferrari logo black. They came out beautifully! Later that week, we went to the Ferrari factory and gave some sweaters to Regazzoni and other team members. We gave some to Forgheri too. I've heard he passed one on to the old man himself. Don't know if that's true, but I like to think that he wears one of my sweaters when he's cold!

"That was the beginning. It was, of course, a long way
(continued on overleaf)

*The 365 GTB/4 was the last front-engined vee-twelve sports car from Ferrari (unless this classic configuration returns at some future date). The pictures on the left-hand page show, bottom, the sleek profile; middle, the original headlight arrangement retained on the European version; top, the covered headlight design for the U.S. market. This page, top, a near-final-version prototype is tested somewhere in Italy. Notice the wheel-travel indicators and the unfinished headlight arrangement. Above and right, Chris Amon drives the 365 GTB/4. (Photographs by Pininfarina and Pete Coltrin, courtesy the Hilary Raab Collection and Road & Track.)*

**D**escribed as a man's car, the 365 GTB4 may just be the ultimate in that category – at least if judged by the strength it takes to turn the wheel at low speeds. But this is deceiving, for the Daytona, so christened by enthusiasts after Ferrari's many victories in that race, only shows its true heritage – that of a race car – at very high speeds. If a woman can master the Daytona under these conditions, then it is a woman's car as well. The Daytona is in fact, more than any other production Ferrari, a driver's car. This 1972 model, chassis number 15175, photographed here high in the Santa Monica Mountains, belongs to Style Auto founder Steve Gilman of Tarzana, California.

from those first sweaters to full-fledged marketing, but the sweaters were the starting point. We then went into other items, like tote bags, driving jackets, hats and so on. But the sweaters were the beginning. There at the hotel room in Bergamo!"

We took off on Reseda and continued up to Oxnard. I asked Steve what he was doing in Bergamo besides coming up with bright ideas.

"This was on the tail end of the good old days when you could still buy inexpensive Ferraris in Europe. We found so many cars, I can hardly begin to recall them all. The rich Italians were afraid of driving them, you know. They had a sensitive political climate with terrorism and so on. It was best not to stand out from the crowd.

"We found one of the first Ferraris made. I think it was number 0012 and may have been driven in the Mille Miglia. The car was for sale. This contradicts what I just said about the situation in Italy, because the car was in Argentina. But the deal had to be made in Bergamo. The money was to be wired through Bolivia somehow — I can't remember all the details.

"We also bought a Bertone showcar made for Agnelli, the Fiat chief. And we bought a Testa Rossa. The most beautiful of them all, at least I thought, was the Neri and Bonacini Coupe. It's featured in the Fitzgerald/Merrit/Thompson Ferrari book. All of these cars were brought to the States where we found buyers for them. It was nice because we always had a lot of Ferraris around!"

We parked the Daytona and walked through the showroom. Gray walls and mirrors made an elegant setting for the Style Auto wares. Steve wasn't quite finished with his story. He sank down behind the desk in his office and continued.

"I think the most fascinating place I saw was an old stable at an ancient castle. It seemed like every stall was occupied by an old Ferrari. Imagine the frame of a 1950 car, just sitting there on the floor, covered with hay and dust. And get this! There was an old speed boat with a Ferrari engine!"

He was suddenly quiet, bending over a stack of red message notes. His mind was definitely on a different track now. He didn't even look up.

"I have too much to do here. Why don't you take the Daytona on your own and keep it all afternoon?"

I was surprised at myself. I had to control my reaction. After a pause I answered casually.

"Sure, Steve. That'll be fine."

The canvas-ripping came very easily, just by touching the accelerator. But the clutch was very hard and the steering was extremely heavy. I was trying to move out

of the parking space. Even if I didn't wear out the clutch, I knew my arms would be shot by the time I got the car moving. And where was the hood? It looked so long from the outside. Now I couldn't even see it.

But these negative characteristics disappeared as soon as I got on the freeway. I found that it doesn't matter if you can't see the hood when you know there is something that powerful under it.

I turned off on Topanga Canyon Road and onto Mulholland, going south. I was still driving in a proper, relaxed way, listening to the harmonious tune of the engine at 3500 rpm. To this day, I still don't know what come over me at the moment I discovered I had left the populated area.

I braked, shifted down to second and put my weight on the accelerator. The rocket took off! I let it wind up to 7000 rpm, then whipped the stick down to third. I can still recall the sound of the lever hitting metal at the end of the slot in the shifting gate. I was doing ninety in third.

Then I did the same thing over again. And again. I must be going crazy, I thought to myself. I had gotten nine tickets during the two years I owned an E-Type; they finally took my license away. And my insurance rates went sky-high. Now I had been clean for three years. Was I prepared to risk it all?

Things got somewhat calmer as the road began curving and climbing like in the Swiss Alps. Now I discovered a new game. I could utilize the enormous power of the car and the excellent weight distribution to whip it around the 360-degree corners. All I had to do was to give the car the right direction going into the curve, then control it with my foot going through it, letting the back end hang out.

For the photographs, I had chosen a spot at the top of the mountain, where the road curved around a cliff, overlooking a rocky moon-landscape. The mountain was rapidly turning violet in the setting sun; I had spent too much time driving. Now it was almost too late to take the pictures. I had to work very quickly. I looked in the view finder and saw the car where I had parked it in the middle of the curve. But there was something missing. I ran back to the car and turned on the headlights. They came up like the sleepy eyes of a giant monster from another world, and I immediately knew that was the look I wanted.

Afterward, when I drove my everyday transportation again, a Volkswagen Jeep, I had proof that the Daytona was from a different world — worlds apart from my Jeep. I found myself wondering what had happened to it. Why wasn't it moving?

*The 365 GTB/4 was a ferocious competitor in long distance events. The photographs on these pages capture the Daytona in racing disguise on its major arenas — Le Mans and Daytona. Top left, Bell/Pillette took eighth place overall at Le Mans in 1972. Pictured left, Chinetti/Migault in car 38 and Posey/Minter in car 6, keep each other company during the 1973 Le Mans. Right, a NART-entered car during the 1974 Le Mans. Above, Paul Newman behind the wheel of Clint Eastwood's car in the 1977 Daytona race (Photos courtesy Road & Track).*

SPYDER

# First and Last of a Breed

Greg Garrison watched with satisfaction as his daughter Pat worked with the young stallion. There's no doubt, he thought to himself, that this horse has all the distinctive features of a pure Andalusian. Look at the eyes; see how intelligent and fearless he is. Look at the way he carries his head and the way he moves — like a nobleman from Spain.

The Andalusian still had the gray shading of a young animal; later, he may turn light silver dapple, or maybe he would become pure white, like his father. Legionario! Grand Champion of Spain! You have a good-looking son!

It was early morning. The sun had only moments ago appeared over the crest of the hills. Its warming rays would soon dry the dew in the fields of Hidden Valley, a horse-breeder's haven. In spite of its back-country atmosphere, it was less than an hour from the metropolis of Los Angeles.

Garrison, a veteran television producer and director, sipped his first cup of morning coffee while leaning against the white fence encircling the training rink. The air was still cool, but he could feel that the morning would turn into another warm day. The winter of 1972 has been mild so far, even for California, Garrison thought to himself, and the pleasant weather sure has continued into 1973, but we could use some rain soon.

Garrison walked over to the patio in front of the ranch house that was shaded by oak trees of the same size

and shape as those dotting the rest of the valley. The trees grew closer together down by the creek, where he kept the mares. The stallions were inside the stable. He sat down in a shaded chair, turned it so he could observe the entire rink, and took a sip of the coffee. He enjoyed the taste of the coffee and he enjoyed the freshness of the early-morning air and he enjoyed watching his daughter as she worked with the horse.

I have been very lucky, he thought to himself, but I have worked hard to make it happen. During those early years at Northwestern University, right after the war, I was already busy shaping my career. I wrote jokes for comedians then. Afterward I became involved with the drama school and after that came the years as an assistant stage manager on Broadway. One thing led to another. Broadway led to Hollywood. Hollywood led to the long and fruitful friendship with Dean Martin, which led to the production of the Dean Martin Shows, the specials with Frank Sinatra and many other television projects. Yes, I have been lucky! I have enjoyed it all and what's more, it has given me the means to pursue my other interests — purebred horses and purebred sports cars.

He looked across the rink, focusing on a sign of a prancing white horse attached to the wall of the stable. If you are a connoisseur of horses, you know that's the symbol of the Andalusians, he thought to himself, but you have to be a connoisseur of sports cars as well to know that the same prancing horse, in black, also decorates the Ferraris.

Garrison has owned a long string of sports cars. Among the British cars, he favored Aston-Martin; he has owned the DB 4, the DB 5, and the DB 6 models. Of the German cars, he was partial to Mercedes-Benz and BMW. He has owned a Gullwing, a 503, two 507s and many others. Of course, he has not escaped the attraction of the most distinctive and exotic of them all — Italy's Ferraris. He didn't own any Ferraris until the early sixties, when he had a Pininfarina Coupe, a Cabriolet, a 250 GTE 2 + 2 and a Superamerica. He purchased all of them as used cars. The new Ferraris came later. Now, in 1973, he had quite a collection of them.

He had known the people at the Ferrari factory since the mid-fifties — since the year he toured Europe with Esther Williams and the Aqua Spectacles. He produced shows in London, Paris, Rome and Milan. It was during this stay that he accepted an invitation to visit the Ferrari factory. He met Enzo Ferrari and Amerigo Manicardi, who was very important to his future dealings with the

(continued on overleaf)

*First shown in 1969, the 365 GTS/4, or Daytona Spyder, was the last true Ferrari convertible. The yellow prototype is captured top left and right on its stand at the Frankfurt Show. In the 1972 photograph to the left, the Spyder shows off its top-up rear quarter view. Although extremely exciting to look at, the Spyder's true character is only fully revealed at speed; the combination of performance, handling, styling, and open-air charm makes it the ultimate drive for the road. To the right, the interior of a Daytona, with its compact cluster of gauges and uniquely-styled seats. (Photographs by Pininfarina and Geoffrey Goddard, courtesy the Hilary Raab Collection and Road & Track.)*

**E**nd of an era! This is Ferrari's last true roadster, Ferrari's last front-engined sports car, Ferrari's last Daytona Spyder. Period. Pictured on these pages, chassis number 17073, delivered in 1974, is actually the last off the line. It belongs to Greg Garrison of Westwood, California, and has been driven less than 400 miles. It is a brand new car – and the owner plans to keep it that way. The styling of the Daytona was both classic and modernistic – a mix of stunning effect. Breathtakingly beautiful from any angle, the flowing simplicity of the enormous hood, the impossible rake of the windshield, the surprise angle of the cut-off rear – it all worked together as a coordinated whole.

Factory. Manicardi was Ferrari's man in charge of sales. They kept in touch over the years, and saw each other as often as possible. Garrison speaks of Manicardi, who has mastered seven languages, as his personal friend and one of the few Europeans he has met who understands and appreciates the American sense of humor.

In 1957, it was time for another visit to the factory. At that time, while he and Manicardi were talking in the courtyard, Pinin Farina happened to walk by, and Manicardi introduced him. Garrison commented on the Nashes that Farina had designed for the American market. Farina turned to Manicardi and told him in Italian that this American seemed to be quite a car enthusiast and that he really should own a Ferrari. Garrison was brought around a corner and there sat the prototype of the new Spyder. It had not yet been shown publicly. Garrison thought it was a most beautiful car, and soon afterward he regretted not having bought it. Many years later, he found the same car in Los Angeles; it is now a part of his Ferrari stable.

Garrison often met Enzo Ferrari during his frequent visits to the Factory, but it was always in passing. He was impressed by the proud posture, the firm handshake and the unyielding eyes. The word aloof is often used by others to describe Ferrari, but on one occasion, when Garrison was accompanied to the Factory by his young son Mike, he saw a different side of the man. Garrison noticed that Ferrari kept his eyes on Mike during the whole conversation. Almost ten years earlier, Ferrari had lost his only son to an incurable disease. The father's grief and the effect it still had on his daily life was well-known to the people around him, but it wasn't until later in the evening that Garrison understood the connection between Ferrari's interest in Mike and the memory of his own son Dino. After dinner, when they had already retired to their room at the Hotel Real-Fini, a large package was delivered, addressed to Mike. It was unwrapped and found to contain a collection of scale-model Ferrari race cars. A personal note expressed the sincere compliments of Enzo Ferrari.

Garrison purchased his first new Ferrari in 1966. He went to the Geneva Salon that year and was so taken by the new 330 GTC on the stand that he told Manicardi that he wanted that car! He didn't get the prototype, however, but he did get the first one off the production line.

Again, in 1968, as soon as Garrison heard of a new model being shown in Paris, he called Manicardi and told him that he was interested in the new four-cam car. A few days later, Manicardi called back and reported that he had spoken to Mister Ferrari about the matter,

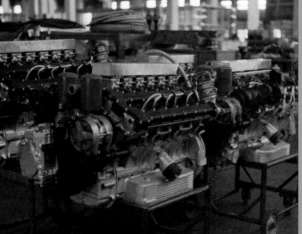

*Pictured above, the Daytona engine compartment, and to the left, Daytona engines at the Factory. To the right, bottom, a one-off experiment from Pininfarina. The Targa top over-complicated the clean look of the Daytona. The remaining pictures on the right-hand page feature the 365 California, a Superfast-inspired four-seat convertible shown at the 1966 Geneva Salon and available on a limited-production basis during 1967. It had the single-overhead-cam engine and a rigid rear axle. The clean styling was marred by pop-up high beams, over-developed taillight treatment, and an out-of-place two-tone interior. (Photographs by Pininfarina and Pete Coltrin, courtesy the Hilary Raab Collection and Road & Track.)*

and that Mister Ferrari wanted Greg to have a very special car — the prototype Daytona. This car was also on display in Geneva and London as well as in Los Angeles. Afterward, it was flown back to Italy, where Scaglietti replaced the interior and Ferrari mounted an engine, since the show car had only a mock-up engine under the hood.

Later, Garrison would own four Daytona Coupes in succession. Because of an old football injury to his arm, the Daytona, with its heavy steering, was a difficult car to drive in the Los Angeles traffic. But every time he sold one of those Daytona Coupes, he immediately regretted it and ordered a new replacement.

There was coffee left at the bottom of the mug, but it was cold now, and he had just decided to go inside for a refill when the telephone rang. He heard it through the open window and answered it on the fifth ring, wondering who would call so early.

"Good morning!"

Garrison immediately recognized the voice. Manicardi was calling from Italy. It was late there.

"Good afternoon, my friend! What's up?"

"I have an offer you can't refuse. We have five Daytona chassis left. I have talked to Ingegniere Ferrari, and we have decided what to do with them. Four cars will go to our Swiss distributor and we thought you might want the fifth!"

"I don't think so, Amerigo! I already have a Daytona!"

"These are all going to be Spyders, Greg! The Swiss distributor said he wouldn't sell theirs for five years."

There was a pause, then Garrison replied.

"Okay, Amerigo! Let me have the last one! I won't sell it, and I won't drive it for ten years! How's that?"

"I'm happy!"

"Okay! Have it painted in the special Pininfarina color, Oro Chiaro. And let me know when it's ready. I want to pick it up myself."

The Spyder will fit perfectly into my collection, Garrison smiled as he replaced the receiver. I already have the first production convertible; now I will also have the last. He walked over to the stable. I better ride Legionario now before it gets too hot. Then I'll take the Daytona into Hollywood.

His daughter was just returning Legionario's son to the stable.

"He really is a distinctive Andalusian, Pat!"

"He is beautiful, Dad!"

Yes, Greg Garrison thought to himself, he has those distinctive features that make him stand out. Just like the prancing horse on the grille of a Ferrari.

365 GTC 4

# A Ferrari Brotherhood

We drive rapidly down Victoria Avenue, the grand old tree-lined esplanade cutting straight through Riverside's valley floor. Orange trees laden with ripening fruit surround us. Long ago, the area between the two lanes was set aside as an equestrian trail. I can visualize the wealthy landowners in their turn-of-the-century outfits, complete with wide-brimmed Panama hats and long cigars, parading on their purebred horses early in the mornings. Somewhere along the way, needless to say in the name of progress, the riding path was replaced by a double row of power poles. And today, in a further erosion of nostalgia, the orange groves are being cut down to make room for mushrooming housing developments.

But Victoria Avenue still has charm and beauty. Majestic crowned palms and gigantic eucalyptus, with branches meeting across the lanes, form long and cool tunnels. The silver-blue Ferrari 365 GTC/4 runs effortlessly through the shadows like a sleek, modern-day horse.

I'm accompanying the Rouhe brothers to Lake Mathews. We plan to do some serious driving on the network of roads surrounding it. It's a hot afternoon. The speed-wind flows soothingly through the open windows. We could have used the air conditioning, but that would have closed out the sound from the four exhaust pipes, and we definitely want to hear that purebred vee-twelve noise. The engine revs at just the right speed, and for some reason I find the exhaust note particularly satisfying around 4200 rpm, in third gear.

"This is a long way from Africa!" Ed says suddenly.

*The styling of the 365 GTC/4 was, in some ways, uncharacteristic of Ferrari; in other ways, it tied in well with the theme of the period. The kinship with the Daytona is obvious in the styling of the long, sloping hood and its air vent arrangement. The hard-rubber bumper was a new approach, but a remnant of the classic Ferrari grille was still there. The interior was very well-appointed, in keeping with the general luxury appeal of the car. A total redesign of the dash layout had taken place, and an attractively-equipped console covered the gearbox, which had now been moved up to make room for small rear seats. (Photographs by Pininfarina, courtesy the Hilary Raab Collection.)*

He is behind the wheel. Richard sits in the passenger seat. I occupy the two small back seats. My six-foot-one body is squeezed in diagonally, equally distributed between the two seats. I had insisted on trying them for myself. In a fold-down position they make an adequate space for luggage, but as seats they are definitely only for children.

"Yes, this is certainly far from Africa!" Richard repeats. "Thirty-five years and eight thousand miles away. Who would have guessed when we were kids and drove that home-built go-cart in the middle of the African jungle that we would end up in Riverside collecting Ferraris?"

"That go-cart was the most primitive vehicle since the invention of the automobile," Ed recalls. "We wrote to friends in the States and asked them to ship us a lawnmower engine. They sent us a Briggs & Stratton. I think it came off a surplus Army generator. Everything else on that go-cart was made out of wood. It had a wooden frame, wooden wheels and a wooden steering wheel. Everything was wooden!"

"Remember that dusty road we drove it on?" Ed asks Richard.

"Yes, we filled the carburetor with gas and went as far as we could on that dirt road. The natives were running alongside, frightened but intrigued. When we ran out of gas, they helped us push the go-cart back for refueling. Then we took off again!"

"Where was this?" I asked.

"In the Belgian Congo — it's called Zaire now — at the Songa Mission," Ed answers. "Our parents were missionaries there. The nearest town was four hundred miles away!"

"A very unusual place for developing an interest in cars!" I say. "What kind of vehicles did they drive there in the Belgian Congo? Land Rovers?"

"No, I never saw any Land Rovers. I recall only American cars," Richard answers. "I remember a gray forty-seven Pontiac that we had there at the Mission."

"I remember one time when the entire family went to Cape Town in South Africa," Ed continues. "We had to pick up two new cars there. One of them was a Plymouth and the other was a Chevrolet; they were forty-eights. We boys helped drive them back. It was a three-thousand-mile trip!"

"We were crazy about collecting brochures!" Richard remembers. "We had our friends in the States send them to us. And we cut out pictures from magazines that we got. They were usually half-a-year old by the time they reached the Congo, but we were still able to keep up with the new models."

*(continued on overleaf)*

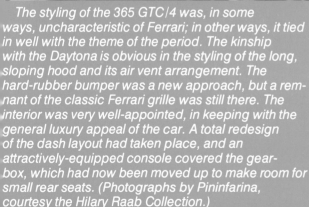

Civilized is the word used to characterize the 365 GTC4. And civilized it is – from the soft leather seats and the effective air conditioning to the power-assisted brakes. But don't be mislead by such amenities. Under the hood hides a very powerful four-cam vee-twelve. It takes two rows of three twin-throat carburetors to feed the 330 horses. The 365 GTC4 is a worthy, often underestimated, touring companion to the Daytona. This 1972 model, chassis number 15653, was photographed among ripening citrus trees and tall palms in Riverside, California. The silver-blue beauty belongs to the Rouhe brothers, Ed and Richard, both experienced Ferrari enthusiasts with a stable to choose from.

We're on the freeway now. Ed lets the Ferrari run free. "I only drive the Ferraris when I know I can go at least 100 mph," he says. "When I'm past eighty, I begin to feel what a Ferrari is all about. 'Aha!' I say to myself, 'this is what a Ferrari was made for!'"

We turn off the freeway now and continue on a two-lane road. I soon see the lake on my left. Ed is quiet while he negotiates a long left-hand curve.

"So, there you are in Africa, driving and getting excited about American family sedans!" I say. "What about sports cars in general, and Ferraris in particular? When did you first become involved with them?"

"Well, we didn't know about them until we got back to the States and started reading Road & Track," Richard responds. Ed is still busy with that long curve. A sharp right-hander comes up ahead.

"I drove my father's MGA to begin with," Richard continued. "Then, I bought an Austin-Healey and later, a Jaguar E-Type. The first Ferrari was a 275 GTB/4. Ed talked me into it; he got one also. They were both red. Then came five 365 GT 2+2s and a Daytona Spyder. All we have right now is this 365 GTC/4, a 308 GTB, and two Daytona Coupes."

"And you own them together?"

"Yes, we started out together as car enthusiasts in Africa; we might as well continue to share that interest. Besides, we're both Ferrari men. We like the same kind of car!"

The road divides in two. Ed goes left. He stops the car after a few hundred yards on the narrower road. I see it continue curving up a hill ahead of us.

"Now it's your turn to drive," he says to me. "I'll sit in the back for awhile!"

I crawl out from behind the passenger seat and stretch my legs while walking around the Ferrari. The styling of the 365 GTC/4 is a curious combination of soft lines and sharp edges. From the rear, for instance, it looks quite square. If you see it from the front and side, on the other hand, it looks rounder. The curving line that starts low at the nose and arches over the front wheel, sinks as it passes the cockpit, then makes another arch over the rear wheels before it sinks again, is mainly responsible for this appearance. The styling of the front bumper also adds to the impression.

"The car is really very beautiful!" I say to Ed as we meet behind it en route to our respective new seats.

"Yes, it is!" Ed says. "There's no question that it was overshadowed by the Daytona while they were both in production. Only now is the GTC/4 beginning to become widely-appreciated."

Ed squeezes into the rear seats. I make myself com-

*The photographs on this page show the 365 GT 2+2, introduced at the Paris Salon in 1967. Produced between 1968 and 1970, it was the most advanced four-seat Ferrari so far, featuring independent rear suspension, ventilated disc brakes, power steering and power windows, as well as air conditioning. In spite of its weight, it could move four persons at a top speed of 152 mph! Pictured on the right-hand page, the latest of the 2+2 Ferraris, the 400 Automatic – a further development of the 365 GT/4 2+2 first seen at the Paris Salon in 1972. (Photographs by de la Rive Box and Pininfarina, courtesy the Hilary Raab Collection and Ferrari S.p.A.)*

fortable behind the leather-covered steering wheel and adjust the seat until I'm sitting the proper distance from the wheel.

The dash, compared with the Daytona's, is totally different. It was designed very tastefully. It's covered with the same dark gray, cloth-like material used in the Daytona. After a few years in the California sun it tends to fade, but in this car it's still perfect.

A rather bulky but attractive console rests on top of the gearbox, which has been moved forward to make room for the back seats. It could more fittingly be called a comfort console; the switches and buttons all have to do with the air conditioning, the radio, the heat and cold air ventilation, the power windows and the front and rear window defrosters. There are even individual fans for each side of the cockpit.

The centerpiece of the console is the gear-shift lever. It's not gated, as it is on the Daytona, and the layout is also different; on the GTC/4, first gear is located forward, which is the position for reverse on the Daytona.

I give it throttle and let go of the clutch. It's the typical Ferrari clutch. You have to be assertive and let it up in one decisive movement, or else you'll be taking off in embarassment. The wheel feels a little too light for my taste, owing to the power assist. I shift to second. Then I make a mistake that has to do with the lack of gate, but mostly with my lack of experience with the car: I go directly from second to fifth! That's a true let-down. It's a painful anticlimax to the normally very-satisfying acceleration process. I slow down and do it over again, getting it right this time. All four of them! It feels very good.

The GTC/4 is smooth and responsive, not as brutally-powerful as the Daytona, but quite adequate. I move up into the curvy and hilly part of the road now. I shift down to second. A particularly inviting turn is coming up. I give the car full throttle in the middle of the corner, and *swish!* The back end spins out! No problem. I just let up a little on the gas and the car takes care of it; I'm back on the track as quickly as I got off it.

"Did that scare you?" I say, and glance over my shoulder with a smoothing-over smile. At that moment I see something red out of the corner of my eye.

"No — not at all! It's hard to do anything wrong with this car," Ed says while struggling to regain his balance in the back seats.

I look in the rear-view mirror. I can't believe my eyes. There's a bright-red Lamborghini Miura right on my tail. It wants to pass. I make room, and it shoots past me in a way that makes me look like a Sunday driver.

"That's our kid brother," Richards says. "He's a Lamborghini man!"

# 246 GTS DINO

# The Dino Legacy

The age of eleven could very well be the magical time for a young man's introduction to the world of motoring. It was at this age that Enzo Ferrari for the first time went on his own to watch the 1909-vintage race cars duel on the highway outside Modena. Together with other similar occurrences, this experience led Ferrari to a career which, in the history of racing, will never be surpassed.

The eleventh-year experience of Bart McGrath, however, having had no effect yet on the course of history, would seem too insignificant to mention were it not for the fact that the retelling of such events serves as nostalgic reminders to all enthusiasts.

Bart grew up in Dartford, an industrial suburb south of London. The family lived a quiet life. They rarely deviated from their established routines, and couldn't afford to spend money on extravagant pleasures. Young Bart could have stayed locked into the same environment had it not been for Mister Bishop, the next-door neighbor.

Mister Bishop was an eccentric and an adventurer. He had been a pilot during the war. Now, when it was over, he found that nothing could match his death-defying experiences in the sky. In 1949, in an effort to recapture some of the excitement lacking in his life, he acquired a 1934 Bullnose Morris.

The car needed extensive work, and Mister Bishop spent all his spare time on the project, sometimes working late into the night. Young Bart assisted in any way he could, but he generally had to go to bed very early. Worried about how Mister Bishop was managing without his help and company, Bart usually never fell asleep until the voice of Mister Bishop's wife shattered the quiet night, demanding that her husband come to bed at once,

*Pictured on this page, the 1966 365 P, a Paris show car and one of several experimentals carrying the pre-Dino look. The 330 P3, at the top of the right-hand page, was typical of the mid-engined sports racers of the era, which provided the basic inspiration for the Dino shape. To the right, a portrait of Ferrari's only son, Dino, as it still hangs on the wall in Ferrari's private Maranello office. To the far right, middle, the rear-window treatment, reminiscent of the Dinos, of a one-off show car. Bottom, far right, a coupe forerunner to the Fiat Dino Spyder, which was also powered by the Dino engine. (Photographs by Pininfarina, courtesy the Hilary Raab Collection. Dino portrait by Gunther Molter, courtesy Road & Track.)*

or else!

One day, the Bullnose was ready to drive. Mister Bishop asked Bart if he would like to come along on the maiden voyage. He was planning a trip to the Daily Express Trophy Race at Silverstone. Bart had seldom been beyond Dartford, let alone seen an international race; he accepted at once, but his parents were very concerned. Are you going in that old car? For sure it will break down! In the end, however, seeing the enthusiasm of the boy, they let him go.

After a trouble-free drive, during which Bart was indoctrinated with talk about British racing heroes, they arrived just in time for the beginning of the race.

Bart was excited as never before. His eyes darted from one point of action to another, then came to rest on the sleek, open-wheeled race cars as they lined up for the start. His level of excitement rose even higher as soon as the race got under way. He was immediately disappointed, however, when a red car took the lead over the green ones and held the position with ease.

Every time this car came shooting toward the end of the straightaway and rounded the corner in a perfectly-controlled four-wheel slide, Bart focused on the driver, who was clearly visible in the low-cut cockpit. The thin fabric helmet and the aviator goggles made him look like the heroes Bart had seen only in photographs. He wore a sleeveless shirt, and Bart noticed the play of the muscles in his tanned arms and the firm grip of his gloved hands on the steering wheel as he forcibly kept the car on its course.

The nose of the car was flat and covered by an egg-crate grille. It had two rows of louvers on each side of the spool-shaped body. The long exhaust pipes came out from below the engine and ran along the bottom of the body, ending behind the rear wheels. The car was attractive in a no-nonsense way, but in Bart's opinion, the sound was the best part. He listened with fascination to its distinctive roar as the car accelerated up the straightaway in front of the bleachers. With every lap his initial resentment gradually turned into admiration.

Mister Bishop told him that this was a new Italian make called a Ferrari. The cars had already won several races on the Continent. It was Alberto Ascari, their top driver, who again drove it to victory! The car had a super-charged engine with twelve cylinders in vee-formation, Mister Bishop told Bart, who did not understand the terminology, but understood that the car had to be supreme in order to have beaten the British. So it was that, at the magical age of eleven, Bart first heard the two names he would forever keep in his memory —

*(continued on overleaf)*

S treet legal? By the mid-sixties, the cars competing in international sports car racing had taken on shapes that looked less and less like the cars available for street use. Consequently, when the Dino was introduced in 1967, first in the form of the 206 GT, it came as a stunning surprise. Enthusiasts wondered if it was really intended for the road. The Dino, named after Ferrari's son, looked just like a race car; it had a mid-mounted racing-proven vee-six and superb handling to match that incredibly low, aerodynamically-effective styling. It was indeed a Ferrari for the road, and Bart McGrath of Huntington Beach, California, owner of the featured 1974 246 Spyder, chassis number 07470, didn't wait long to make up his mind. He wanted one – or two, rather! He now owns one Coupe and one Spyder – a great idea when you can't decide which one is the most attractive.

Ferrari and Ascari.

Alberto Ascari captured the World Championship in 1952 and again in 1953, both times in Ferraris. Two years later he was dead, the victim of a freak accident at Monza. He had borrowed Castelotti's Ferrari for a few practice laps. Driving without a helmet, he died instantly when the car, for reasons never established, overturned in a long left-hand curve. Ascari had driven for Ferrari as early as 1940, and although he was not on the team at the time of his fatal accident, his death was a terrible blow to Ferrari. But the tragedy would not come alone!

Ferrari had become a father relatively late in life. His only son, Dino, was his pride and joy. Dino had inherited the passion for cars and racing, and his father groomed him for an active part in the business. But Dino, who had long suffered from poor health, fell victim to an incurable kidney disease. He died on June 30, 1956, just over a year after the death of Ascari.

Dino, however, left a legacy. Before his death, even at his bedside, father and son had worked together with Vittorio Jano on plans for a new engine. Following Dino's suggestion, a vee-six configuration had been chosen. After Dino's death, Ferrari announced that the engine would carry Dino's name.

This engine was first planned for the new Formula Two class introduced in 1957, but the original 1489 cc displacement was soon enlarged to 2417 cc. In this form it became the power source of a new Formula One car, the 246 Dino. Mike Hawthorn captured the 1958 World Championship in this car.

After two unsuccessful seasons, the engine was placed amidships in a new car for 1961. It carried Phil Hill to a World Championship. After a disastrous 1962 season, which saw the demise of the vee-six Dino as a Formula One engine, it made a comeback in 1965, now used solely for sports-car racing, and it won the European Hill-Climb Championship Series twice. The 206 S was, with its mid-engine configuration and its distinctive styling, the direct inspiration for the soon-to-follow production version.

The new regulations for the 1967 Formula Two class required that the engine used be produced in no less than 500 examples. This was an impossible task for Ferrari; he turned to Fiat for help. The design was a Rocci-developed version of the original vee-six. The light-alloy components were produced by Fiat, but assembled by Ferrari. The new engine saw use in Ferrari's 206 SP sports racer, and appeared in two Fiat sports cars introduced in 1967.

Pininfarina had in 1965 already displayed a styling

exercise based on the Dino. Ferrari now assigned the final design work for the production car to the Turin firm. The 206 GT, first shown in 1966, had the engine mounted parallel to the length of the car. The light-alloy-bodied production version 206 GT was introduced in 1967. The engine had been turned to a transverse position.

The final version, the steel-bodied 246 GT, became available in 1969. Only minor styling details set it apart from the 206 GT, but mechanically there were important differences. It still had the same four-cam engine, but it had been enlarged. The block was now made from cast iron, and the transmission arrangement had been changed.

The 246 GT became the first "low-priced," "mass-produced" Ferrari. Its exotic styling and mechanical sophistication, combined with superb handling and excellent performance, made it a worthy monument to the memory of Ferrari's son.

I drove Bart McGrath's yellow 246 Dino Spyder southbound on the Pacific Coast Highway. The sun had long ago disappeared into the ocean. When it had become too dark to take any more pictures, Bart and I had gathered up the polishing rags and the film wrappers, and we were now on our way from the shooting location in the Santa Monica Mountains back to Huntington Beach, where Bart lives nowadays, far from his native England.

The 246 felt marvelously stable and massive. Its go-cart-quick steering wheel and spine-thrilling accelerator made it a pure pleasure to drive. Equally enjoyable was the view from the tightly-hugging driver's seat. I glanced at the illuminated gauges, neatly organized within an ellipse of brushed aluminum. In front of the wide, curving windshield, I noticed only a hint of the hood, but the ballooning fenders were adequate compensation They made me feel like I was driving the original Ferrari 206 racer!

We had removed the roof panel, and as I accelerated, I felt the cool, salt-smelling ocean air tugging at my hair. It was the perfect medicine after a day in the burning California sun. Bart, for once demoted to the passenger seat, turned to me with a big satisfied grin on his face.

"Any doubts about this being a Ferrari?"

"The heritage is there, the look and feel are there, but the name badge is missing!"

"That's the way it was planned. The small Dino is the offspring of the big Ferrari. A son is the offspring of his father, but he still has his own identity. Sentimental, but that's the way Enzo wanted it!"

*All the sensuous beauty of Pininfarina's styling, translated into steel by Scaglietti, decorates these pages. To the right, bottom, the 206 GT, the first production version introduced at the 1967 Turin Show. This model was not available on the U.S. market. To the left, bottom, the 246 GT, introduced in 1969. Although it was built on a 40-mm longer wheelbase in addition to many other technical changes, its exterior was distinguishable from its predecessor only by minor details. The Spyder version, with removable roof panel, followed in 1972. (Photographs by Pininfarina, courtesy the Hilary Raab Collection and Ferrari S.p.A.)*

# BB 512 BOXER

# A Boxer In The Wild

I stand in the middle of a narrow road, somewhere east of Kiowa, southeast of Denver. I hold my heavy camera with both hands. I look down at a point in front of my feet, focus on the yellow divider line, and follow it with my eyes as it stretches along the center of the arrow-straight road. I follow it until it becomes too faint to separate it from the gray asphalt surface, when I instead follow the road itself, until it also becomes too faint.

I'm waiting for the red Boxer to return. I have already photographed it from behind. Now I want to shoot the front view. The road was too narrow for the Boxer's turning radius, so John made a run down to a crossroad three miles ahead.

Besides the gray of the road and the yellow of the divider line, there's only the endless green of the surrounding prairie, the even-greater vastness of the blue sky, and the almost-transparent white of the clouds. They sail slowly in a northeasterly direction. The warm wind blows the same way, producing the only sound and movement in the quiet stillness as it shakes and shifts the tall grass. The road is the only man-made element in sight, until suddenly a red object appears on the horizon. I watch it grow.

The red Boxer belongs to John Dekker, thirty-six years old, nightclub owner, big-game hunter and race

driver. He drove cars when he was fourteen, built "street-rods" when he was sixteen, and raced "funny cars" professionally for eight years, four times becoming Division-Five Champion of the National Hot Rod Association.

During his active "hot-rod" racing career he piloted cars that accelerated from zero to 240 miles per hour in less than seven seconds. Lately, in an effort to recapture some of that thrill, he has again taken up racing, now driving a new Lola T 540 in Formula Ford.

When he wasn't racing, he was selling cars with the same success. One year, he became the leading new-car salesman in a region covering eleven states. Step by step, he invested his earnings in a business with a great potential; he also got himself a Ferrari 308 GTS, and took up big-game hunting in Africa and South America, always looking for excitement and new fields of challenge.

The red object becomes larger and larger. It looks like a scene in a movie, shot with a telephoto lens. The car bounces with the changing elevation of the road. I measure the light and check the setting; sixteen and a sixtieth. I can now vaguely hear the sound of the Boxer engine above the wind.

Last January, John decided to sell the 308. It wasn't that he didn't like it; in fact, he enjoyed this Ferrari so much that he wanted to take the step up to the ultimate Ferrari — the Boxer. He made his plans for the purchase, as always, with great care. He visited several of the shops which specialize in legalizing exotic cars. He compared prices and quality of workmanship. He wanted to be able to follow the work process and make sure that it all conformed to his standards.

*Ferrari's super-car, the mid-engined Boxer, was first displayed at the 1971 Turin Show. The production version of the 365 GT/BB became available in 1973. The unique picture at the top of the left-hand page shows an early scale model. Compare this with the final shape of the prototype photographed on Pininfarina's "turntable." Above, the Boxer is undergoing aerodynamic testing. The 512 GT/BB was unveiled at the Paris Show in 1976. Among the exterior changes was the well-louvered rear deck, which improved the ventilation of the engine bay; compare the two bottom-row pictures, the 365 to the left, and the 512 to the right! (Photographs by Pininfarina and Pete Coltrin, courtesy the Hilary Raab Collection and Road & Track.)*

The Boxer closes in quickly now. I hear John downshift to fourth, and now again to third. He's still going fast. I wave him over to the middle of the road. He understands and lines the car up along the center line. I see the Boxer move sideways with typical mid-engine quickness. The sound becomes strong and good now as John revs up and down-shifts to second. He's still going fast. Too fast? Maybe he has brake failure? Maybe he wants me to move? Now he brakes hard and comes to a stop twenty feet in front of me. I move up close; the fifty-five-millimeter wide-angle lens is on the camera. I look in the viewfinder, moving up and down and sideways, searching for the right angle and the right reflection. The all-red Boxer looks perfect. John ordered

*(continued on overleaf)*

**C**olorado's wide-open roads, cutting arrow-straight through the unpopulated prairie, were the perfect testing grounds for this brand new Boxer. Here the top speed of Ferrari's fastest, close to 190 miles per hour, could be reached without the risk of certain costly and irritating interruptions. John Dekker of Denver, owner of this 1980 BB 512 Boxer, chassis number 31157, took delivery at the Factory. He then made sure his treasure got safely on the plane to Los Angeles, where the necessary legal conversions were made. The graphic starkness of the surrounding prairie effectively contrasts Pininfarina's exquisite styling; masterfully-sculptured forms make the Boxer look just as resourceful as it is.

it that way from the factory. It looks much better than having the lower half of the body painted black. I take two rolls of ten shots each, bracketing up and down, then walk up to the car on the passenger side, open the door and sit down. I want to wait until later, when the sun is lower, to take the remaining shots.

"Were you testing me or the brakes?"

"Did you think I was going fast there at the end? I was just checking to see if you were paying attention."

"Good thing I was," I kidded. "How's the car running?"

"Perfect. But I'm taking it very easy. It's the first time it's been driven, you know."

"You picked it up in Italy, didn't you?"

"Yes, at the Factory. Well, in Modena, actually. Vern Lindholm was with me. He owns the shop where the legalizing was done, Ferrari Compliance in Santa Ana. We flew into Milan and took the train to Modena. The sales manager, Mister de Franchi, took us on a tour of the plant. During the tour we could hear the sounds from the test track nearby as the race cars were being set up for the Long Beach Grand Prix. We were introduced to Scheckter and Villenueve afterward in the restaurant across the street."

"Did you drive your car in Italy?"

"No, unfortunately not. We had planned to drive it to Rome, but something was wrong with the insurance papers. The Ferrari people just started it up there in the courtyard so I could hear it run. They then took it on a transporter to the Rome airport."

"You had it flown back?"

"Yes, I was on the same plane. I supervised the loading as well. We flew it directly to Los Angeles, so Vern could start on it right away."

"What all had to be done to make it legal?"

"Well, there are two sets of regulations you have to comply with. Structurally, first, you have to strengthen the doors and the bumpers to make them more crash-resistant. Fifty-pound steel bars are normally put inside the doors, but Vern has designed units that use corrugated eighteen-gauge sheet metal that weigh only five pounds and are just as strong. He's also designed special sheet metal assemblies that fit perfectly inside the original resin bumpers. With Vern's approach, you can hardly see any difference from the outside."

"What about the engine?"

"Well, that's the other set of regulations you have to comply with. You have to install a catalytic converter. Vern has a special unit manufactured to his specifications. You also have to install an air pump, designed to force air into the exhaust manifolds to improve the burning of excess fuel. A pair of doors also has to be installed

*This view of the Boxer, top left, shows the dam below the grille and the vent in front of the rear wheel. Both were new elements that had been added to the 512 model. To the left, the luxurious cockpit, comfortable and surprisingly spacious. At the top of this page, John Dekker's Boxer is pictured while being towed to a waiting 747 at Rome airport for direct transportation to Los Angeles. Above, Dekker's car in the courtyard at the Factory. Notice how good the single color looks – a Dekker request. To the right, John Dekker during a tour of the Factory, captured beside a Boxer engine. (Photographs by Pininfarina, John Lamm and John Dekker, courtesy the Hilary Raab Collection and Road & Track.)*

inside the air cleaners to prevent fuel evaporation. They actually shut the carburetors airtight when the engine isn't running. I also had Vern replace all the rubber hoses and lines in the cooling and fuel systems with aircraft-type steel lines. That was my contribution."

"It sounds like quite an involved operation!"

"Wait, it's not over yet! The halogen headlights have to be replaced by sealed-beam lights. There also has to be a seat-belt buzzer, and a buzzer that comes on when the door is open!"

"And a buzzer that comes on when you're going faster than fifty-five, right?"

"That'll probably come next!"

"Well, John, do you feel up to showing me how fast a Boxer can go? It should be safe out here in the middle of nowhere."

"Yes, probably. But I'll go slow."

He fires it up and takes it through the gears without straining it. We soon pass the 100-mph mark, still in fourth. I hardly feel the speed; the Boxer is as stable as a locomotive on its track. I enjoy the picture before my eyes; the all-tan, leather-covered interior, specially-upholstered for John, is a most pleasing place from which to watch the road and the grass as they rush toward me in out-of-focus streaks.

I become fascinated by the thought of the air that flows around the car, how it envelopes it and presses on it, and twirls and twists behind it. I imagine the air suddenly being split by the nose of the car, one stream flowing under it, and another, the stronger one, flowing up over the wide hood, pressing the car down, continuing across the windshield, over the roof, and then being split again, now by the aileron-spoiler mounted just behind the roof, allowing a small stream to escape down into the space behind the rear window, between the fins, to feed the hungry carburetors.

I feel the speed now! John is in fifth, still pressing on, still looking calm and collected, when he suddenly sees the only turning point within ten miles, the cross-road, come up only a few hundred yards away. He jumps on the brakes. The front sinks low, the rear lifts high, but the car stays steady on its track. We come to a stop, overshooting the cross-road by about fifty feet. Smoke bellows out from the wheel wells.

"The car has gone less than sixty miles, you know," said John. "It's only normal that the brakes smoke a little the first time you use them real hard!"

It takes my brain a moment to collect itself and formulate what I feel.

"One hundred and fifty-five miles per hour! You call that going slow?"

# 308 GTS

# A Sculpture Of Speed

"It's the rake of the windshield," I told myself. "When the roof panel is removed, you can really see how much that windshield slopes," I mumbled as I bent down to examine the low silhouette of the car.

The white 308 Spyder reminded me of a sculpture on display. It looked like it had been placed there on the abandoned road by a committee of art lovers. The flowering desert west of Palm Springs, with its massive blue mountains and dramatic clouds, could not have been surpassed in beauty and grandeur by any exhibition complex in the world.

"It's the thin, pointed nose and the turned-up undercarriage," I continued, still talking to myself, still trying to pinpoint the reasons for the distinctive expression of speed in Pininfarina's Spyder design.

"It gives the car an appearance of lightness. Even when it stands still, it looks like it's flying. The speed theme is probably more pronounced in this than in any other design Pininfarina has done for Ferrari. The Boxer has it too, but in that design the element of power is the most prominent. With the Spyder, it's all speed," I reasoned to myself.

"It's the arrow-shape that does it, more than these individual isolated elements. That's what makes the Spyder look like it's always going full speed!" I concluded the discussion; but I immediately regretted having come to that conclusion. "That, and all the other things. They all work together!" I corrected myself, realizing that it was no easy task to decide what exactly makes a design work.

I stood up and walked over to the other side of the Spyder, where Chic Vandagriff and his son Cris were waiting. I had just taken the last shots of the car, and the sun was almost hidden behind the mountains to the west.

"Good-looking car!" Chic commented.

"It sure is!" I agreed. "The more you look, the better it gets. But what do you think — is it better-looking than, say, the Lusso?"

"It's too early to tell. The Lusso was very beautiful, but it belongs to a different era. It's always difficult to judge the classic qualities of a model while it's still in production. Nostalgia has a lot to do with the way we feel about a design, you know. One thing that I have always been impressed by, though — and I don't know how the Ferrari people do it — but they always manage to improve every new model, inside and out. The cars just get better and better!"

"Well, you should know!" I told him. "You've owned and driven all of them, haven't you?"

Chic Vandagriff, owner of Hollywood Sport Cars, and one of the first and most successful Ferrari dealers in the country, has deep roots in the world of automobiles. His grandfather was a riding mechanic for Barney Oldfield, and the feel for speed and excitement was transferred to Chic. He grew up in Burbank, a native Californian, and he spent the war years in high school. At the age of fifteen, after his father's untimely death, young Chic attempted to join the Navy. The age limit was seventeen, but he managed to get as far as the shipyard in San Diego before his actual age was discovered and he was sent home.

Without his father, the family had to manage on a limited income. But Chic wanted a car badly. He took to buying and selling horses, until he finally had enough money to get a 1931 Ford Model A Roadster. It didn't run, so Chic had to *make* it run! From then on his career was firmly connected with automobiles.

*At the top left of the page, the flight-filled, uninterrupted profile of Pininfarina's 308 GTB, first seen at the Paris Salon in 1975. To the left, a bird's-eye comparison between the GTB and the GTS. The Spyder was introduced at the Frankfurt Show in 1977, and was received with much approval, immediately turning into a Ferrari best-seller. On this page, top, the European version of the four-seat 308 GT4, styled by Bertone and now replaced by the new Pininfarina-styled Mondial. Above and right, an interesting if not too successful attempt by Pininfarina to give the GTB a racing-machine look. This experiment was displayed at the 1977 Geneva Salon. (Photographs by Pininfarina, courtesy the Hilary Raab Collection and Ferrari S.p.A.)*

"Yes, you're right! I've had just about all of the production cars," Chic said. "I liked them all, but I've always liked new cars. I traded for the new ones as soon as they came out. I guess that's natural when you're a dealer, but it also had to do with my background. I had my own clunker sales-lot when I was twenty-one, and I got plenty fed up with old beat-up cars!"

"It's quite a step from a used-car lot to a Ferrari dealership. How did it happen?" I asked.

"In the late fifties, when I worked as a salesman for a sports-car dealership in Burbank, I was able to buy an Austin-Healey 3000. I prepared it for racing and went to driver's school, then I drove it at Riverside and Willow Springs. At that time I got an offer to take over Hollywood Sport cars, and those responsibilities cut my racing career short. But I kept the Healey, hired a full-time racing mechanic, and got Ronnie Bucknum to drive it. We won thirty-five firsts and the Pacific Coast Cham-
*(continued on overleaf)*

**S**tyled in such a fashion as to reflect the looks of the 246 Dino as well as the Boxer, the 308 GT, powered by a vee-eight which was a further development of the original vee-six Dino engine, carries Ferrari's mid-engine concept into the eighties. The brand new Spyder pictured on these pages, chassis number 30101, was supplied by Hollywood Sport Cars of Hollywood, California. The early-evening sun filters through approaching clouds, casting soft shadows on Pininfarina's space-age sculpture – a striking contrast to the surrounding Palm Springs desert landscape.

pionship in 1962.

"It was during my years in racing that I first became involved with the early Ferrari enthusiasts on the West Coast — guys like Bill Doheny, John Edgar, Otto Zipper and others. At that time I also sold my first used Ferrari. I remember it well. It was a Boano. But it wasn't until 1964 that I began selling new Ferraris. That was the year of the Lusso. I drove one myself for a couple of years. Then, in 1965, I became the first of Bill Harrah's dealers when he took over the Ferrari distributorship for the West Coast. I got myself a GTS at that time."

"I've heard that you have a very good relationship with the Factory, and that you even took classes in Italian to be able to communicate better with them," I said. "When did you first go there for a visit?"

"I went there for the first time in 1968. I met Amerigo Manicardi then, Ferrari's commercial director in charge of sales and marketing. I count him as one of my best friends. I also met Ferrari himself at that time. I might tell you something of interest that happened on one of my trips to the Factory. I know Ferrari claims not to speak or understand English, but I think he does! How else can you explain this?

"We were sitting around a table in the restaurant across the street from the Factory, having lunch. Ferrari, Manicardi, Gozzi, and many others were there, among them the organizers from Le Mans. Ferrari kept up an involved discussion with them in French. Everybody talked to each other about something. I talked to Gozzi in English. I told him about a new race car that Jerry Titus and I were developing that had no suspension. When I said that, Ferrari, without interrupting the conversation with the Le Mans people, leaned across to Gozzi and asked him in Italian to please take notes, because he wanted to know all about this race car that didn't have any suspension. I was impressed. Not only was he able to keep up a detailed discussion in French, but he was also aware of everything else that was being said around the table. I got the impression that it didn't matter whether it was said in English, Italian or French — he heard and understood it all!"

"Have you seen him lately?" I asked.

"I last saw him in 1978, in his office at the test track by the Factory. He's getting older, like everyone else, but he's as vigorous and sharp as ever. Still going strong!"

"During your visits to Italy, did you drive Ferraris, or did you drive Fiats, like Mister Ferrari does?"

"Sometimes I drove Ferraris. I remember one time especially well; it was during my first visit in 1968. I drove a 275 GTB/4 that time. I remember taking it on a trip to Naples. On the way back to Modena, I drove the Auto-

Pininfarina has, over the past three decades, held a virtual monopoly on formulating the Ferrari look. Featured on these pages are styling exercises that show what could have become — and what will become? At the top of this page, the engine-less P6, displayed in 1968 at the Turin Show. The Boxer and the 308 GTB lines can already be detected. Above, the most exciting of them all, the 512 S, featured at the Turin Show in 1969. To the right, top, the Modulo, unveiled at the Geneva Salon in 1970. Right, the 1974 Cr 25, photographed in Pininfarina's wind tunnel. To the left, its extremely well-designed interior. (Photographs by Pininfarina, courtesy the Hilary Raab Collection.)

strada. I made it in less than five hours, which works out to an average of about 165 mph. When I told Manicardi about it, he just looked at me with a stone face and asked what had caused the delay. It's true, by the way; Ferrari does drive a Fiat. Well, nowadays he's chauffeured — in a Fiat!"

"You've been a Ferrari dealer for fifteen years now. Has the excitement worn off?" I asked.

"The best way to answer that question, I guess, is to tell you of an experience I had at the Factory, also in 1968. One of the first Daytonas off the production line was sitting there ready for preferred delivery. It had Chinetti's name written in big letters on the windshield. I asked what I had to do to get that kind of treatment. The answer was, 'You have to be our man for twenty years, like Chinetti!' I still remember those words.

"Yes, I've been at it for fifteen years. But I still have the ambition to improve. I'm talking about areas like customer relations, sales volume, Factory relations, service and so on. My contacts with the Factory are already excellent; for instance, I'm one of the first to see the new models, and I often have the opportunity to influence things in a small way. Another step I've taken recently is to put Cris in charge of the Service Department. To say it all in one sentence: my goal is to become better and better — just like the Ferraris!"

He opened the door and sat down in the open cockpit. I knew he had a dealers' meeting to attend in Palm Springs that night. The shooting had taken longer than expected, and I could see he was anxious to leave. I just wanted to get in one last question.

"With all the Ferraris that have passed through your hands, have you kept any of them?"

"Yes, I still have a 365 GTC/4. I really liked that car. Cris is almost done with the restoration. Well, I guess I have to be on my way now. You'll go back to Hollywood with Cris, right? See you!"

The vee-eight came to life with a well-muffled but unquestionably exotic sound. The racing heritage could not be hidden behind a set of mufflers. He drove off, taking it easy at first, then sped up, turning east toward Palm Springs. The car soon disappeared beyond the fields of yellow desert flowers, but its sound hung in the air awhile longer.

"It's really funny," Cris said with a smile. "That GTC is mine. He gave it to me a couple of years ago; he said I could have it if I restored it. Now, when it's almost finished, he gets excited and thinks it's his. I'll have to remind him!"

"I didn't think he liked old cars."

"He does — when they're like new!"

# The Survivors Series    By Henry Rasmussen

"Ferraris For the Road," fifth in the Survivors Series, was photo-graphed, written and designed by Henry Rasmussen. The Model Re-sumés in the content section, as well as the Chronology of Production, were written by Larry Crane. Assis-tant designer was Walt Woesner. Copy editors were Barbara Harold and Kathy O'Brien. Typesetting was supplied by Tintype of San Luis Obispo. The color separations were produced by Graphic Arts Sys-tems of Burbank. Zellerbach Paper Company supplied the 100-pound Flokote stock, manufactured by S.D. Warren. The special inks were for-mulated by Spectrum Ink Company, Los Angeles. LithoCraft of Anaheim printed the book, under the supervi-sion of Brad Thurman. The binding was provided by National Bindery of Pomona. In addition to the skilled craftsmen associated with these firms, the author wishes to thank the own-ers for their time and enthusiasm.

Special acknowledgements go to Larry Crane of Santa Barbara, for his excellent writing and invaluable help with technical information; to Hil-ary Raab of Chicago, for supplying the majority of the black and white photos from his extensive collection in such an unselfish manner; to Cris Vandagriff of Hollywood Sport Cars, for his inspiring support and inventiveness in locating cars; to Tom Warth of Motorbooks Interna-tional, without whose actions of confidence this book would not have been done.

The author also wishes to thank Tony Anthony, Dean Batchelor, Steve Earle, John Gaughan, John Hajduk, Vern Lindholm of Ferrari Compliance in Santa Ana, Mike Lynch, Tom Martindale, Larry Menser, Ed Niles, Giancarlo Perini, Chuck Queener, Robert Resler of Rapid Color in Glendale, Dyke Ridgley, Chuck Smith of Road & Track, Henry Smith, and Henry Wolf.

# Mercedes For The Road

## By Henry Rasmussen

MERCEDES FO

First published in 1983 as
*Mercedes For The Road*

The 220 was the first new body style from Mercedes-Benz after the war. The old 170, although similar, had been introduced in 1936, and then reintroduced in 1946 when postwar production started again. The classic grille was retained on the 220, but the headlights were now mounted inside the fenders instead of on top of them. The six-cylinder overhead cam engine displaced 2195cc, had one Solex carburetor and gave 80hp at 4850rpm. Acceleration from 0-60 took about twenty-one seconds. Top speed was 90mph. The Cabriolet came in two styles: A) Front seats only, without rear quarter windows; and B) Front and rear seats with rear quarter windows. The wheelbase was 112 inches and 6.40X15-inch tires were used.

Both the Sedan and the Cabriolets were introduced in 1951. The last Cabriolet in the series was made in 1955. A total of 2,360 220A and 220B Cabriolet were built. A hardtop Coupe was made available in 1954. The 220 received a new body in 1954 — known as the 220a only available as a sedan.

The original 220 frame was shaped like an X and made of oval tubes. Fully independent suspension was utilized. The transmission was fully synchronized, had four speeds, and had the lever mounted on the steering wheel column. The price in the United States was just over $5,000.

The styling of the 220A Cabriolet was not as dramatic as that of the 300S. Nevertheless, the engineering and the workmanship was excellent, carrying forward the classic Mercedes-Benz tradition.

A modern interpretation of the famous prewar 540K, the 300S model was at once prestigious and sporty. It was first shown at the Paris Salon in 1951. *Road & Track* supplemented a road test of the 300 Sedan version by saying, "breathes there an enthusiast, who after driving a superb piece of machinery, has not started dreaming of modifications? A little more power. A little lightening of the body here and there. A touch of this and that to add to the sporting characteristics." The S model was the answer!

The 300S was made from 1952 till 1955. The 300Sc — small letter "c" signifying production modifications — was made from 1955 till 1958. The Sc was similar to the S, but had fuel injection and single-pivot swing axle. The X-shaped frame was mounted on a 114.2-inch wheelbase; the 2996cc straight six engine produced 175hp at 4300rpm and a top speed of 112mph; the 0-60 time was fourteen seconds. Only 200Sc units were built — in 1957 only fifty-two!

The external difference between the S and the Sc lay in two small areas — the rubber strips on the bumpers were eliminated and louvers were added to each side of the hood. At a price of $12,500 when introduced in New York, it was not your everyday utility runabout!

The superb quality that has become synonymous with the Mercedes-Benz name is everywhere evident on this model. With its conservative styling and high-quality craftsmanship, it has an aura of timeless elegance.

## 220A Cabriolet

## 300Sc Roadster

The 300SL Gullwing Coupe — with doors that open up instead of out — was born on the racetrack. The unorthodox manner of access was necessary because of the side-members of its advanced multi-tube frame. The wheelbase of 94.5 inches would be repeated on the 190SL and the later 230-250-280SL Roadsters. Independent suspension is the rule for Mercedes-Benz automobiles. The 300SL engine is the same 2996cc straight six-cylinder that powered the rest of the 300 series. With Bosch fuel injection, power was 240hp at 5800rpm. Top speed was about 140mph with 60mph reached in about 7.4 seconds. A four-speed transmission, with synchromesh in all gears was used. Tire size was 6.70X15. The production 300SL Coupe was introduced in 1954 and was replaced by the 300SL Roadster in 1957. A total of 1,400 Coupes were built, with the majority of 867 built in 1955. The price at that time was $7,463.

After the many victories of the 300SL factory racing team in 1952, the production version was eagerly awaited. *Road & Track* said, "just when we were beginning to suspect that the 300SL Coupe would prove to be a mediocre performer, we got one for a full scale road test. The new car turned out to be far beyond our boldest expectations." The magazine finished the article by saying, "The sports car of the future is here today."

Few automotive creations have achieved the degree of visual impact as has the 300SL Gullwing, its powerful looking, yet elegant forms inspire admiration from enthusiasts and non-enthusiasts alike.

The 300SL Roadster was a definite improvement over the Coupe; it provided better all-around vision — and, of course, better ventilation — a shortcoming of the Coupe. Actually, the Roadster should be called a convertible, since it had roll-up windows. In late 1958, an optional hardtop became available and in March 1961 disc brakes became standard equipment.

The Roadster kept the basic tube-frame format of the Coupe, but it was modified to allow conventional doors. A new low-point swing axle improved handling. Independent suspension, six-cylinder, single overhead cam, three-liter engine with fuel injection, and four-speed transmission, remained. Power was up, 250hp at 6200rpm. Speed varied with rear axle ratio; *Road & Track* got a faster 0-60 time of seven seconds but a lower top speed of only 130mph with the Roadster compared to the Coupe. In a later test, the magazine said, "To those who can afford the initial cost it offers a car they can be proud of, and they will be secure in the knowledge that not many cars on the road are better built or can cover ground faster with as much safety."

A total of 1858 were built from 1957 to 1963 (only fractionally fewer Coupes were made). In 1958 only 324 were made; each costing $10,970. The Roadster did not have quite the charisma of the Coupe. The Gullwing was indeed a difficult act to follow, quickly creating an almost cult-like enthusiasm for itself. The Roadster was a more practical automobile than the Coupe — easier entrance and exit, slightly heavier but more powerful and with better handling.

# 300SL Coupe

# 300SL Roadster

Introduced at the same time as the 300SL, the 190SL was always outclassed by its big brother. Indeed, the 190SL was an altogether different automobile. Although it had the same wheelbase as the 300SL, 94.5 inches, it had unit construction derived from the 180 Sedan. The suspension was as on all Mercedes-Benz cars, independent all around. Thirteen-inch wheels were used.

*Autocar* tested a 190SL in 1958 and found that "The overall impression was one of comfort and of sparkling performance with a very reassuring level of safety. It is necessary to make full use of the well-designed four-speed gear box if maximum performance is to be obtained." Rightfully so, since the 190SL had a single overhead cam, four-cylinder engine displacing 1897cc. Power was 120hp at 5700rpm using dual Solex carburetors. Performance was 0-60 in thirteen seconds and a top speed of 102mph could be reached.

The 190SL was introduced in 1954, but 1955 was the first year of production. By the time the last one had been built in 1963, 25,881 units graced the roads worldwide — ample proof that Mercedes-Benz' marketing strategy worked. The price in 1955 was $3,998.

Conceived in the shadows of the 300SL, the 190SL has always remained there. The large numbers produced and its relatively sluggish performance collaborated to keep it there.

All of the side windows of the 300d could be lowered — the windows in the front and rear doors as well as the rear quarter window (the latter was lifted out) — creating an uninterrupted opening much like a prewar phaeton. Yet, it was not a primitive tourer — it was a formal limousine! The 300 series was the most exciting line of cars to come from any manufacturer in the fifties. Racing car, sports car, two-seat luxury tourer, distinctive limousine — they could all be found in the 300 series.

Introduced in 1951, the 300 Sedan stayed in production until 1962. The 300d Sedan was produced from 1957 till 1962. A total of 3,077 Sedans were built; in 1962 only 45 were made. A convertible was also available.

With a fuel-injected, six-cylinder engine displacing 2996cc, the power output was 180hp at 5300rpm. The wheelbase was an impressive 124 inches and 7.60X15 tires were used. Three-speed automatic transmission was standard. Performance included a top speed of 105mph and a 0-60 time of eighteen seconds. The price in the United States was approximately $10,000.

The frame was X-shaped, using oval tubes. But the styling of the 300d differed from the earlier 300 Sedans in several areas; the front fenders protruded farther forward and had larger rings around the headlamps; the rear fenders and the trunk were more pronounced; the rear quarter windows were enlarged. The 300 series finally brought all that prewar prestige back to Mercedes-Benz.

## 190 SL Roadster

## 300d Sedan

There were two different body-style versions of the 220S and SE Cabriolets and Coupes. The style featured here was produced from 1958 to 1960; the later version from 1960 to 1965. The early model still carried a hint of rear fender in spite of the slab-side styling.

Powered by the overhead cam, six-cylinder engine of 2195cc, it produced 120hp at 4800rpm — the same as the later 220SEb. The 0-60 time was about fourteen seconds, with a top speed of 107mph. The "E" stood for "Einspritz" — fuel injection. The Bosch system was used.

These models all had unit bodies with traditional independent suspension and sat on wheelbases of 106.3 inches — some 4.7 inches shorter than the sedans. Four-speed transmission with the gear lever mounted on the steering column was standard on the 220 S and SE versions. Small, 6.70X13 tires were used. Price in the United States was about $8,500. Total production of 220S Coupes and Cabriolet was 3,429 units from 1956 to 1959; and of the 220SE, 1,942 from 1958-1960. The 1960 production was 1,200.

As a small concession to the current trend, the windshield curved back slightly. The distinctive grille raised with the hood when engine maintenance was due, rather awkward, but necessary. When the top was lowered and the boot installed, it presented a fairly flat look. This was something relatively new for German coachbuilding, especially on a touring model.

"The Mercedes 600 is not an ordinary car," said *Road & Track*. It went on to quote from the factory announcement that stated, "The new car takes up the prewar tradition of the company which was to have at least one model which would be included whenever ultra-prestige cars were considered." The magazine continued, "Its sheer bulk is imposing and because the mind's eye is not accustomed to such grand dimensions, it takes a while to encompass it — like a statue that is larger than life. Or a cathedral."

The 126-inch wheelbase is indeed enormous, but the 9.00X15 tires help to camouflage the size. The general looks of the car show the kinship to the regular Mercedes-Benz line. The makeup of the immense auto is also similar — independent suspension, low-pivot swing axle, unit construction, fuel injection — but the 600 goes beyond with a self-leveling suspension system, ground clearance and ride softness that could be adjusted by the driver, pneumatically operated windows lifts, seat adjustments, door locks, trunk lid and so on.

Power was by a V-8 engine with an overhead cam for each bank. It displaced 6329cc and produced 300hp at 4100rpm. In spite of the 5,434-pound weight, performance was rapid — to 60mph from a standstill took just ten seconds; top speed 127mph. In 1969, the price of the 600 Limousine was close to $21,000, and 279 were made that year.

The 600 series was introduced at the Frankfurt Auto Show in 1963. Until the end of 1979, 2,613 units had been produced.

## 220SE Cabriolet

## 600 Limousine

A convertible selling for more than $14,000, with a hand-operated top, styling from 1960 and a short 108.3-inch wheelbase — only Mercedes-Benz could do it and be successful! This was the 1971 280SE 3.5 Cabriolet. The 280SE Coupe and Cabriolet models carried the same body as the 250SE, which in turn carried the same body as the 220SEb of eleven years previous.

In the beginning it had the familiar six-cylinder, 2195cc, single overhead cam engine. Later, the enlarged 2496cc was fitted, as well as the fuel injected 2996cc unit, the car now being labeled 300SE. Later yet, it received the 2778cc engine before it was finally outfitted with the new 3.5 V-8 powerhouse in 1969. It produced 230hp at 6050rpm. Top speed was 127mph and 0-60 time was about nine seconds.

The suspension was the by now well-proven independent type front and rear, with the diagonal-pivot swing axle. Unit construction provided solid, rattle-free motoring. Tire size was 185H14. As always, included in every Mercedes-Benz was superior quality and solid engineering. It was done right, or it wasn't done at all.

But the 3.5 proved to possess another quality as well; the powerful 3.5 engine provided the final impetus to a model that had symbolized the utmost in styling and comfort for more than a decade — now it became an instant classic. Altogether, since its introduction in 1960, 36,000 Coupes and Cabriolets of the 220, 250, 300, 280 and 3.5 types were made — in 1971, only 1,026 units.

"The Mercedes-Benz 300SEL 6.3 holds the top honor among sedans because of its scorching performance that is blended with the usual traits of comfort, longevity and dignity. The best description of it is that it comes close to being all of the Ten Best Cars of the World in one great package." Those are the words of *Road & Track!* What more needs to be said?

In 1971, at $16,275, one could, of course, have expected more than a 112.8-inch wheelbase. But what fools these mortals be. Look at today's market and today's prices! The 6329cc V-8 put out the same 300hp at 4100rpm as the 600, but because of the lighter weight (3,828 pounds) performance was 6.9 seconds for 0-60 and top speed was 131mph. No wonder *Road & Track* labeled the performance "scorching." And no wonder that it concluded, "If we had to choose one car, regardless of cost, to serve all our automotive desires, it would have to be the 300SEL 6.3."

This fabulous sedan was produced from 1967 till 1972. In all, 6,526 units were made, just 670 in 1971. It was truly understated. The only way you could tell the 6.3 powerplant was to look for the small numerals on the trunk lid. *Road & Track,* in its road test, said, "But in every one of the lesser Mercedes, we've always felt a little apologetic for the lack of power. No so with the 6.3."

A gentleman's hot rod indeed, and today still surprisingly affordable.

## 280 SE 3.5 Cabriolet

## 300 SEL 6.3 Sedan

Tradition can be a Pavlovian kind of thing! It is doubtful that the 280SL ever won a road race — but it sure looked like it could. It had the lines of the 300SL, down to the grille. It even had the same wheelbase, 94.5 inches. At $7,469, in 1971, it sold only 830 units; but from 1967, when it replaced the 250SL, until the last 280SL was produced in 1971, it sold 23,885 units. Added to some 25,000 previously built 230SL and 250SL models it became another "right car for the right time!" Maintaining the Mercedes-Benz theme of unit construction, independent suspension, low-pivot swing axle and fuel injection, the personal-sized Mercedes again hit the spot. Powered by a 2778cc six-cylinder engine producing 180hp at 5700rpm, performance was a creditable 9.9 seconds 0-60. Top speed was 114mph with four-speed automatic transmission. The stick-shift might have taken a second off the 0-60 time.

The 230SL, 250SL and 280SL line continued the Mercedes theme of elegance mixed with sportiness; it would not be out of place at the yacht club or the supermarket. But, a Mercedes is first of all meant to be driven. *Road & Track* said, "The ride, over all sorts of roads, is fantastic. The body is absolutely rigid and rattle free, and the supple suspension just works away down there without disturbing the superb poise of the SL." The 230SL, 250SL and 280SL — already classics, already increasing in value.

The 3.5-liter 350SL could not be imported into the United States. The imported 350SL always had a 4520cc engine — a V-8 producing 190hp at 4750rpm. The California version produced only 180hp because of stringent smog regulations. Bosch fuel injection helped keep the carbon monoxide and nitrous oxide levels down. Performance was 10.2 seconds 0-60 and top speed was 124mph. The usual Mercedes-Benz arrangement of unit construction, independent suspension and diagonal-pivot swing rear axle were retained — but the 350SL and 450SL was an all-new design. It was heavier and longer than the 230SL, 250SL and 280SL models it replaced.

In 1977, the European market received the 450SL 5.0 with front and rear spoiler. Currently, the body houses the 3.8-liter engine in the United States and is known as the 380SL. The 450SL was introduced in 1971 and in 1974 its price was $17,056. Production that year was 6,093 units.

*Road & Track* compared the 450SL to four other roadsters. The 450SL was tested against the Corvette, Dino 246GTS, Jaguar E-Type V-12 and the Porsche 911 Targa. The testers pointed out, "these are five very different cars." It was a test with no winner intended. They said, "The 450SL is in a class by itself: not as we said, a sports car — but fast enough for almost anyone and a wonderful two-seater for someone who wants quality but not necessarily excitement." They also said, "it's a two seat luxury car for driving fast in supreme comfort and avoiding the bulk of a big sedan."

## 280 SL Roadster

## 450 SL Roadster

# The Best or Nothing!

Although this is the eighth volume in The Survivors Series, I have never before done a book on a marque I have actually owned.

My first Mercedes was a 190SL that I acquired in 1967, while I still lived in Sweden. The second was a 250SE Cabriolet that I possessed for too short of a time, after I had moved to California.

Having owned Mercedes automobiles does not mean that I can claim to be well familiar with their inner workings; engineering was never my forte. It only means that I know firsthand what it *feels* like to *own* a Mercedes; I am referring to that special feeling — a blend of pride and invulnerability. and it means that I know what it feels like to *drive* a Mercedes; anyone who has driven one will always remember that solid, tight, massive feeling transmitted through the steering wheel. It even means that I know what a Mercedes *smells* like; somewhat naively I brag about being able to tell a Mercedes apart from other automobiles while blindfolded inhaling the fragrance of the leather.

So, what makes Mercedes-Benz so special?

Well, they were the ones who started it all — the first to manufacture and market an automobile. No other car company has been around for so long, surviving both wars and oil gluts as well as depressions and recessions.

A tradition as long as theirs has come about as a result of — but has also helped dictate — a formula that has been followed in the creation of every new design. It is a formula that has produced sound engineering and dignified styling; a formula concerned with both safety and economy as well as comfort and elegance; a formula that is perfectly expressed in the company's own credo; The Best or Nothing!

The following pages endeavor to communicate the result of this formula, illustrating it impartially, with cold facts and photographs that do not exaggerate, but also — and may the reader forgive — partially, through the owners' and my own irrepressible enthusiasm. Enjoy!

One of the world's most recognized symbols, the Mercedes Star was first seen in 1909. The three points symbolize the threefold application of Daimler products – on land, at sea and in the air. The pictures on these pages illustrate a few of the many uses of the Mercedes Star. Above, it graces the rear deck of a 300SL. To the right, it crowns the radiator of a 300d. On the opposite page, it is seen incorporated in the 300SL grille. To the far right, it is imbedded into the horn button of a steering wheel, and below, it is seen as a part of the bodybuilder's badge on a 220A Cabriolet.

**M**ercedes designers always seem to succeed in creating interiors with just the right blend of function and elegance. Above, the racecar-inspired cockpit of a 300SL Roadster – a curving chrome strip outlines its inviting shape. Above right, the lounge-like cabin of a 300d Sedan – the wide seats are covered with smooth leather, the dash and windows lined with rich wood. To the right, a 280SE Cabriolet in the driveway leading to the suburban Chicago home of a wealthy publisher. Opposite page, a 220A Cabriolet on a dusty plantation road near Caracas, Venezuela. Far right, the snug airplane-like accommodations of a 300SL Gullwing.

ub caps changed very little over almost three decades – illustrative of the conservative evolution of design at Mercedes. Above, the cap of a 1952 220A had a small diameter, covering only the hub. As was the style, it was painted the color of the car, leaving very little chrome showing. On a 1957 300Sc, right, and a 1962 300d, opposite page, the hub caps remained basically the same, but were now surrounded by separate vented chrome rings. On a 1960 220SE Cabriolet, far right, the restorer left the cap unpainted. On a 1974 450SL, the cap is a one-piece affair, covering the entire wheel. Throughout, the Star remained the decorative element.

or sheer beauty, few headlight designs can compete with that of the European version 300SL Roadster, left. Its smoothly rounded shape seems to form the perfect beginning of the fender, but not only esthetically, also aerodynamically – Mercedes engineers never design things just to look good! The headlights of the 300SL Gullwing, upper right, had a conventional design. Pictured above and to the lower right, the headlights of the 280SL and the 300SE, both shown in their American versions. In the photograph to the far left, the classic headlight shape of the 300d Sedan.

**D**etails make the whole – and attention to detail has always characterized a Mercedes. The pictures on these pages, although only a few, are evidence enough. From the studied shape of the door handle on a 300SE Sedan, to the harmonious symmetry of the gauges on the dash of a 300SL Gullwing, to the speed-evoking slant of the louvres in its body side vent, to the smooth curves of the wood and the intricate folds of the leather on the door panel of a 220SE Cabriolet, to the perfect fit of the chrome moldings around its windshield – it all shows that Mercedes never left up to chance the design of even the smallest detail.

**M**an and his machine — a reflection of the owner's personality. Opposite page, Alex Dearborn unveils his choice machine, a 300SL Gullwing. It peers out from behind the garage doors of a converted New England carriage house — old-world perfection. This page, far left, Jose Harth admires the flowing forms of this 300SC Roadster — flamboyant elegance. It is parked in the courtyard of an old Venezuelan hacienda. Above, Lee McDonald sits ready for take-off in his 190SL. The beams of a sinking Florida sun reach into an always-open cockpit — gallant audacity. Left, Jay Pettit makes himself at home in the backseat of his 300d — conservative class. The fertile plains of Illinois draw an uninterrupted horizon line.

# Short Resumé of a Long History.

## By Gene Babow.

"The sight of Stuttgart was heart-rending. No newspaper report could convey what the eyes beheld. I kept asking myself where the people I saw lived — the houses were almost all bombed out or damaged.

"The next morning I drove to Untertürkheim, to the factory. I found a field of rubble there. They were clearing the rubble away, everyone was shoveling and carrying off debris. All of the employees of the firm were helping, voluntarily and without pay, regardless of rank or position. 'Our' factory had to be rebuilt, 'our' star had to rise again."

This was how Rudolf Caracciola, perhaps the greatest of the Mercedes-Benz racing drivers, later described his reactions to seeing firsthand the terrible destruction caused by allied bombing raids during the final phase of World War II. Assessing their losses, the Board of Directors stated: "Daimler-Benz has ceased to exist."

But, miraculously, the "star" would rise again.

Adopted by the Daimler Company in 1909, the three-pointed star had already survived for almost four decades, including a world war and a great depression. The symbol was introduced nine years after founder Gottlieb Daimler's death. His two sons, who managed the company, chose the symbol, recalling that their father had once drawn a guiding star over a picture of his home in Deutz.

Daimler-Benz Aktiengesellschaft, which now manufactures Mercedes-Benz automobiles, trucks and buses, as well as engines used in all forms of transportation, is the ultimate result of a merger between "Daimler Motoren Gesellschaft" and "Benz and Cie" that took place in 1926.

Daimler had patented a small, light, high-speed engine in 1883. The same principle of design is still fol-

lowed today. Starting in 1886, Benz had begun manufacture of a two-stroke, stationary engine. It had gas-throttle control and enabled him to begin work on a self-powered vehicle. The same yer, Benz introduced his gas-engined vehicle. It was a three-wheeler, specially designed for the purpose — not a motor-powered horseless carriage. If Daimler's first effort, on the other hand, closely resembled the horseless carriage, it was because it actually was a converted horse-drawn carriage. Self-powered vehicles had been seen before Daimler and Benz' time. These two men, however, foresaw the future of the automobile and started actual production.

Just before his father's death in 1900, Paul Daimler had developed a small 8hp car. It had a honeycombed radiator up front and formed the basis for a new model, the Mercedes.

This new car was named after the daughter of a Daimler agent in southern France, Emil Jellinek. It was Jellinek who had proposed the new car, put up the money, and insisted on the name.

The new car had the engine up front, was lower and longer than its contemporaries, and had a more favorable power-to-weight ratio. These features would soon be copied by almost all automobile manufacturers.

The engineer responsible for the actual design of the Mercedes was Wilhelm Maybach. More than anyone else, it was Maybach who influenced Daimler to produce a complete automobile, rather than just engines for boats, trains and commercial vehicles.

Maybach was followed by Paul Daimler, who had inherited the engineering prowess from his father. At Benz, Hans Neibel was their counterpart.

In 1908, the Grand Prix of France was won by a Mercedes. The four-cylinder, 135hp car reached an average speed of 69mph. Benz cars were second and third. When Mercedes dropped out of racing, the Neibel-designed "Blitzen Benz" took over. Neibel even raced the car himself with notable success.

Mercedes came back in 1914 and won again, but the war put a damper on racing and development, especially at Mercedes and Benz. It took several years after the war, in 1923, before a four-cylinder, supercharged Mercedes was built. It ran at Indianapolis, but was not a winner. The development of this car was entrusted to an engineer from Austro-Daimler — Ferdinand Porsche. The following year, this same car won the Targa Florio. Porsche went on to develop the supercharged "K" sports car, as well as the legendary SS and SSK models.

When Porsche decided to open his own consulting

*In 1945, at the end of World War II, much of Germany lay destroyed – the Mercedes plants included. But production was resumed already in 1946. The first units were similar to prewar models. To the left, an example of the 170-series is seen beside a ruin in an unidentified location – for our purpose it symbolizes past destruction and new beginnings. The 220-series was shown in 1949. It resembled the 170-line. By now foreign travel was again possible – a 220, above, is seen on the French Riviera. The 300-series, right, shown in 1951, was the first all-new postwar design.*

firm, Hans Neibel became the chief engineer. Neibel specialized in suspension and chassis design. He was responsible for the 1934 Mercedes-Benz Grand Prix cars. Regrettably Neibel died before he could see the formidable success of his creations.

A part of this engineering period was Fritz Nallinger. In a Mercedes-Benz press release dated 1978, he was credited with "the application of independent suspension to all four wheels, friction free springs, self-supporting frame floor unit with sub-frame, high speed, light Diesel engine for trucks and autos and direct gasoline injection into the cylinder."

He also raced and, therefore, had a feel for cars that handled well. It was he who suggested the 300SL for 1952. He had also been instrumental in the creation of the 500K and 540K of the late thirties.

Enter Rudolf Uhlenhaut, the next generation Mercedes super-engineer. He was responsible for racing successes as well as improved passenger car handling and safety. Alfred Neubauer, director of competition at Daimler-Benz commenting on Uhlenhaut's contribution said, "Up until then [1937] every designer assumed that a racing car must be tightly sprung and noisy. As a result, drivers were tossed about like a dry martini in a cocktail shaker. Uhlenhaut introduced soft springs and a quieter engine. The new Mercedes was as comfortable as an easy chair with 600hp purring beneath it."

Although not a competition driver, Uhlenhaut's capacity behind the wheel has become a legend. An example often mentioned is the occasion when Juan Manuel Fangio tried out the W196 Grand Prix car at Nürburgring. Fangio was finally satisfied with his lap time, but Uhlenhaut was not. He went out and bettered the time, according to this account.

No history of Mercedes-Benz, however brief, could be complete without mentioning Alfred Neubauer, the team manager. He was a master of strategy and also introduced the signals between pit and driver.

Prewar production from 1936 until the outbreak of the war was about 90,000 of the Type 170, 20,000 Type 230 and 300 540K. In 1938 alone, automobile production totaled 27,762.

In 1946, it was time to pick up the pieces and start over again. At first, only repair work was done. Then the plant at Mannheim, which suffered the least damage, resumed commercial production.

In 1946, only 214 passenger cars were built. In 1947, production increased to 1,045 units. In 1948, came the currency reform which brought stability to the new German Republic. A total of 5,116 cars of the

170 models were produced that year.

Early in 1951, Mercedes wished to return to Formula One racing. The then current formula of 1.5-liter supercharged or 4.5-liter without supercharger, would run until 1954. Mercedes could not have a new design ready until 1953. It was meaningless to produce a car for just one year of racing. Neubauer tried to get the formula extended, but failed.

Nallinger then came to the rescue. "How would it be if we developed a sports model out of our latest passenger car, the 300?" he suggested. The resulting 300SL put Mercedes back in racing. But it was the new Formula One, the 2.5-liter unsupercharged, that Mercedes wished to compete in. The W196 was the result, with lattice-type tubular frame, eight-cylinder engine, and desmodronic valve gear. With Uhlenhaut, Neubauer and Fangio on the team, the W196 was a winner. When Fangio drove the car, he said, "From the very first test, I was sure that I had in my hands the perfect car, the sensational machine that drivers dream about all their lives." He won the first race that the W196 appeared in, in 1954, at Rheims, France. He also won the German, Swiss and Italian Grand Prix races that same year, along with the championship in 1954 and 1955.

Now a few words about nomenclature. The numbers used to label passenger car models usually referred to engine size; 170 was 1.7 liters, 220 was 2.2 liters. The lower-case (a, b, c and d) letters signified further development of a model. Upper-case (A, B and C) letters signified body style; the 220A was a two seater convertible, 220B had a rear seat and a rear quarter window. There were exceptions, however, especially when the V-8 engine was introduced. The SL in 300SL stood for super light or "super leicht" in German. The letter S usually meant super. The E stood for "einspritz," or fuel injection in English. L meant long. D was usually reserved for diesel. The letter C originally meant a two-seater convertible for four passengers, without rear quarter window; but was later used to denote coupe, as in the 250 series.

The styling of Mercedes-Benz automobiles can be characterized as "non-trendy." True, there were vestigal fins at one time, but they were quickly removed. "Form follows function" is perhaps the best way to describe Mercedes styling. Yet, there has always been instant identification of any Mercedes automobile.

In recent years, Mercedes styling and size has been copied by almost every automobile maker. But it is really not styling that has placed Mercedes ahead of much of its competition, it is the faithful adherence to

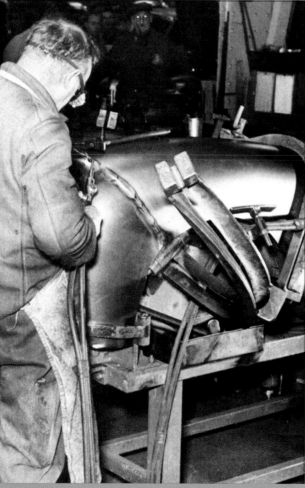

*The pictures on these pages are from the early fifties, and show the Mercedes facilities bristling with activity. Note the absence of automation – the individual craftsman was king. To the left, the assembly area for the limited production covertibles. The profile in the foreground belongs to a 220A Cabriolet. Above, getting the piping of the seat just right requires careful attention. To the right, a fender takes shape. Top of the page, a 300-series engine is monitored while running on the test bed.*

the meaning of the words safety and quality.

This book deals with the 1946 to 1974 models. At the end of that period, total annual production was 331,682. In the United States, 41,865 were sold through about 380 dealers. Prices ranged from $6,662 for the 220D to $16,498 for the 450SLC.

For comparison, the figures for 1981 show total production at 440,778. Sales in the United States totaled 63,059 through 409 dealers. Prices ranged from $21,858 for the 240D to $51,956 for the 380SEC.

Mercedes-Benz now ranks fifteenth in motor vehicle production, worldwide. Besides the factories in Stuttgart/Untertürkheim, Sindelfingen, Mannheim, Gaggenau and Berlin/Marienfelde, there are plants in Düsseldorf, Bad Homburg, Worth/Rhine, Munich, Friedrichshafen and Nürnberg. There are also assembly plants in Argentina, Brazil and Turkey.

The following is a brief look at the first three decades of Mercedes-Benz models with regard to their collectability. For the most part, the four-door sedans have been omitted. While these are fine automobiles, they were the plebeian transportation. Almost by definition, any two-door Mercedes-Benz will be collectable. The demand factor rates high. Simple economics dictate ever-increasing values.

**170SA and 170SB Cabriolet.** The Model 170 was first introduced at the Berlin Auto Show in 1936. The same design was also to become the mainstay of early postwar production at Mercedes-Benz, beginning in 1946. The last of the dozen or so variations on the 170 theme was built in 1955. Due to the relatively low production numbers of these cars, especially during the first years, the 170 in all its various forms, must to some extent be considered collectable. But it is particularly the A Cabriolet, the convertible two-seater, and the B Cabriolet, the convertible four-seater, that are desirable. A total of 2,433 between 1949 and 1951.

**220A and B Cabriolet.** Introduced at the Frankfurt Auto Show in 1951, the 2.2-liter sedans were the first new automobiles from Daimler-Benz after the war. These cars, along with the 220A and B Cabriolets and a later Coupe, still had fenders front and rear. Styling-wise, they were basically a facelift of the Model 170, with the headlights now in the fenders. Only 2,360 Cabriolets were made between 1951 and 1955. The Coupe came in 1954.

**300a, b, c, d Sedan and Cabriolet.** This prestigious line of automobiles was also introduced at the 1951 Frankfurt show. No attempt was made to join current styling trends; therefore, the model took a long time to become dated. Refined elegance was the

keynote. Obviously, the Cabriolets are the most rare — only 707 were made from 1951 to 1962. The total number of sedans built during the same period was 10,723. These automobies were elegant and luxurious, but are not as sought-after today as their sportier two-seater counterparts, even though they were built with the same attention to quality.

**300S and Sc, Coupe, Cabriolet and Roadster.** Movie stars like Bing Crosby and Clark Gable were quick to snap up the sporty 300S two-door model. In concept it was a modern 540K. Only 560 units were made. A rare Sc model (fuel-injected) was also built — only 200 units. The S and S came as fixed Coupes, Cabriolets with irons and folded top visible, and as Roadsters without landau-irons and the top hidden when folded. The S was produced between 1951 and 1955, the Sc between 1955 and 1958. The latter is now the most sought-after of all postwar Mercedes models.

**300SL Coupe and Roadster.** A classic from introduction, the production 300SL was an outgrowth of the all-conquering competition 300SLs. The gullwing doors of the Coupe were a necessary novelty due to the space frame chassis. Only 1,400 units were made between 1954 and 1957. The Roadster (with reworked space frame and conventional doors) sold 1,858 units from 1957 to 1963. The Coupe, with its gullwing doors, reached a higher visibility than any other Mercedes, and with that came instant collectability. The Roadster, after a slower start, is now close behind.

**190SL Roadster.** A junior 300SL, based on the 180 Sedan, was for the affable, less racing-interested clientele. Only 120hp, but high in quality, production was 25,881 units, showing that the concept of a comfortable, less-powerful touring car was a winner. For a long time a relative sleeper, the 190SL is now gaining popularity as a collector Mercedes in its own right. It was produced between 1955 and 1963.

**220S and 220SE Coupe and Cabriolet.** The styling of this model was not far removed from the earlier 220, but the slab side was new. A grace of line, regal perhaps, typified these cars. Only 3,429 220S units were made from 1956 to 1959. The 220SE, which had fuel injection, was made between 1958 and 1960. Production was 1,942 units. This model was always appreciated by the enthusiast. It possessed the timeless lines that made it look expensive and elegant long after production had ended.

**220SEb Coupe and Cabriolet.** This is a modern classic. Unlike the 220SEb Sedan, the Coupe and Cabriolet did not have fins. Simple lines, beautiful and

*In 1952, racing fans were stunned by the revelation of a new Mercedes sports racing car. Entered in Italy's Mille Miglia, it took second place. Left top, the coupes parade through the streets of Brescia. Entered in Switzerland's Bremgarten, they took a triple victory. Fritz Reiss is seen to the right. In France's Le Mans, the 300SL's took first and second. Norbert Niedermeyer, captured at speed, to the lower left. In Germany's Nürburgring, a row of four roadsters crossed the finish line. Reiss shows his style above. Added to these successes was a victory in Mexico's Carrera Panamericana. A fantastic record year – setting the stage for Mercedes' magnificent postwar comeback.*

restrained, made it an enduring favorite. Introduced in 1960, 16,902 units had been sold when production ended in 1965. This model is still relatively affordable, but available examples may require restoration too costly to be justified by their present value.

**300SE Coupe and Cabriolet.** Basically, this model has the same look as the 220SEb, but with the larger engine, air suspension and four-wheel disc brakes, it is a more advanced piece of engineering. In this case, because of the unique suspension, the Sedan may also be considered collectable. Production figures for the Sedans: 6,848 units; for the Coupe and Cabriolet: 3,127 units. In 1965, a new body appeared on the Sedan. Another 5,106 units were made of this model. the same rule of collectability is valid for the 300SE as for the 220 SEb, except that with the more complicated suspension, and maintenance, it will be even more expensive to restore.

**230SL, 250SL, 280SL Roadster.** This is the model that replaced the 190SL. Personal transportation in sumptuous elegance was still the theme. This car is timeless in its classic simplicity. Introduced in 1963, it went through two displacement increases and was built until 1971. Production numbers were: 230SL 19,831; 250SL 5,196, and 280SL 23,885, for a total of 48,912 units. The cars came with four-speed automatic or manual, or five-speed optional. Many units were produced, but not enough to meet the demand. A sound and enjoyable investment.

**600 Limousine and Pullman.** This automobile brought back the term "Grosser Mercedes" or "Grand Mercedes," recollecting the 7.7-liter Limousines of the late thirties. The Limousine and the stretched Pullman versions are both magnificent automobiles, conceived for executives and heads of state. Introduced in 1963, only a total of 1,960 Limousines and 364 Pullmans had been produced by 1973. The last 600 is believed to have been completed in 1981. Prices for examples in prime condition stay high. The 600 is looked upon as the finest automobile of its type ever built.

**250SE and 280SE Coupe and Cabriolet.** More power is found in both cars, as compared to the 220SEb, but virtually identical looks. Production of the 250SE Coupe and Cabriolet was 6,213 units; of the 280SE 5,187, from 1965 to 1972. Conventional suspension makes these models less expensive to restore and maintain. Also, examples of later years can still be found in excellent original condition.

**300SEL 6.3 Sedan.** The connoisseur's muscle car was available only as a sedan. What a shame. As such, it will probably not hit the stride that a two-door

model would have. But with a production of only 6,526 units from 1967 to 1972, it could do better than expected. Maybe it is a sleeping giant. Two facts are clear, however: It is the most desirable of the Mercedes sedan, and still the fastest sedan on the road.

**250C and 280C Coupe.** These sporty little hardtops still had the six-cylinder motor. They had the same wheelbase and overall length as the 250 Sedan, but looked somewhat better. Relatively high prices indicate a potential sleeper. Production figures: 250C 42,290, 280ZC 23,576. About half were fuel-injected, but these were not sold in the United States. Made from 1968 to 1975.

**280SE 3.5 Coupe and Cabriolet.** This model has the same body style as the 220SEb, originating way back in 1960, but comes with the 3.5-liter V-8. A lower and wider grille was used. It was also faster. Only 4,502 units were made between 1969 and 1971. This is the ultimate Mercedes four-seat coupe and convertible. As such, the convertible holds the position as the third most desirable of the postwar Mercedes models, surpassed only by the 300S and SC, and the 300SL Coupe and Roadster.

**350SL and 450SL Roadster.** The replacement for the 280SL was the 350SL, first shown in 1971. Even though it was a totally new design, it did carry on the family resemblance, but now it was bigger and heavier, and also looked it. In Europe, the 350SL actually had a 3.5-liter engine. In the United States it had a 4.5-liter power source right from the beginning, but was still labeled 350SL. From 1973 on, it was correctly called 450SL.

Between 1971 and 1973, 11,230 350SLs and 18,258 450SLs were built. An attractive feature of this model was that it always came with both the soft and hard top. The 450SL still has a few years to go before it will be replaced. As always, collectability increases when production stops. Of the U.S. version, the early years, with the small bumpers and the hubcapped wheels, are most desirable to the collector.

**350SLC and 450SLC Coupe.** The Coupe was fourteen inches longer than the Roadster counterpart. It had a rear quarter window with decorative vertical louvers and a real back seat that could carry two more passengers. It had the same engine as the Roadster, and was also introduced the same year, 1971. There were 9,318 350SLCs made between 1971 and 1973 and 6,294 450SLCs were made in 1972 and 1973. From a collector's viewpoint, the Roadster is the more desirable of the two, mainly because of its sportier looks and open-air option.

*With the publicity generated by the racing victories, came a need for new products. New generations of bread-and-butter cars were soon introduced and the facilities took on a more automated look, top left. The 180-line was first shown in 1953, its diesel version seen to the right. The following year a more luxurious range, the 220-series, left, was introduced. The 190SL, above, built between 1955 and 1963, hardly seems to qualify as a bread-and-butter model; but conceived to capitalize on the success of the 300SL, this small brother did the trick, with more than 25,000 units produced.*

# 220A CABRIOLET

# Sugar Cane, Palms and Other Exotic Species...

There was almost total stillness inside the narrow valley between the hills.

Above the valley, moving like gigantic cotton floats, were woolly-white clouds. They moved very slowly. And when they passed in front of the sun, the huge dark shadows they made drifted, also very slowly, across the fields of tall ripening sugar cane that covered the valley floor.

Above the floor, if you looked closely, you could see that there was a breeze. It moved up there among the palm crowns. The palms grew towering and tall-trunked in long, arrow-straight columns that lined the sides of the narrow roads crisscrossing the Santa Teresa plantation. The breeze stroked the long branches very gently, making them shiver just enough so you could see it.

But there was no breeze near the ground. Only the hot air moved, vibrating with heat as it rose from the burning soil. Every time there was a shadow the vibration stopped and it was gone as long as that merciless sun was gone.

It was siesta time on the plantation.

José Harth, owner of the 1953 Mercedes-Benz 220A Cabriolet parked in the middle of the road, lounged beside it on the grass, his head and shoulders propped up against one of those wide-bellied old palm trunks. His eyes were closed.

Alberto, the Chilean chauffeur, sat in the shade underneath the open hatch of the Wagoneer. He sipped

(continued on overleaf)

The 170V, left, was produced in ninety thousand examples between 1936 and 1942. When production was re-started after the war, in 1946, this model again became the bread-and-butter line. It had a four-cylinder engine that produced thirty-six hp. Top speed was sixty-two mph. Early production consisted mainly of utility vehicles, such as delivery vans and ambulances. The model remained in production until 1953. Its most successful year was 1951, when almost thirteen thousand units were made. Already, in 1949 came improved versions with stronger engines, better weight distribution and smoother styling of the hood. From a collector's viewpoint, the Cabriolets are the most desirable. Above, a 170S Cabriolet A, the two-seat version, parked on a street in Cannes, France. To the upper right, an offical factory photo of the same model. Note the separate, fully chromed headlights. To the right, the 170S Cabriolet B, the four-seat version.

**P**alms, planted almost two hundred years ago, line the narrow roads cutting through the Santa Teresa sugar plantation, east of Caracas, Venezuela. The 220A Cabriolet stands out like a magnificent sculpture of steel and leather. The tall radiator, the narrow hood, the swooping fenders, all reflect its prewar heritage. Jose Harth obtained his Survivor, chassis number 187.012.031.32/53, in 1975 from a doctor who had owned it since new. Built in 1953 – one of 403 convertibles produced that year – it still has only 87,000 kilometers on the odometer.

from a bottle of Coke while his eyes wandered across the hillsides, looking for nothing in particular.

I had just put away my camera; it seemed like a crime against local custom to work in the middle of the day. I walked over to the silver Mercedes sitting there like a shining sculpture of steel and leather.

Now, thirty years after it had been built, the car still looked very beautiful, maybe more so, I thought to myself as I slid in behind the big white three-spoked steering wheel. The door opened suicide-style, making entry easy.

The leather that covered the seats, door panels and dashboard was still bright red, except where sun and wear had faded and polished it. The wood was perfect. The radio in its wooden console was still the original one.

The two knobs on each side of the ashtray located on top of the dash — the left controlling the windshield wipers, the right containing the cigarette lighter — and the knobs governing the ignition setting, the headlights, the instrument lights and the choke — all located on the lower edge of the dashboard — were all chromed. So were the levers controlling the heating and ventilation settings, the airflow nozzles, the door handles and the window cranks — all chromed, so that they all matched.

Everything you could see was made from basic, honest material — leather, wood, steel, glass, rubber — all, except the steering wheel. It was made from some kind of plastic that looked like ebony. The small knob on the end of the column-mounted shift lever was apparently made from a different kind of plastic — it had turned yellow.

There were two large gauges on the dashboard, one on each side of the steering column — a clock to the left, a speedometer to the right. The odometer showed 87,000 kilometers. Original mileage, José had told me.

He had bought the 220 from its first owner, a doctor, and had himself put only about ten thousand kilometers on it during the past seven years.

Today's trip would be the longest, he had said.

We had started early in the morning from José's home built right on top of the highest ridge of the mountain to the south of Caracas. The undersides of the clouds had brushed the roof of the house and, sitting there on the veranda, it had felt like sitting in an airplane coming in for a landing, the city sprawling long and narrow in the valley below, white in that mild forgiving morning sunlight, blue mountain ranges on all sides, the mass of office skyscrapers and apartment highrises looking like vertical brush strokes in an impressionist painting, the brick-red shantytowns showing vaguely on

The 220 model appeared in 1951. It was a vastly improved vehicle, now sporting a new six-cylinder engine that developed eighty hp. Top speed was about ninety mph. The model carried on the basic styling theme of the 170, but was now larger and roomier, and also had a much more luxuriously appointed interior. The headlights were mounted inside the fenders instead of outside, as on the 170. To the left, a 220 Sedan captured against the background of Monte Carlo. Above, a 220 Cabriolet B on tour through the Schwarz-wald region in Germany. To the right, for both the 170 and the 220, fitted luggage was an option, so that, if so desired, the trunk space could be utilized to its maximum.

the hillsides to the east and west, the Atlantic shimmering brightly through an opening in a mountain chain.

In back of the house, inside a high wall, behind a gate, under protecting roofs, stood two rows of the most desirable postwar Mercedes collector cars you could assemble — a 300SL Gullwing, a 300SL Roadster, a 300Sc Coupe, a 300Sc Roadster, just to mention a few.

José Harth was foremost among a handful of super-enthusiasts in Venezuela. He had begun cultivating his interest in cars many years ago — while his friends were still laughing at his eccentric passion. He had searched towns and villages for cars as he traveled the country in his business. He had become familiar with nearly every old car in existence. He knew their whereabouts, their conditions, their owners — and what it would take to obtain them.

José had told me all this with great excitement, as if it had pleased him much to finally meet another enthusiast just as car crazy as himself.

He had met me at the plane arriving from San Juan at midnight. Driving back, it had taken more than an hour to get up the hill — traffic had been heavy in spite of the late hour. When we arrived at his home, the rows of those beautiful cars had become another obstacle — enjoyable, of course. Then there had been more talk in the library — between sips of French cognac so fine we never got a headache, between cooling breezes from windows open to city lights far below, between music from sapitos — those tiny frogs that sound like they carry their own little marimba, constantly hitting the same high note. We had been up till three in the morning. That was only a few hours ago, I thought to myself, sliding a little deeper into the comfortable seat. I had driven the 220 up from Caracas. We had passed through the city on the freeway that runs the length of it, then continued on a highway to the southeast, passing through thick-foliaged forests and green fields.

Driving the 220, I realized it was indeed a postwar link with the prewar past. The steering, the controls, the handling — all reminded me of classics I had driven. Even the view from the driver's seat was classic — the flat dash that narrowed, like on a boat; the long, slim, tall hood with the star way out there; the swooping fenders...

I felt myself slide farther down. Comfortable, I thought to myself. Those Mercedes designers sure knew how to make a car comfortable. I let my neck rest against the top of the seatback and reached up to adjust the visor so the sun would not shine in my eyes. Comfortable, I repeated...

It was siesta time on the plantation.

# 300Sc ROADSTER

# Up That Last Long Hill to Caracas...

The road snaked through the jungle like a narrow river. Here and there the jungle opened up and you could see traces of man; fields had been cleared long ago and bamboo planted around them. The bamboo grew thick and impenetrable now, like the jungle itself.

The Mercedes rolled like a boat in heavy seas as it charged ahead. Two cones of spinning dust came shooting out from behind the rear wheels and united farther back into a cloud that continued to twist and swirl until the turbulence went out of it, leaving the dust to sink slowly into the foliage. The ice chest with the beer and soda inside, the short wooden step ladder and my aluminum camera cases were making noises as they slid around on the fold-down seat behind us.

José Harth, owner of the 1957 300Sc Roadster, was at the wheel. I was in the passenger seat. He had driven very slowly going the other way earlier. But then it was important to keep the car clean for the pictures. Now we were in a hurry to get back to Caracas before the sunlight would be gone.

Between potholes and curves I was thinking about the location we had just left. It was a stroke of luck to have found it; like finding the needle in a haystack. I had described to José what I saw in the back of my mind. He had a vague mental picture of having seen such a place: Hacienda Iscaragua, built in 1837. It said so, right above the gate. A ruin now, coffee beans had once covered the slopes. When the profit went out of lowland-grown coffee the hacienda had been abandoned and the buildings left to deteriorate.

I was lucky, too, that I was dealing with an owner like

*(continued on overleaf)*

The 300S and Sc models were handbuilt automobiles, even though these photographs from the factory give an impression of assembly line procedures. Of course, it is all in the speed with which the line moves! Judging from the number of cars in presence, the photographs were probably taken during the latter part of 1952, just after production had reached a serious pace. At that time the average production was one car a day. Later, in 1954, 1955 and 1957, production averaged barely one car per week! The photographs show the stage where body panels were checked for final fit. As can be seen, the lowly file was still an important tool then.

Styling, craftsmanship and performance of this 300Sc Roadster brought back the glory-days of prewar 500K and 540K Roadsters. It is remarkable that Mercedes was again able to create an automobile that rivaled what had already become the standard of excellence. The fuel-injected Sc even outperformed its prewar counterparts. This beautiful 1957 Survivor, chassis number 180015-7500021 – all original except for the paint – was photographed in Caracas, Venezuela. In 1978, Jose Harth was finally able to obtain it from its second owner, an airline pilot, after having been on its trail for several years.

José, I thought to myself. Altogether, there were fewer than two hundred of these cars, the most valuable of all postwar Mercedes models. What were the odds in favor of finding an owner with José's philosophy? An owner who was willing to drive wherever the best location took him? Willing to take the risk a great photograph often requires?

We even had to build a primitive ramp of bricks and dirt to get the car into the courtyard. Where the mossy old tiles were. Where the pillars were. And the white-washed walls with the layers of old paint showing through here and there. Lavender.

It had been tough going getting in there.

Don't worry, José had said, when I looked sick from hearing the frame scrape against the bricks. Don't worry! This car is built like a railroad car. It was meant to be driven hard. This car you can't kill driving. It was built like a tank. Not like a railroad car. Like a tank! Sí, Señor! It should be driven. That's what it was built for. For what else would you use the car? You can't let it sit around. That's what makes it go bad!

I liked his philosophy.

Not that he was careless. Far from it. He kept all his cars in top shape. Not in concourse shape; but clean. Working properly. And he was fanatical about authenticity. A car was always better when it was used. The patina gave the car charm. Like a walked-in pair of shoes. Of course, there had to come a day when restoration was necessary. But that day should be postponed as long as possible.

I hope it was all worth it, I thought to myself as we came to the end of the dirt road. If the picture came out as good as it looked in the viewfinder, it would be worth it. Maybe a cover shot, I thought. But it should really have had everything in it. The stream on the other side of the main building. The jungle rising beyond it. And the parrots.

José wanted me to drive now. I slid in behind the wheel, found first gear, and accelerated out onto the paved road. There was that column-mounted shift lever again, same as on the 220. I just could't get used to it. It was as if I was stirring a pot of oatmeal. And then there was the gigantic steering wheel. Also a little hard to get used to. Especially since it required great movements to keep in touch with the direction of the wheels. I was moving my arms like you would when making fun of an old lady in her '52 Olds.

But those were unimportant observations. The overpowering fact was that almost no other car in the world could have given me the feeling of flying high as did this magnificent machine. I'm not talking about putting on

The 300S and Sc models were available in three different body styles: the Cabriolet, pictured above, which had the decorative landau irons and a roof that folded down in the traditional fashion, leaving it protruding from the rear deck; the Coupe, above right, which had a steel top that could not be removed; the Roadster — the last of the cars lined up in the picture to the lower right — which was equipped with a top that disappeared completely behind the seats, allowing for an uninterrupted rear deck line. The car pictured in the background is a 300 Cabriolet B. To the left, the instrument panel of the 300S.

the helmet and the driving suit. I'm talking about sliding into a tuxedo on a Monday morning!

After a few minutes on the paved road we reached the three-lane highway between Caracas and Guarenas. José told me to turn left. I accelerated through the gears with the engine purring quietly. Only at the end of each gear, when I kept the pedal down a little longer, letting the revolutions come rolling, did the engine give off an excited snarl. The wind was flowing briskly across the open cockpit now, grabbing our clothes, pulling our hair. The air was warm, and smooth as silk. I figured the sun had about five more minutes to go. Ahead, there was a long sweeping turn before the highway began to rise slowly, turning uphill, rising for ten or fifteen miles, leading to a summit and a final approach to the city.

José suddenly turned to me, shouting, "This is my favorite time of the day. I wanted to hurry back so you could have the pleasure of driving up this hill with the sun going down."

I smiled a thank you without taking my eyes off the road. We were doing about ninety kilometers an hour. In fouth. I shouted back to José, "Does it beat the 540K?"

"Sí, Señor! Claro!"

"Let's compare. The 540 had a straight-eight. Right? Pushrod. One hundred eighty horses!"

"But remember, that was with the supercharger going. This one has a straight-six. Overhead cam. One hundred seventy-five horses! And it's two thousand pounds lighter! You know what that means."

"Okay. But the frame is about the same, isn't it? Suspension too. Swing-axle. Right?"

"Yes, but this one has the single-pivot axle. Like on the 300SL Roadster. Handles better. And it has fuel injection. What was the top speed of the 540K?"

"One hundred sixty."

"Give it full throttle, Henry!"

I downshifted to third and pushed the pedal to the floor. The car surged. The speedometer needle swung to one hundred twenty. I shifted to fourth when the snarl got angry. The car continued to surge, passing new cars with expressionless look-what-I-am-driving types behind the wheel, passing old cars with neck-turning, surprise-faced passengers, passing over-crowded buses with lots of faces, a look-at-that-old-car expression on them, the owners of the faces hanging out through the open windows, smiling, waving, shouting, all while the old workhorses spewed out clouds of exhaust, laboring hard in low gear.

I looked at the needle again — one hundred sixty.

"It's doing it uphill!"

"Sí, Señor!"

300SL COUPE

# By the Grand Piano, a Gullwing!

"The Gullwing!"

Even before Alex Dearborn answered I knew I had asked an unnecessary question. How could a man who had built a business and a lifestyle around a single automobile — who even kept an example of it in his living room — be expected to say anything else?

We sat quietly, both looking at the silver Gullwing parked over by the grand piano. It was placed there like an art object. Which it was!

No ordinary car, the Gullwing, I thought. And Alex, no ordinary man — no ordinary living room!

The home of Alex Dearborn was the former carriage house of a large estate located one-half-hour's drive northeast of Boston. It had been built by a railroad tycoon in the early part of this century. Some years ago the land and the various buildings on it had been split into smaller parcels. The carriage house itself was grand enough for a king.

Alex and his family occupied the upstairs portion. One end of it alone was so roomy the kids used it for a basketball court. Downstairs, in the middle of the facade, were the entrance doors, themselves magnificent examples of old-time craftmanship. Inside, to the right, were the stables. But, where horses used to be kept, now stood rows of Mercedes collector cars. To the left, with floor and walls and ceiling covered by Southern pine, was the hall where the carriages used to stand — now the living room!

It was a huge room, more like a grand ballroom, with high ceilings and an enormous fireplace. In the old days it was where hunting parties gathered before and after the day's activities. Now there were oriental rugs, plush sofas, comfortable chairs, coffee tables, antique lamps and large desks — stacked high with automotive literature.

Alex had a fire going. The light from the flames

Above top, the very first version of the 300SL. Note that the gullwing doors have not yet been cut down into the side panels. Left, the design of the space frame was arrived at through experiments with models. Above, the engine compartment of the racing version. Opposite page, top, Rudolf Uhlenhaut, responsible for the technical development of the 300SL, photographed beside the chassis. This picture clearly shows the angle of the engine. To the left, the interior of the open cars raced at the Nürburgring. To the right, the interior of the car displayed at the New York Auto Show in 1954. Bottom right, the first prototype of the production version 300SL. Note the different treatments of nose and hood.

flickered, making patterns that danced on the paneling and colored and warmed our faces. His looked like that of an English gentleman, fair-skinned and honest-eyed, with features that had been molded by a stubborn strength.

We were waiting for the other guests to arrive; Alex had invited a few car-enthusiast friends for an informal get-together.

"The Gullwing was always your favorite?"

"Yes, as long as I can remember. But to begin with I didn't know enough about Mercedes cars to know about the Gullwing, from a technical viewpoint, I mean. I had to learn the hard way. The first Mercedes I owned was a 1954 220 Sedan. Still have it, matter of fact! Bought it for six hundred dollars. It needed a lot of work. Trouble was I couldn't find anyone competent to do it! That's how I discovered there was a need. So, I decided to open a shop. But I would specialize in Mercedes cars from the fifties. No other models! No other marques! That was in 1972."

"It obviously worked very well!"

"Very well indeed!"

"And now you've sold that business?"

"Yes, in 1978 I sold it to my employees, headed by Paul Russell. The Gullwing Service Company they call it. My own business is still named Dearborn Automobile Company. You see, I was faced with a dilemma! I got more and more involved with the brokerage of cars. It was finally too much to handle both businesses. Besides, I saw an opportunity to realize an idea I'd had for some time. So I bought a larger building in Topsfield. The original business was moved from Marblehead to the new facility. There we had room for an additional four businesses, all catering to Mercedes cars — but all independently owned and operated! You see the advantages? I also formed a new company, specializing in the leasing of old and new Mercedes cars. It's called Boston Leasing Company. So now we have — all under one roof — a service shop for newer models, a body shop for older models, a body shop for newer models, the original restoration shop, and my showroom..."

There were sounds from cars driving up in front of the house. Alex left to greet the guests. I was too exhausted from two days of photographing the Gullwing to even attempt to get up from the deep of the sofa. I let my eyes return to the bulky, bulbous, brutish-bold shapes of the Gullwing, standing there in the room, big-wheeled and beautiful.

Everything about the car is extraordinary, I thought to myself. Just to sit inside that cockpit is extraordinary, the *(continued on overleaf)*

One of the most talked-about automotive designs of all time, the 300SL Gullwing hardly needs an introduction. This 1955 Survivor, chassis number 198040-550042, belongs to Alex Dearborn of Topsfield, Massachusetts, who has received international recognition for the fine Mercedes automobiles he restores and purveys. A remarkable quality of this track-proven sports racing car is that it not only looks awesome but also elegant, as evidenced by these photographs, taken in front of the carriage house Dearborn has converted to garage his inventory as well as his personal collection.

seat grabbing a hold of you so firm, the ledge and the tunnel surrounding you so protectively, those two big gauges staring back at you so invitingly, the doors curving above you so curiously, their chromed telescope tubes shining brightly. Even entering the car is extraordinary, I thought, the way you have to do it just right: treading one leg in first, placing the foot far back on the floor board, then sitting down on the leather-covered ledge, then leaning in at the same time as you grab hold of the tunnel — placing your hand far enough back so as not to lose your balance when you let yourself drop into the seat — then following with the other leg, bending the knee, grabbing the ankle with the left hand, pulling the doubled-up leg back toward you while you sweep it over and across that ledge — not hitting leather!

You could tell from scratch marks whether owners had bothered to learn the technique or not.

And, of course, driving it was extraordinary, I thought to myself: pulling the choke, turning the key, the gauges coming to life; then pushing the start button while pressing the pedal lightly, the engine coming to life, a little unsure of itself, clearing its throat, then straightening up when you patted the pedal a few times; the engine rumbling sound and deep-voiced, then taking off with that whining sound from the transmission; accelerating out onto the open road; listening to that open-mounted hissing from the engine sucking in air when you floored the pedal; going through the gears; and when you let up between shifting, listening to that sound from behind you, sounding a little like when you were a boy and you ran along a picket fence with your stick . . .

Yes, the Gullwing was extraordinary all around. A race car for the road! Was Ferrari first with that concept? I asked myself. No, of course not, the world's oldest car company had done it before, in the twenties, I remembered, with its SS model.

The Gullwing had to be counted among the three top postwar sports cars, I decided. What about the other two? The Ferrari GTO was worthy. And a Jaguar? The XK120? Too many made? The XKSS? Too few made?

The guests were introduced. Terry Bennett. Paul Russell. Christopher Smallhorn.

"Name the three most outstanding sports cars of the early postwar period."

It was a challenge that caused enough thought and discussion to outlast the evening. To outlast Alex's supply of fire wood. As well as his Dubonnet.

There was of course no agreement. We were all of different temperament. But one car kept cropping up!

How could it not? Especially with one sitting right there in the living room!

Featured on these pages is a unique series of photographs from the factory, showing various steps during the assembly of the 300SL. To the far left, the jig is used to check the form of the body panels. Top left and above, it took a lot of skill to make the gullwing doors fit perfectly. Note the lighter color of the hood, together with the doors and the trunk lid, made from aluminum. To the near left, the engine is lowered into the chassis. The fuel injection side is toward the front. To the right, the body, with all its panels fitted, but still lacking paint and interior trim, is mated with the chassis, lacking only wheels.

# 300SL ROADSTER

# Promising Beginning, Regrettable Ending.

When you make your living photographing cars, as I do, you spend a lot of time thinking about the sky and what you see up there. Where is the sun coming up? Going down? Is it going to shine at all or is it going to be overcast?

On the day I had arranged to take pictures of Manfredo Lippmann's 1958 300SL Roadster the weather report had promised partly cloudy skies with a chance of rain in the late afternoon. Especially in the foothills. Snow in the mountains.

The location I had chosen, Red Rocks, west of Denver, was located in the foothills. Rain isn't welcome when you take pictures of an open car. But it was still my number one choice; the rough red rocks would look very dramatic behind the smooth red roadster.

I had spent the morning making a final check of the location. The sky was good, a haze covering the sun cast an even light on the formations. The Rockies rose blue and fuzzy-peaked in the distance.

When I arrived at the warehouse where the 300SL was stored, it turned out that the caretaker had no time to come along; my chaperone had more important things to do. It meant I could have the 300SL all to myself. You always have a better time without a chaperone, I thought to myself as I took off.

Driving it along the backroads up into the foothills, I had a strong sensation of doing something I had done before. I coudn't remember where or when. Only that there was something uncomfortable connected with the experience.

But it felt good to be back behind the wheel. It was good to feel that fifties feeling again; that big and heavy feel of the steering wheel, feeling the suspension kick-

*Captured at speed on the Nürburgring, above, is the open version 300SL sports racing car. Driven by Fritz Reiss, it came in third in a victorious row of four such cars. To the left, Rudolf Uhlenhaut, in charge of racing development — as competent behind the wheel as any of the competition drivers — gets ready for the first test in the open version 1955 300SLR. Two years later came the open version 300SL — one could have wished for a development of the SLR, rather than a refinement of the SL. Opposite page, American Paul O'Shea, seen at Bridgehampton, successfully campaigned a factory-prepared Roadster during the 1957 season, capturing the SCCA title.*

ing you innocently in the seat, that typical 300SL feeling, rather trucklike — less so in the Roadster, but still there.

When I arrived at the location, the sky had changed. There were big clouds up there so that part of the time the sun was bright, making dark definite shadows, and part of the time obscured, making weak fuzzy-edged shadows.

I preferred to shoot when the sun was gone. It meant I had to wait for long periods. While I sat there, my back against a rock, looking at the sensous shapes of the Roadster, I felt that strange sensation again. The disappointment too.

It was a pity the Roadster turned out to be the last true Mercedes sports car, I thought to myself. There should always have been a high-performance machine in the model line-up!

The excitement began with the original 300SL, that first racing version running away from its competition in 1952. It had the innovative space frame that made it so light. And it had those round, smooth shapes that allowed it to shoot through the air like a bullet. The first version had the gullwing doors end at the bottom edge of the windows. The next version got the doors cut down a ways into the body side panels. There was also a Roadster version. Altogether only ten cars were made. Then there was the pre-production version — only one made — with slightly different front-end styling. Next came the production Gullwing, fourteen hundred made, and finally the Roadster, about eighteen hundred.

The Roadster differed from the Gullwing in more ways than it first appears to, I thought to myself. They didn't just cut the roof off. The front and rear ends were made one inch longer, adding two inches to the overall length. The rear fender was made higher, the trunk more drawn out, the splash shields above the wheels longer, the chrome strips coming out from the side vents also longer. And, of course, the headlights were now vertical with smoothly shaped glass covers. And then there was the wraparound windshield.

But it was really under the skin that it differed the most. That original racing car had three downdraft Solex carbs. The output was 175 hp. Top speed about 150 mph. The weight was less than 2,000 pounds. On the production car the carbs had been replaced by fuel injection. The output was now 215 hp, but the weight had increased by almost 1,000 pounds! Top speed was about 140 mph. The frame was the same as on the racing version. So was the suspension and the wheelbase. But front and rear tracks were almost four inches narrower on the Gullwing.

*(continued on overleaf)*

**D**ecoratively pitched against the rough shapes created by the Hands of Nature are the smooth forms made by the Hands of Man; dramatic cliff formations in Red Rocks National Park, west of Denver, Colorado, is the setting for these photographs of Manfredo Lippmann's 1958 300SL Roadster, chassis number 198042-8500126. A recent restoration has returned it to the same condition it was in when Lippmann took delivery of it brand new. The unique knock-off wheels are still there – a reminder of the days long ago when he piloted the 300SL over tough road racing courses all across Central America.

The Gullwing had two major flaws: handling and brakes. And two major drawbacks: lack of adequate ventilation and lack of adequate luggage space. The Roadster was an improvement in all areas. It had the new single-pivot swing axle. In 1961 it also got four-wheel disc brakes.

The frame of the Roadster was basically still the same — but now more compact across the side-members. The engine and transmission sat slightly lower in the frame. The front and rear tracks had increased slightly. The fuel tank was smaller, the spare wheel relocated and the trunk, therefore, larger. The ride was a little softer and the steering less direct — the Gullwing took two turns to lock, the Roadster, three.

Unfortunately, engine output was left unchanged. Unfortunately, because the car had become almost four hundred pounds heavier. So the Roadster actually had a little lower top speed than the Gullwing. It was a deliberate move, I thought to myself. It was a continuation of the concept of "the Mercedes luxury sports car," first applied to the 190SL.

Why didn't they go the other way, I asked myself? They already had the engine and the styling available in the 1955 300SLR. A straight-eight developing 300 hp. Top speed 175 mph! And the styling! That drawn-out nose with headlight covers á la Ferrari Testa Rossa. Only two made of the one with the gullwing doors. As far as I'm concerned a car never had to look any better, I thought.

It looked like there would be no more shooting that day. The clouds had suddenly become thick and unpenetrable. The Rockies were dark gray and washed blurry, like on a watercolor painting. It was snowing up there. That meant it would soon rain down here. I had better get out.

I stood up to collect my camera gear. And just at that moment I suddenly remembered: It was in 1969, in Sweden. I had been looking at a 300SL Roadster to buy. Twenty thousand Swedish crowns; five thousand dollars then. The owner let me have it for the day to try it. I had taken it out in the country, parked it beside the road, against some granite rock formations. Then I had sat down in the grass to look at it. Yes, I remembered now. Later I had driven back on the motorway to Stockholm. I had been doing 225 kmph. Suddenly there had been a ripping sound coming from behind me. I was scared to death and didn't dare to turn my head. Not until I had slowed considerably. The sides of the soft top had broken loose and were flapping in the wind like the flaps of an old-timer's leather helmet.

I never bought the Roadster. It was that feeling of disappointment I still felt inside.

If the Roadster looks longer than the Coupe, as in the picture to the upper right, it must be an illusion — or is it possible that one extra inch up front and one in the back can be seen? The optional hardtop became available late in 1958. The extreme wrap around of the window gave excellent rear vision. In the picture to the lower right, can be seen the vertical headlights and the long chrome strips extending from the sides vents — two of the most obvious styling changes. To the left, the dash of a 1957 prototype. The extremely attractive steering wheel, with its recessed horn button, was unfortunately never placed in production.

190SL ROADSTER

# A Scientific Study of Shapes at Sunrise.

It was five in the morning and still pitch dark. A gentle breeze from Cuba came tip-toeing up along the shore. It hardly moved the black branches of the palms that lined Fort Lauderdale's long sandy beach, separating it from the four-lane highway that ran parallel to it.

Lee McDonald and I sat quietly inside his 190SL. The air flowed through the rolled-down windows, feeling crisp but a little nippy from the pre-dawn chill. I felt frozen from having just gotten out of bed. I clenched the white foam-plastic cup with its steaming hot coffee from the all-night coffee shop on the corner of Las Olas and Sunrise Boulevard. Sipping from that cup and warming my hands on it seemed to be the only life-supporting systems in operation.

We were waiting for the sunrise.

Lee was originally from Pennsylvania. He had been a sales manager with the Algar Ferrari dealership before he embarked on a career in auto racing; successful, but cut short from a lack of funds. He had then established Prova, capitalizing on his connections among Ferrari owners, as well as realizing a desire for being his own man and for living where life was pleasant.

Prova specializes in the sales of high-quality collector Ferraris. Right now Lee was trying to find a home for the one-off 250GT Spyder Pinin Farina shown at the Geneva Salon in 1957. It featured a cut-down door on the driver's side and was purchased after the show by Ferrari team-driver Peter Collins. Lee is also working on a film documentary on the life of Enzo Ferrari for Gar-Mac Productions.

Lee had run across the 190SL by accident, at the time not on the lookout for a car, but having always been attracted to its elegant lines. He felt it could be worth-while to try a new set of wheels for cruising around Fort

Lauderdale where the climate certainly favors year-round top-down motoring. The car was also exceptionally well preserved having been pampered since new by its owner Haddon Judson, a prominent name in automotive circles and a manufacturer of super-chargers and magnetos. The paint had faded a little over the years, so Lee had Durland Edwards give it a top notch paint job. The car is one of the earliest cars produced, number 240, to emerge in 1955.

Looking out across the waves I became aware of a slight bluing of the sky. It was reflected in the glossy never-still surface of the Atlantic. The surf landed on the beach with a slow, soothing rhythm. But I knew from experience that it would all happen very quickly when it finally did happen. I decided to get my camera in position at once. I had found a portion of the beach where two lone palms leaned their slim bent trunks, making long lazy expressions against the lightening sky. The 190SL stood parked in front of them, carefully positioned so as to counterbalance the weight of the still-black palm crowns.

I had decided to place the Mamyia low, in fact, right on the pavement of the opposite far-left lane. Never in the habit of using a tripod, I folded one of Lee's polishing rags and placed it under the camera so it could be easily angled. Flat on my stomach — Lee watching for early-bird traffic — I checked the viewfinder. It looked good.

All I needed now was a colorful sunrise.

I sat down on the edge of the sidewalk, waiting for it to come, when I suddenly remembered the photographs stowed away in the back of my camera case. I got them out and lit my pen-size flashlight.

"Hey, Lee! Ever seen these? The 190SL prototype," I said. "See that strange nose? Angular. More protruding. And that hood? Opens up all the way down to the grille. There's a hood scoop too! And look at the shape of that rear fender. Flatter on top."

Lee bent down to take a closer look, then straightened to check his own car, sitting there across from us, subtly illuminated by the street lights.

"There's no splash shield above the rear wheel arch on that prototype car!" he said. "See that?"

"Yes. Look at yours. Yours doesn't have any chrome trim on those splash shields and no chrome trim along the bottom edge of the side panel either, below the door. Typical for the early cars! Yours probably didn't come with a hardtop. That option came later and those cars all had the chrome trim."

I shuffled the photographs until I found one of the interior. Lee bent down again.

*(continued on overleaf)*

*The photographs on these pages show the 190SL prototype as it was introduced in 1954. The most obvious differences were found in its styling: slightly more protruding grille; the hood scoop; the hood that opens all the way down to the grille; the shape of the rear fender; the lack of splash panel above the rear wheel. To give the 190SL a more sporty image, a version geared to the weekend racing enthusiast was also made available. It featured low-cut aluminum doors that lacked windows and had a small screen in front of the driver. The idea was that these items could be easily exchanged for the everyday doors and windshield.*

arly morning sunlight floats across the waves of the Atlantic, tinting the silver surfaces of Lee McDonald's 1955 190SL Roadster, chassis number 5500230. It is parked beside the main beach in Fort Lauderdale, Florida, where McDonald operates Prova Automotive, an organization specializing in the purveyance of Ferraris and other fine automobiles. The prototype 190SL was first seen in early 1954, but production did not begin until early 1955. Less than 1,800 units were made that year. With its low chassis number, McDonald's is one of the first to emerge from the production line.

"The gauges are arranged differently," he said. "And there's no leather on top of the dash, just a thin strip, padded, it looks like, running all along that upper edge. And look at that bent, long shift lever. Looks like one of those palm trunks!"

"This is the car exhibited at the New York Auto Show early in 1954," I said. "It was featured with one of the first production Gullwings. A curious thing was that both cars had the same rear axle at that time. The old swing axle, you know. But about a year later, when the 190SL production car was introduced, it had the improved low-pivot-point swing axle. Same as on the later 300SL Roadster, but without that big compensating spring. Curious thing is that they kept the old axle on the Gullwing, in spite of the fact that it didn't handle well . . . By the way, the specs for the prototype 190SL called for a column-type shift lever. You could also have the car with a bench seat instead of the buckets!"

I shuffled the photographs.

"Look at this, Lee! You could get cut-down racing doors for it! Aluminum. And a small racing screen, too. The big one came off with two screws. The bumpers came off easily, too. Those were the days of the dual purpose sports car, weren't they!"

"It shows their marketing strategy, too!" Lee said. "Shows that they tried to squeeze as much as possible out of the 190SL looking like the 300SL. There was no way it could have been competitive on the track though! It was way too heavy!"

"Yes, too heavy and too sluggish!" I said. "That racing stuff was only image. It wasn't even needed. The 190SL was a success because of what it was — a classy, comfortable, sporty-looking two-seater!"

I happened to look up at the sky. It had suddenly turned bright yellow to the east. There was a cloud bank sitting heavily on the horizon, hiding the sun that had already risen behind it. The cloud was a dusty pink and had fuzzy orange edges. I knew the picture would change quickly now. Lee and I jumped into action. I laid down flat on the street, looking through the viewfinder. The curved trunks were in there and the crowns, silhouetted black against the sky. And the car was in there, a thin burning outline of orange flowing along its contour.

"Hey, Lee! Turn on the lights!"

It would have to be a time exposure. I pressed down hard on the housing of the Mamyia, holding it perfectly still while I pushed the shutter release.

A moment later the rays of the sun shot across the edge of the cloud and everything became light, all colors consumed now by the brightness of morning.

The 190SL came both as a Roadster and as a Coupe with removable hardtop. Pictured on the opposite page, bottom, is the second version hardtop, introduced in 1959, featuring an enlarged rear window. The 190SL was seldom seen on a racetrack, but here, opposite page, top, the factory has dropped a diesel engine into its smaller sports car for an all-out attack on the world speed record for diesel cars, Class E, under 2000cc. The new record over the standing kilometer was fixed at 98.6 kmph. The seats of the Roadster, above, were inspired by racing buckets. To the right, a Roadster photographed on a picturesque cobblestone street in the German wine-growing community of Pleisweiler.

300d SEDAN

# Plain Setting for Fancy Automobile.

The road runs straight like a cutting edge. There are few trees. Fewer houses. Fields, a faded ocher color from the lifeless stubble of last year's crop, extend their planes seemingly all the way to the horizon. Like on an ocean, the curve of the planet is almost there to see.

I am driving a 300d. The engine sounds like it is working too hard, like there should be another gear to engage. I glance at the speedometer. Seventy. When the model got the automatic transmission, an American Borg-Warner unit, it was not well adapted. Jay Pettit, owner of the car, had told me about it earlier. Curiously, the American-market version got a 5.11 rear axle ratio instead of the standard 4.67. It meant lower top speed and higher revs during normal cruising. I slow to fifty and feel the engine settle down to a peaceful hum.

The skyline of Decatur is slowly vanishing behind me as I continue on my way to a location I had found the previous afternoon. The primitive simplicity of the fields would be an effective contrast to the urbane elegance of the 300d. I could visualize the car in front of the ornate entrance to a hotel or the monogrammed awnings of a restaurant. But what would it look like out here? I just hope there will be no unpleasant surprises; like that time in Italy when I had found a place with columns and arches and wild grass in front of them. I had especially liked the grass, growing tall, leaning lazily in the wind. When I came back to photograph the Alfa the next day, the grass had been cut!

The 300d was introduced in 1957. Production began late that year. It was basically a 300 of 1951 vintage, but it now had new styling. The trunk lid and the rear fenders, as well as the front fenders, had been extended, all made possible by a four-inch longer wheelbase. There was also the pillarless window design, a

The photograph above was taken in August of 1957 — before the 300d was officially available. Factory engineers, visible inside the car, are engaged in fine tuning the new automatic transmission. The 300d was even more formal than its predecessor. The rear, left, with its larger trunk and wider window, was an area where obvious changes had been made. Mercedes-Benz, in 1960, presented Pope John with a special 300d — a Landaulet. This version had a convertible top that began just behind the divider window, and a throne-like chair that occupied the entire rear seat. To the right, the Pope gives the car its official blessing.

feature allowing an uninterrupted open window area. The engine, on the original 300 producing one hundred thirty-five horsepower, was now fitted with fuel-injection, which increased power to one hundred eighty horsepower. There was also power steering and, optional from 1959, air conditioning. Jay's example is from 1962, the last year of production, when only forty-five cars were made.

The plains of this part of Illinois are cut up into huge squares separated by the kinds of roads I am driving on. It had been difficult to locate one without power poles and power lines; the poles would destroy the simplicity and the lines would reflect in the polished surface of the car. Where is that road? Have I passed it? I decide to continue straight, searching both sides carefully.

Driving on, I remember something else Jay had told me, something about the power steering. I can feel it. It feels like the assisting impulses are not coordinated with the movements of the steering wheel, causing the car to wander off and you have to correct it. Only the car will then wander off in another direction, so that you have to correct continously. I cannot be sure that it is not a peculiarity to this particular car. Jay seems to think that it might be a characteristic found in all early cars fitted with power assisted steering.

Another element of the 300d that also seems not up to par is the air conditioning. I am not thinking of the way it works — I do not care to try it out, slightly frozen as I am from the pre-spring coolness — but of the way it looks. Two enormous scoops protrude from the rear window deck; they are made from ugly-looking black bakelite and do not at all fit the styling theme of the interior. Below these scoops, inside the trunk, sits the evaporator, taking up a lot of space. It looks a little like the one in my motel room, I think to myself.

Those three elements, the automatic transmission, the power steering and the air conditioning were obviously concessions to American tastes, overtures to an all-out attack on the rich market on the other side of the Atlantic. On subsequent models these elements would be fully developed, but on the 300d they remain curious mementos from an infantile stage.

But there is nothing underdeveloped or immature about the rest of the car, I think to myself as I continue to look for the road. The engineering is built on decades of research and development. The styling is superb. The standard of workmanship is on an exceptionally high level.

It has never been a tradition at Mercedes to give credit to stylists. But they have always touted their
(continued on overleaf)

**R**epresenting one of the most prestigious luxury automobiles of its era, this 1962 300d Sedan, chassis number 189.011-12-003131, belonging to Jay Pettit of Decatur, Illinois, retains its majestic elegance even on a narrow farm road, surrounded by freshly plowed fields. In its day the 300d was the means of transportation for dignitaries such as German Chancellor Adenauer as well as President Kennedy on his state visit to Mexico. Pettit, who maintains his beautiful example in perfectly original condition, values it as one of the most outstanding examples of postwar automotive craftsmanship.

engineers. Fritz Nallinger and Rudolf Uhlenhaut, top names during the early postwar period, were always given credit for their innovations. If one searches Mercedes literature with dedication, one will run across the name Karl Wilfert. He was responsible for the styling department during these years. Responsible. Not necessarily the creator of the actual shape! One might also stumble upon the name of Paul Brac, a Frenchman employed at the Mercedes styling department. He was supposedly the man who created the 300SL Gullwing. If this is correct, I think to myself, if he actually did do the 300SL, and if he actually is French, it is ironic that a design always thought of as being typically teutonic, came from the pen of a Frenchman!

I suddenly realize I have forgotten to look for the road. Where is it? Did I pass it? I must have. I decide to turn back.

I remember another subject Jay and I discussed. I had asked him why he was so attracted to the fifties and sixties Mercedes cars. Why that period in particular? The chrome plated brass, he had said. Not the brass itself, of course, but the quality of workmanship and the limited production it symbolized.

The 300d, for instance, he had said, has chrome plated brass stampings and extrusions all over: the windshield and window frames, the radiator, the head-light rims and all the chrome trim. The radiator grid is aluminum. All the die castings are, from necessity, made out of white metal: the star, the door handles, the model identification trim and so on. The bumpers and the hubcaps are pressed steel.

The brass period began to deteriorate with the 280SL, where the side moldings were of aluminum, chemically brightened and anodized — a necessary move to facilitate mass production. But the 280SL is still looked upon as belonging to the brass period.

The 280SL, by the way, is one of Jay's particular favorites. And he should know what he is talking about. A 300Sc Roadster as well as a 300SL Roadster and a 600 Limousine that once belonged to the Shah of Iran are among the other Mercedes cars he owns. Of course, they all have their particular purposes. The 300Sc is the car to use when you go to the club. The 300SL is the car for the track. The 300d is the car to drive to a formal dinner. The 600 is the car in which to pick up business acquaintances. But the 280SL, is the car for the road!

The road! Hey! There it is!

But right where I had planned on placing the car, right there, a tractor was busily plowing the field, destroying it, sending a cloud of dust into the air . . .

In 1951 — after a ten-year respite — Mercedes-Benz was again able to offer a big, impressive, limousine-type automobile. The 300, first shown at the Frankfurt Auto Show, was the embodiment of this theme. The conservative styling, the luxurious interior and the powerful engine, made this model perfectly matched to the demands of such a car. The 300 was most often seen in dark colors, but even in a light color, as in the picture above, it retains its formal elegance. What about when it carries skis on its roof? As in the picture to the left. The photograph to the right, shows the Cabriolet version, of which 642 units were built.

# 220SE CABRIOLET

# The World, According to Mr. Price.

Right beside the Red River, before it joins the mighty Mississippi, right in the heart of Louisiana, there is a city, and in that city there is a big, square, two-story industrial building built from brick, once a Coca-Cola bottling plant, now, without any signs of use, standing there alone in a deteriorating neighborhood. There has been talk about tearing the building down to make room for a new thoroughfare, and if that ever happens Walter Price will have to look for another place to keep his forty Mercedes cars.

Walter Price grew up in that town. And he never left it to live anywhere else. True, he was away while studying architecture at Georgia Tech. And he was gone for a few years during the war. In the Air Force. Navigator on a B-24. After two missions to Anzio (we hit it from the sea . . .), he was shot down over Steyr on his ninth (we took a direct hit in the number two engine and bailed out from twenty-five thousand feet . . .) and was taken prisoner. He was lucky — not all of the men made it (we left two dead in the tail section and one was killed when the plane hit the ground . . .). But except for those detours, (a man has got to learn a profession and he has got to do his duty in wartime . . .), he stayed faithful to the city by the river.

When Walter Price takes you to his building to show you the cars, he will invite you to ride with him in his 1971 280SE Sedan (have had this one since new . . . has got two hundred thousand miles on it now . . .). He will drive

*(continued on overleaf)*

*Featured on these pages is the work of Kurt Wörner at its best! Almost all the excellent black and white historic photographs in this volume come from his prolific Leica camera, via Road & Track, which purchased the entire collection a few years ago. Wörner chose to capture the essence of the beautiful light-colored 220SE Cabriolet by placing it against the magnificent Swiss Alps, the Brünigpass and the Süstenpass, to be specific. These photographs reflect the pleasure of motoring the way it once used to be — both in Europe and America — when the automobile was not only a means of everyday transportation, but a way to explore the land.*

Chromed brass, wood, leather – true materials of the classic automobile – abound in the 220SE Cabriolet. In this perennial favorite, the materials were combined to create one of the most lavishly comfortable models to emerge from Mercedes. The pictures on these pages, photographed on the grounds of a plantation in Louisiana, show the splendor of this 1960 Survivor, chassis number 128.030-10-003042, belonging to Walter Price. The model could not be complemented for speed and power – its attraction lay solely in the areas of styling and comfort – areas in which it could be sure to draw superlatives.

fast, and when you arrive at the building, he will drive right up in front of the tall delivery door, honk three times, and when the door rolls up, rattling and squeaking — seemingly before it has risen high enough to let the car under — he will drive inside, fast. The door will roll down and close behind the car, and, from the outside, everything will look as before — as if the door and the building were never used.

It is dark inside and it will take a while before your eyes are used to it. But soon you will begin to recognize rows of familiar shapes; 220SEb, 250SE, 280SE Sedans and Coupes and Cabriolets, even a few 300SE Coupes and Sedans, sitting there on their knees from the suspensions being shot, all just resting there quietly idle (my brother bought a Mercedes and he told me I ought to get one too . . . he liked it real well, he said . . . I drove his for a week and I couldn't believe what I had missed out on . . . I used to buy a new Lincoln Continental every year . . . no more . . . it was like a religious conversion . . . I had to tell everyone about Mercedes and what a great car it was . . .) Next he will take you past rows of 180 and 220 Sedans in another part of the building, opening hoods and doors on some, wiping a patch of paint clean on others (all this one needs is a new water pump . . . this one has to have the driver's seat replaced . . . see how the paint on this one is still pretty good . . . amazing how well they hold up . . .).

Then he will take you around to the back of the building where engines and axles lay lined up in orderly rows, and hoods and doors and trunk lids stand stacked against the walls, and wrecks sit oily-black and rusty-brown with their guts removed (it got to the point where I thought everyone should drive a Mercedes . . . but I figured not everyone could afford to buy new . . . so I started buying up old ones . . . figured it was my duty to provide people with the best car there was . . . in the end I had six mechanics working for me, full time, just fixing them to sell . . . and I was traveling all over buying every old Mercedes I could lay my hands on . . .).

Then he will take you to another area where there is shelf upon shelf stacked high with trim details, seats, dashes, gauges, steering wheels, wheels, hubcaps (trouble was, the public wasn't ready . . . they were ignorant . . . they were too caught up in this new-model-every-year business . . I've bought and sold about two hundred cars, I figure . . . but I never made any money on them . . . not that that was what I was after . . . but the public just wasn't ready for it . . . have about forty left . . .).

And then there is yet another part of the building, over to the side, the white bottling-plant tiles still covering the

floor. This is the area for the chosen ones — his own collection. There is one 300S Cabriolet, one 300S Coupe, one 600 (this is my second... bought my first new in '72... should have never sold it...), one 190SL, two 280SL Roadsters, one 280SE 3.5 Cabriolet, one 300SE Coupe, one 280SE Coupe, and several 280SEL and 300SEL Sedans (I'm going to have to thin out among those... I'll keep the best one of each...).

Just as you think you have seen it all he will take you over to a big elevator. It is big enough to hold a car and... yes, you guessed it. He will lower the prison-bar gate, slamming it shut, and the elevator will begin to rise, shivering, shrugging, finally coming to a halt, jerking. Up there it is light and airy. There are wooden floors and antique furniture — the former executive offices. He will bid you to exit the elevator first (after you, sir...) and as you round the corner your eyes will be dazzled by an astonishingly well-preserved 300SL Roadster (knew of that one for a long time... finally got it last year... seven thousand original miles...). Beside it stands an almost equally good 300S Cabriolet. And beside it, in the last spot — there is only room for three — an immaculate green 220SE Cabriolet (got a Gullwing under restoration... Don't know where to put it...).

He will talk at length about the green convertible (this is one of my favorites... it's a '60 model... they made only twelve hundred that year, handmade... it was their top of the line model... you could buy the 300 Cabriolet, true, but that was a limo... look at all this wood, more wood than in any other Mercedes... the new model, the 220SEb, came in '61, was nothing like this... this one is the epitome of luxury and craftsmanship...). He will invite you to sit behind the wheel and you will understand his enthusiasm, sinking deep into the leather aroma, surrounded by the sight of wood, wood on the dash, burled walnut, four and a half feet of it, solid, so solid it helps stablize the cowl, wood around the windshield, wood on the armrests, leather seats, wide and soft, leather on the door panels, he points (wood, leather, wood, wood...).

Now he will turn around and with sweeping gestures tell you what he wants to do up there (I'm going to have car seats set up... groups with tables... and I'm going to have books and artifacts like a museum... and over there I'm going to have a car rotating... so you can sit here and look at it from every angle...).

Afterward you will know that you have been with a true enthusiast, one of the few who still have an honest regard for what is good and right (those Mercedes cars are built right... and I like that...).

*The 220S and SE came in two luxury versions: Cabriolet and Coupe. The hardtop of the latter was non-removable. The Coupe, pictured above, was even more restrained in its appearance than was the Cabriolet — truly a car for the distinguished lady or gentleman. Its interior, same as that of the Cabriolet, shown to the left, matched the elegance of the exterior. More wood and leather was used than in any other Mercedes of its size. Pictured to the right, the 220S, from which the luxury versions were derived, was also an elegant car. It began life in 1954, and was produced until 1959, at which time more than eighty thousand units had been made.*

# 600 LIMOUSINE

# Perfection, for the Sake of Perfection.

I am intrigued to discover yet another oasis, yet another of those refreshing havens of appreciation of quality and craftsmanship that still remains on this desert planet, where sometimes only the crass and the superficial seem to survive.

This particular oasis is flourishing inside an unpretentious gray building in Escondido, a community located twenty miles northeast of San Diego.

Thomas Kreid, a German descendant from Illinois, is the well of this oasis. He would not want to describe himself in those terms, but he is nevertheless, with his two decades of experience, one of the most knowledgeable Mercedes experts around. He has spent the past four years exclusively involved in researching the prewar classics, the 500K and 540K (particular emphasis has been on the Special Roadster, of which one example exists in his collection), and the postwar greats, the 300S and 300Sc, as well as the modern Mercedes giant, the 600.

Inside this oasis I encounter five cars, all in such excellent condition that I have seldom seen a collection like it under one roof.

The first is a metallic-silver 280SL (a restoration exercise, Thomas tells me). After a virtual remanufacture, which took only nine weeks, it was entered in the 1982 National Meet of the Mercedes-Benz Club and was chosen Reserve Best of Show.

The second car is a twelve-thousand-mile 300SL Roadster, probably the best preserved original example in the world. The original whitewalls, Continental Super Record High Speeds, are still on it — not even the weights have been touched! It has unusual color combinations (California colors, Thomas calls them): bamboo interior, ivory exterior, beige hardtop (like coffee with cream, he tells me). This car was the centerfold of

*(continued on overleaf)*

In spite of all its impressive elegance — as evidenced by the photograph to the left, picturing the 600 Limousine by the shores of Lago Maggiore in northern Italy — there was still an automobile that could top it! That automobile was the bigger brother of the 600 Limousine, the truly majestic 600 Pullman. It was built on a twenty-seven-inch longer wheelbase and was intended for heads of state and other dignitaries. Above, the Pullman, and to the right, the Landaulet (a Pullman with a convertible roof above the rear seat) are pictured during a parade in 1964.

**N**amed the "Grand Mercedes," the 600 Limousine was certainly more grand than anything else Mercedes had ever produced, bringing back memories of the prewar 770K. In the 600, however, classic craftsmanship was combined with modern technology to a degree that had never before been seen – and possibly never again will be. The 1969 600 featured here, chassis number 100.012-12-001481, was photographed in front of San Diego's Del Mar racetrack, and belongs to Thomas Kreid of Carlsbad, California – a connoisseur whose taste for perfection has brought him a reputation as one of the finest restorers around.

the Silver Anniversary issue of *Star*, official publication of the Mercedes-Benz Club.

Third in this lineup is a magnificent burgundy 300Sc Roadster, also restored by Thomas and his team: Stephen Azola, Michael Neuman, Michael Biener, Fidel Gonzales and Axel Jensen. (The skill levels of these men are as high as those of the men who built these cars in the first place, or higher, Thomas feels.) The car won Best of Show at the 1983 Orange County Tribute to Mercedes-Benz, in a field of 130 vehicles.

Another two 300Sc cars, both in the process of being restored, occupy the opposite side of the building. They remind me of a factory scene from the fifties, looking as if they were under assembly there, every component shiny and seemingly new. Rows of shelving, containing a great variety of parts, cover the near end of the building; the far end, is used for painting and for manufacture of fenders and other body panels, formed over jigs made from original patterns.

Next in the lineup come two examples of the 600, one dark blue, the other light metallic-beige, both so exquisitely well preserved they look exactly like they did on the day they were delivered new.

Thomas is called away to the phone, and I sit down behind the wheel of the light-colored car. There is an original British-market sales brochure left on the passenger seat. I pick it up and scan the pages. A headline, "Basic Equipment," catches my eye.

"Lighting: Asymmetrical dipped beam; fog lamps; front and rear limit lights; flashing direction indicators; parking light; reversing light; instrument lights, dimmer-switch controlled; socket for inspection lamp; light in glove box; map-reading light; boot light; foot well lights: two in front, two at rear; roof lights at rear; two adjustable lamps in rear roof pillars.

"Signalling equipment: Headlight flasher; wind horn, and two electric horns; additional high-volume horn available; automatic cancelling of flashing indicators.

"Instruments: Speedometer; rev counter; gear-selector indicator; oil pressure gauge; petrol gauge; engine thermometer; indicator lights for battery charge, flashing indicators, headlight beam, hydraulic system, air pressure, petrol reserve; clock; mileage recorder; trip recorder; outside-air thermometer.

"Locks: Four hydraulically-operated, safety door-locks; central control for locks on doors, boot and petrol-filler cap; manual operation of all door locks from the inside, and of front doors and boot from the outside; steering lock combined with ignition switch, starter and device to prevent accidental starter operation; lock on glove box.

"Hydraulic press-button system: Press-button hydraulic opening and closing of door windows; rear seat and center armrest fully adjustable hydraulically by pressing a button; front seats horizontally and vertically adjustable hydraulically by pressing a button; front backrest rake infinitely adjustable hydraulically down to horizontal position by pressing a button; hydraulic adjustment of shock-absorbers by lever.

"Heating and ventilating system: Front: heating and ventilating system with two heat-exchangers and blower; Rear: heating and ventilating system with one heat-exchanger and blower; fresh air system for front and rear; temperature selector with electronic control to compensate for effect of different driving speeds; defroster for side windows; defrosting for rear windows by electric heating elements embedded in the glass.

"Miscellaneous: Oddments tray between front seats; pockets on all four doors; parcel shelf in the front over transmission tunnel; parcel net on front seat backs; anti-dazzle rear view mirror; two exterior rear view mirrors adjustable from the inside; two padded sunvisors, with vanity mirror on passenger side; four handrails in the roof frame; grab-handles on all doors; four coat hangers in rear (two each side); armrests on all doors; independent centre armrest for each of the front seats; folding armrest in the rear; two adjustable headrests in the rear; ashtrays on all doors; automatic cigar lighter on all doors; safety steering wheel adjustable for rake; two foot rests in rear; curtains on rear window and rear side windows.

"Optional extras: Centre partition with hydraulically operated glass screen, bar, shelf for vanity box, and at right and left, folding tables with indirect lighting; steel sliding roof hydraulically operated by press-button."

Thomas returns and proceeds to show me how all these things work — and why: the engine with its twin alternators, the hydraulic system, the ventilated disc brakes with their doubled-up lines, the suspension — adjustable for both height and stiffness...

With all these overwhelming facts jammed into my head, I realize that the 600 is the ultimate expression of automotive perfection, the epitome of engineering virtuosity, workmanship, comfort and elegance. I also realize, with frustration, that no matter the words, no matter the pictures, my presentation will be inadequate — an entire book is needed to do the 600 justice!

But I am comforted by the thought that cars like the 540, the 300, the 600 — the likes of which we will never again see — are safe in the hands of men like Thomas Kreid, to whom the quest for perfection is not a mirage...

*Of the 600 model, there were 2,677 units built. Of these, 428 were Pullmans. Of these, fifty-nine were Landaulets, and of these, seven were of the Presidential type — with the convertible top starting immediately behind the divider window, and otherwise equipped according to the special wishes of the customer. The example featured in these pictures belongs to Kenneth C. Smith of La Jolla, California. It was originally purchased by an Australian businessman. Other customers of Presidential Landaulets include Pope Paul, Queen Elizabeth, marshal Tito, and curiously, Chairman Mao. The price was in the eighty-thousand-dollar range — almost three times as much as a normally equipped Pullman.*

# 280SE 3.5 CABRIOLET

# The Man Who Preserves the Memories.

As a boy, Karl knew the river well. Every day he would watch the traffic on the Rhine: the long low-floating barges that came and went in a steady stream, the white yacht-like excursion ships, packed with tourists, and the small pleasure boats, sprinkled in-between like the beans in a boiling vegetable soup. Some were headed upstream toward Koblenz, working hard against the current, looking as if they were almost standing still. Others were headed downstream toward Cologne, floating swiftly, effortlessly.

Karl also knew the autobahn well. Every time he accompanied his father to Cologne or Bonn or Frankfurt he would watch the traffic: the long dark limousine-type cars that came roaring by in the fast lane, looking like express locomotives, their horns howling, and the low, smoothly shaped sports cars that appeared so suddenly in the rearview mirror, looking like small dots, and then, just as suddenly, had passed and were gone beyond the horizon, leaving only a memory to be stored away somewhere deep inside the brain.

Karl Keller was ten years old when the first Gullwings began to appear on German roads and highways. He was sixteen when Mercedes introduced the new beautiful 220SEb Coupes and Cabriolets. Three years later Karl had a car of his own, not yet a Mercedes, but an Opel — one time on the autobahn that year he drove the Opel as fast as it would go just for the pleasure of watching the exciting lines of a 300SL.

Also that year, 1964, Karl moved to America. The 220SEb Coupes and Cabriolets were indeed new cars despite the fact that only a small "b" distinguished them from the earlier models. They were constructed according to the same principles as before,

but they now rested on a two-and-one-half-inch longer wheelbase and were also longer overall (eight inches), wider (about three inches), and lower (three inches).

When the 220SE Sedan was discontinued in 1959 the old Coupe and Cabriolet models were kept in production until the new ones were ready to take their places. But they were fitted with the updated engine, producing one hundred thirty-four horsepower. When the new Coupes and Cabriolets appeared in 1961, they were equipped with the same engine.

The new "b" model was fitted with disc brakes up front, which was an improvement over the earlier model and its drum brakes. Top speed was 107mph. Fourteen seconds were required to reach sixty.

If the 220SEb Coupes and Cabriolets were not entirely new under the skin, the skin itself was certainly brand new and very pleasing. It was a style that would last for a decade — another one of those Mercedes favorites that seem to vanish when they are at the height of their popularity. The trouble was that these cars were semi-handbuilt, particularly the Cabriolet with its padded top; nowadays, with automation and robot efficiency there does not seem to be room for the old-school craftsmen. Altogether nearly 36,000 units were built over the ten-year period.

The styling of the new model was a superb blend of traditional and modern lines. It had lost all the somewhat stodgy look of its predecessor, but was still just as elegant. The front end, especially when the less-cluttered, European-version headlights were fitted, was simple and slightly rounded. Without looking dated, it managed to carry on the traditional Mercedes theme — the classic radiator. The rear was also only slightly rounded with a smooth-ending fender line. The fins of the Sedan version were fortunately not incorporated into the styling of the new Coupe and Cabriolet. The front and rear ends harmonized extremely well. Two creases ran along the length of the body, tying the two ends together with long, sweeping lines. The interior, while lacking much of the wood of its predecessor, was still well enough appointed to be one of the most luxurious cars of its day, including cars that cost twice as much.

One thing the model always lacked was power! But something was done about that in 1963 when the 300SE came out with an enlarged engine, producing one hundred eighty horsepower. The 300SE had an air-suspension system and disc brakes all around. A chrome strip along the body side and around the wheel arches set that version apart from the regular model.
*(continued on overleaf)*

*The 220SEb Coupe — as well as the subsequent 250 and 280 versions — were outstandingly beautiful automobiles. So classically timeless was the styling that it seemed just as appropriate at the time it was taken off the market in 1971, as it did when it was first shown a decade earlier. In 1969, with the introduction of the new 3.5 engine, a subtle styling change was made: The hood and grille were lowered three inches and the grille also widened four inches. Compare the two pictures, the 220 to the left, photographed in Baden-Baden, Germany, and the 3.5, above — subtle indeed! To the right, the comfortable reclining seats.*

**S**ome automobiles never become classics. Others have to wait a long time. The 1971 280SE 3.5 Cabriolet was an instant classic! The decade-old design already had the looks – mated with the new V-8, it also got the power and speed. Photographed on Chicago Tribune-founder Colonel Robert McCormick's estate in Wheaton, Illinois, this Survivor belongs to Karl Keller. He was assured by its first owner that the top had never been down. Keller always kept it that way – until it was lowered for the photographer. With 16,000 miles on the odometer, chassis number 111.027-12-001533, is certainly one of the most pristine examples to be found anywhere.

The injection system was improved in 1965 and a little more power was extracted. The model was built until the end of 1968.

When production of the 220SEb ended in 1965, the 250SE took over, now with a one hundred seventy horsepower engine. It was built until 1968 when the 280SE continued the theme. The engine was again more powerful, now one hundred eighty horsepower.

The final, and best, version came in 1969 when the all-new 3.5 vee-eight was dropped into the 280SE. Power was now up to two hundred thirty horsepower and top speed was 127mph. Zero to sixty took less than ten seconds. The hood was lowered to modernize the profile (made possible by the flatter engine). The radiator was also lowered (by about three inches) and widened (about four inches). Just then, 1971, when it was most desirable, production was halted — creating an instant classic!

Karl Keller went on to prove that America is indeed the land of opportunity. With the success of the company he started, came soon the resources necessary to realize a dream; he now has a garage full of Mercedes' best: Gullwings, Roadsters, a 600 and a pristine example of the 3.5 Cabriolet, which has only 16,000 original miles on the odometer and the top has never been down!

Pristine is the watchword! Karl is the sort of collector who insists on owning only the best — the perfect car of each model. He searches with extreme patience and miraculously seems to find that particular car nobody thought existed. When he has found the perfect example of the model he wants, he puts it away! He does not show his cars. He does not drive them — except for one, a 300SL Roadster he uses in his business when making sales calls on prospective customers.

When Karl puts his cars away, he puts them away — in an insulated garage that has a special system for keeping the temperature and the humidity at a constant level all year round. Inside the garage, all the cars have the proper covers, neatly stretched and spotless. There are also shields placed on the floor between the cars, behind each exhaust pipe, so that when he fires them up (on a regular basis), the car behind and its cover will not become stained. And to show how serious he is about not driving his cars, he built the garage without a driveway!

A childhood dream has come true for Karl Keller; owning the best of the best and keeping them that way forever!

(I forgot to ask him if he also collects Rhine river barges!)

The 280SE Cabriolet was certainly the last of the classic models from Mercedes-Benz. It was, to a large degree, handcrafted. And it had the kind of styling that expressed taste and affluence in an understated way. The photograph to the right, shows the basic Cabriolet body style in its 1962 300SE guise. Note the chrome strip that runs the length of the body side and the molding that follows the edge of the wheel arch. These are exterior clues to recognizing the top of the line of those early years. The flagship of the last of the line is recognized by the lower and wider grille, above, as well as what hides below the hood — the powerful 3.5, pictured to the left.

# 300SEL 6.3 SEDAN

# The Six Point Three Illusion.

It was still raining when I came out from the Guggenheim Museum. I hesitated for a moment and then retreated to below the overhang. It looked like the shower was fizzling out, so I decided to stay where I was for a few minutes. The clouds of mist, whipped up by quickly passing buses and taxis, blurred my view of the naked-limbed dark-trunked trees in Central Park, rising on the other side of the street like a dead dripping jungle.

I rolled up the magazine I carried in my hand and stuck it safely inside my jacket. It was a special issue of *Road & Track*: the 1969 Road Test Annual. I had had a bite to eat in the museum coffee shop and afterward, since there had still been half an hour until my meeting with Peter Lewis, I had spent the rest of the time reading the magazine.

There were three road tests that interested me in particular. The first of those tests featured a car with a two-hundred-forty-cubic-inch vee-twelve producing four hundred horses. It covered zero to sixty in six point three seconds; zero to one hundred in fourteen point three. The top speed was one hundred sixty-three. The weight was well below three thousand pounds.

The car was a Lamborghini Miura.

The second test reported on a vee-eight with a three-hundred-twenty-seven-cubic-inch capacity producing three hundred fifty horses. It took seven point seven seconds to reach sixty; the zero-to-one-hundred time was not listed. The top speed was one hundred twenty-eight. Weight was about four hundred pounds more than the Miura.

*(continued on overleaf)*

The 300SEL 6.3 was first shown to a group of automotive journalists early in 1968. The photograph to the right, shows the fast sedan circling Germany's Hockenheim track during that press preview. To the left, the photographer has turned his camera to the instruments as the 6.3 nears top speed: 210 kmph. Note the speedometer needle! The hands on the wheel belong to none other than former team driver Karl Kling. Pictured above, are the proud parents, with their new child (from left to right): Uhlenhaut, responsible for engine and suspension; Scherenberg, in charge of overall development; Wilfert, responsible for styling.

**S**eemingly wanting to prove that, although they had chosen not to produce a true sports car any longer, the know-how was still there. Mercedes dropped the big 600-engine into a long sedan, creating the 300SEL 6.3 — a sedan so strong it could out-accelerate almost anything on the road. The 1971 Survivor shown here, chassis number 109.018-12-004623, belongs to Peter Lewis of Greenwich, Connecticut. It was photographed in front of an old granite garage on the family estate — a fitting backdrop for an elegant machine with subtle potency.

The car was a convertible Corvette.

The rain had stopped now. I left my refuge and started to walk down Fifth Avenue. Peter lived almost right across from The Metropolitan Museum of Art, further down on Fifth. It would take me awhile to cover the distance by foot but the air was cool and new-smelling and a brisk walk would do me good. Straight ahead I noticed that the turrets of the skyscrapers were hidden inside dark clouds.

There would soon be more rain.

The third car was also a vee-eight. The size was three hundred eighty-six cubic inches. It produced three hundred horses. Zero-to-sixty took six point nine seconds; about half a second slower than the Miura but almost one second faster than the Corvette. It weighed four thousand pounds; the heaviest of the three. Top speed was one hundred thirty-one; faster than the Corvette.

If the three of them had lined up for a quarter-mile drag contest there would have been very little separating them at the end of the race; the Miura would have covered the distance in fourteen point five seconds; the third car would have done it in fifteen point one seconds; the Corvette would have needed fifteen point six seconds.

The Miura had an extremely low body, sleek and posing very little air resistance. But it could seat only two people and it had very little room for luggage; about five cubic feet. The Corvette also had a low profile; it also held only two; its luggage space was less than seven cubic feet. The third car, on the other hand, could seat five people and there would still be lots of head and leg room, as well as about seventeen cubic feet of trunk space.

The third car was obviously not a sports car, even though the performance figures seemed to indicate so. It was in fact a sedan! The Mercedes-Benz 300SEL 6.3 Sedan! The best sedan in the world, according to *Road & Track!*

Now everything suddenly happened all at once; it started to rain again and I caught sight of Peter's metallic-gold 6.3 parked on the street in front of the canopy of the apartment building where he lives, and the doorman came out carrying my camera case that I had left with him earlier for safekeeping and behind him came Peter himself.

Peter Lewis is a super enthusiast. Super in the sense that his car interest covers a wider range than most. Super also in the sense that he owns more cars than most. Super, as well, in the sense that he is fortunate to be able to afford any car he desires.

Take Ferrari for instance. He has a Dino. And a 275

GTB/4. And a brand new black Boxer. Maybe also others. (Things could change between the writing of this story and the printing of the book!) Take another of his favorites, Mercedes-Benz. He has an old 300Sc Cabriolet that has been in the family since new. He has a 3.5 Cabriolet. He has an SLC. And, of course, he has the 6.3. (He has, in fact, had five of those). And take Aston Martin, yet another favorite. He has a Volante. And several others.

We enter the 6.3 as quickly as possible, trying to avoid getting wet. The doorman loads my camera case and Peter's briefcases in the trunk and we take off, heading north toward Greenwich, the water splashing around the tires, the rain drumming on the roof. Inside, the rich, dark brown leather seats smell like they should in a Mercedes; they also feel like they should — smooth from just the right amount of wear. The dash, walnut burl or South American Walnut — there are some dark swirls in it — shines rich and lustrous. We accelerate and decelerate, using the power of the engine and the power of the brakes to our advantage, darting in and out, occupying gaps in the traffic as they occur, avoiding both cars and potholes — there are too many of both in New York!

"Did you know this car will almost stay even with a Miura on the quarter-mile?" I ask Peter.

"I've never tried. But I believe you!" Peter says.

"It will beat a Corvette with a full second!"

"That I've tried!" Peter says with a wry smile. "They never seem to learn what those numerals on the rear deck lid stand for, do they?"

"What do you say is the reason for this incredible performance? Only the engine?" I ask Peter.

"The engine is it!" Peter answers. "They lifted it straight out of the big 600 and dropped it into the fifteen-hundred-pound-lighter 300. That engine was already a performer with the fuel injection and all. But in that lighter chassis... dynamite! I wish I could show you what this baby can do, but the roads are too wet! For instance... you cruise at twenty or thirty and suddenly stab the pedal... swish... the wheels spin... the tires smoke rubber! Maybe it won't rain in Greenwich so I can show you!"

"Let's hope it won't!" I say, now fully realizing the intriguing concept of the 6.3. "An illusion!" I add. "The car looks exactly like any other big Mercedes sedan, elegant and refined. But not showing, is a brute of an engine, so powerful it will beat most sports cars. And all that power is there for you to use as you choose. But only you know it. Marvelous!"

It did not rain in Greenwich...

*The most powerful engine developed by Mercedes to date — for use in a production car — was the 6.3 unit, intended at first only for the magnificent 600 Limousine. The photograph above shows the unit in all its massive glory. When this engine was mated with the much lighter 300 Sedan, a most potent combination resulted — a combination that created the world's fastest production sedan. The photograph to the left, shows the engine compartment of the 300SEL, with the 6.3 unit fitted. To the right, a photograph of the instrument panel. Note the tachometer, small, but strategically located right in the center of the driver's field of view.*

# 280SL ROADSTER

# The Right Thing at the Right Time.

"Well, it was the last year of that body style," Andy says, giving me one of the reasons he added the 1971 280SL to his collection. "And it was also the last of the six-cylinder two-seaters," he says, pausing for a moment as if searching for words to express his feelings in a more profound way. "The 280SL was still built according to the old-time principles of excellence. You can see it in the choice of materials and in the way things were made and put together. I'm not saying that Mercedes isn't a great car today. But things are not the same now. The 280SL was the last of an era!"

Andy Cohn and I stand in front of the open doors of the ten-car garage he built a few years ago. Inside, in the back row, stand some thirties Fords. To the left sits a Ferrari Daytona Spyder, a Daytona Coupe and a Dino Spyder, all black — Andy likes dark cars. To the right stand other cars, all under cover — his company is the world's largest merchandiser of car covers. Straight ahead, just uncovered, its dark maroon surface sparkling from a recent polish, stands the 280SL.

Behind the garage the hill falls off steeply, straight down toward North Hollywood. On the other side, behind us, the hill slopes more gently, falling off gradually toward Beverly Hills.

Eight years ago, Andy, together with his partner Jim De Frank, decided on a joint venture; they bought an already well established auto parts store located on Robertson Boulevard in Beverly Hills, not far from Wilshire Boulevard.

Four years later they sold that business but kept the location and the building, opening Beverly Hills Motoring Accessories. As the name indicates, the company specializes in auto accessories, marketing them in all

*(continued on overleaf)*

The extremely unique photographs on these pages came from the camera of a certain Dr. Siefert, and were taken in the styling department at Mercedes-Benz. To the left, a one-to-ten-scale model in front of one of the first actual units to come off the assembly line. Note the vent on the model's side panel — similar to the one found on the 300SL! To the right, a comparison between the old 190SL and the new 230SL. Above, two one-to-ten-scale models beside a final full-scale model. Note the Mercedes-Benz script on the body side, behind the front wheel. The model closest to the camera, is the earliest, unpainted plaster version.

**R**eplacement for the aging 190SL was the 230SL, arriving on the scene in 1963. It was an all-new design, with improved performance and with styling that matched its now firmly defined purpose of being a "sporty luxury automobile." In the subsequent 250SL and 280SL, engine capacity and performance grew further. This 1971 280SL, chassis number 113.044-12-022130, was photographed in front of the decorative French chateau facade of a private home in Los Angeles, California. Andy Cohn, co-founder of Beverly Hills Motoring Accessories, is the owner of this last-year-production Survivor – one o the best preserved examples you will ever find.

their various forms: everything from seats, covers, bras, wheels and exhaust systems to jewelry, watches, sun glasses and key fobs. The bulk of business comes from a nationwide mail order effort — most car enthusiasts are by now very familiar with their ads in *Road & Track*.

It turned out to be the right business at the right time. Interest in accessories soared during the past decade and the company has grown to become a leader in the field, thanks to high-quality products, personalized service and modern marketing techniques. The success of the company provides Andy with means to build a collection of his favorite cars.

"I searched a long time before I decided on this one," he says. "I wanted a last-year model. And I wanted a one-owner car, one with low mileage, and one that hadn't been repainted. I also wanted a dark color. This one has only thirty-three thousand miles on the odometer. It has never been parked in the sun, never been driven in the rain, and it has all the documents: original bill of sale, service records, manuals — everything — even the new-car sticker for the window. The car is just like it was when it left the showroom!

"I wouldn't have minded having one with the manual transmission," Andy continues. "But those cars are all run-down. The owners must drive them very hard! The five-speed is even more desirable. But you only find them in Europe. And all of them are rust-buckets!"

When the Mercedes development people began work on the car that would become the 230SL, they faced quite a challenge. It was clear from the outset that the 300SL could not, and was never meant to be, a big-volume seller. It was too much of a sports car. At its peak, in 1957, the 300SL Roadster was produced at an annual rate of five hundred units. For the rest of the run, annual production was about half that number. It was also clear that the 190SL was not all it should be. The main drawback was a lack of power. But the 190SL had proven one thing: the concept of a luxurious, rather than spartan and sporty looking, rather than sporty acting, two-seater was definately viable. At a seven-thousand-unit annual production rate, during its peak, the brother of the 300SL (or maybe more correctly, the sister), was a sales success.

So, the challenge facing the engineers and the stylists was that of creating a car that would occupy a position somewhere between the 190SL and the 300SL. But was it possible to please both the gentleman racer and the lady shopper? Was it possible to satisfy the need for superior handling at highway speed as well as for luxurious comfort at an urbane pace, for sparkling temperament as well as for dull flexibility?

When the 230SL arrived in 1963, it certainly seemed as if Uhlenhaut and his staff had hit the nail right on its head! The new car was indeed reminiscent of both its predecessors; it had the same wide, squat look and similar grille. But it was more elegant; finer, lighter looking. The unique element of the styling was the concave roof line of the hardtop. Like most styling innovations from Mercedes, this new look seems to have sprung from practical considerations: Structural strength was improved and larger windows and entrance openings were achieved. The interior was also more elegant than on its predecessors, imitating the style of the Sedans with their wide, comfortable seats.

Technically, the 230SL was no wonderchild. It was constructed according to the old proven ideas: unit frame and unit body. Although the improved swing axle was still used, the suspension had been carefully tuned to work with a new kind of tire, developed in cooperation with the manufacturers. The 230SL had drumbrakes in the back and discs up front; the 250SL got discs all around. The engine was the new six-cylinder unit, now slightly enlarged and producing one hundred fifty horsepower. Top speed was around 120mph. Zero to sixty took eleven seconds. The 280SL, which had an even more enlarged engine, producing one hundred seventy horsepower, made the zero-to-sixty run in just under ten seconds. All these performance figures were higher than those of the 190SL, but lower than those of the 300SL — right on target!

During the eight years of production 26,000 units of the 190SL were built. Of the 230SL, 250SL, 280SL, twice as many were made, also during an eight-year period — another bull's-eye for Mercedes!

But a curious thing happened over the years. When the 230SL was first introduced, its sporty character was emphasized. It was even winning tough rallys — a well publicized fact. And indeed, in the beginning the 230SL was driven by a more sporty clientéle. But then came women's liberation — and the car that helped that movement along was the little roadster from Mercedes! How could the Mercedes officials have been so far-sighted? (Just in case someone thinks I'm serious: I'm not!)

"I wouldn't go as far as to say that the 280SL is a feminine car!" says Andy. "All you have to do is to drive it closer to the limit than most drivers do and you will discover the tremendous response of the engine and the superior grip on the road. I would say that the 280SL is a car for the sophisticated man as well as for the liberated woman!" adds Andy with a wink.

The right car for the right time!

*The photographs on these pages, also from the camera of Dr. Seifert, show the interior styling of one of the pre-production models on display in the styling department at Mercedes-Benz. To the left, a suggestion for a third, transversally located, passenger seat. This picture also shows a different design of the backs of the normal seats. To the right, two suggestions for design of the door panel with its map pocket. Above, the instrument panel. Note that, at this stage, there were still areas of variation from the final product: the shape of the fresh-air outlet, the location of the clock, the design of the heating and ventilation controls, etc.*

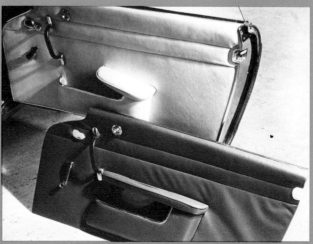

# 450SL ROADSTER

## *Of New and Old, of Good and Bad.*

The orange trees stand ripe with fruit. It is the richest harvest in years and the branches bear it out, hanging heavy and full. The oranges look like bright stars sprinkled across a lush, green heaven. The groves extend from the road, spreading their endless abundance on both sides of it, and, looking at them from the car, the nearest rows of trees appear blurred because of the speed. It all feels very pleasant and rich and blessed, and I press down hard on the gas pedal causing the front to raise, the speed to surge, the car to accelerate briskly along the straightaway leading out of Fillmore and up into the mountains.

I am driving Bob Scudder's light-green 450SL. Bob sits beside me in the passenger seat. We had taken off the hardtop before starting out this morning, leaving it hanging from the rafters in Bob's garage. The soft top was off too, neatly stowed away underneath its lid, behind us. The crisp spring air, laced with the intoxicating fragrance of the citrus flowers, comes rushing past us in the open cockpit. The day's shooting is over and I can relax now, letting my senses settle down to enjoy the feel of the car on the road.

"First time I've driven a 450SL!" I say as I prepare for an approaching turn, a left-hander, the first of many turns, the road beginning to climb the mountainside now, winding in and out of steep-walled ravines, looking like the long body of a snake. "I'm really impressed!" I add, turning my head just enough to register Bob's contented smile.

The Mercedes sweeps around the corner in a smooth, stable, predictable manner. Moving out of the curve, I press the gas pedal again, feeling the tires dig into the road surface.

"I'm also surprised!" I say. "I thought it would feel more like the 280SL!"

*(continued on overleaf)*

The 450SL had an all-new interior; only the classic star in the center of the steering wheel revealed that the car was a Mercedes. There was nothing else left of the style that had characterized the cars from the world's oldest car maker for so many years: the wooden dash, the leather and wood combination, or the leather and steel. That is not to say that all was lost; the new interior was an excellent design, from a viewpoint of styling as well as ergometrics. Above, the 450SL from its best angle, and to top it off, the simple, good-looking European-style headlight covers. To the right, a comparison between new and old — the blood line is evident!

By 1971, the time had come to replace the 280SL – the 450SL was the machine to do it! It still carried forward the theme of "sporty luxury automobile," but it now looked even sportier thanks to the steeply raked windshield and the sleeker overall lines. Bob Scudder of Camarillo, California owns this well-preserved 1973 450SL, chassis number 107.044-12-011142, photogaphed in front of the church built by the Camarillo brothers in the early part of the century. One of the most desirable years to a California collector is 1973 – last year for the small bumpers.

"No! The 450SL is really quite different!" Bob says emphatically. "It's a new car all the way. Styling too. Obviously!"

"I like the feeling behind the wheel!" I say. "The driving position is excellent. Feels more sporty than the 280SL. I'm not talking about driving characteristics now. I'm talking about environment. It's the raked windshield that does it. And the big console between us here. It feels like I'm sitting deeper. More encapsulated. I like that! Yes, the 450SL is definately more sporty than the 280SL. But not as elegant!"

"I agree!" says Bob. "That is true for the overall styling, too. Sportier. But not as elegant."

"They carried that pagoda-like roof line over to the new hardtop, though," I say, letting the steering wheel slide back through my hands after a sharp right-hander. "But it doesn't seem as tall as on the 280SL. I always thought that roof was too tall! The entire car looks rounder and heavier. Especially the body sides and the hood. The rear deck lid, on the other hand, is slightly concave, repeating the roof line. The fact that the rear wheel arch is cut so low makes the car appear even heavier. Another thing, quite nice I think, is the ribbing below the doors. It's not there for looks. Is that right?"

"Yes, that's right!" Bob says. "Like everything else Mercedes does, it has a function. It's supposed to affect the airflow so that the side windows are kept clean from dirt and water when it rains. Same thing with the ribbing on the rear lights, I understand!"

"Overall, I think it's a very good looking car!" I say. "A classy looking car!" I add. "But not a *great* looking car! A matter of taste, of course!"

"Yes, those things are sometimes hard to discuss. One thing though, it does look like a Mercedes. The traditional relationship is there!"

"Yes, the Mercedes stylists are good at that. Always have been!" I say. "But the interior is quite a departure from old. No wood on the dash anymore. And no leather. It's plastic now. I feel bad about that. Not genuine. Look at this!" I point at the door panel "Fake stitches! But at least all the pieces fit well together. The workmanship is still tops. And the instrumentation is great. I like the way the upper half of the steering wheel is empty, leaving an unobstructed view of the gauges, and the way the instrument pod is styled, repeating the shape of the opening in the steering wheel. That's very good!"

I am moving in and out of the curves now, the road rising steadily. I am not driving hard, not pushing it, just letting the car flow with the road — the 450SL performs superbly. The ride is smooth and even. The steering is

*The 450SLC — the four-seater coupe version of the 450SL — was introduced at the same time and in the same place as its shorter brother — the 1971 Geneva show. It rested on a fourteen-inches-longer wheelbase, and was also longer overall with the same measurement — evidence that a section had simply been added behind the seats of the 450SL. The louvres mounted inside the rear quarter windows set the SLC apart from the SL, at the same time as it gave the SLC a more elegant appearance. Under the hood, pictured to the right, they were both the same.*

practically neutral. The resistance in the wheel feels absolutely perfect.

"The handling must be the greatest improvement over the 280SL," I say. "It's fabulous!"

"Yes, they finally got rid of that swing axle!" Bob says. "They have semi-trailing arms now."

"What about the transmission?"

"New too. It's a three-speed automatic with torque converter. Very smooth. They were never imported with manual transmission."

"And the engine?" I ask. "I know it's a vee-eight. But what about performance?"

"The engine was new too. In Europe, they brought it out as a 3.5. But for America, with those emission laws and all, the engine was fitted with a taller block so that the stroke could be longer. But still, power was about the same in both cases. About two hundred horses. Acceleration was down a little compared to the 280SL."

"Too bad it had to be that way."

Bob Scudder grew up in Washington, Indiana. He can trace his interest in cars back to the time when his father took him to see the factory in Evansville, where they assembled the Plymouth Fury. Later, when that time came, he decided to study mechanical engineering.

The 450SL was Bob's first Mercedes. He looked at seventeen of them before he decided on this one. A real-estate saleswoman in Lancaster had owned it before. She had only driven it nineteen thousand miles. Bob specifically wanted a '73 model — because of the small bumpers.

Mercedes ownership soon turned into more than a passing interest; Bob became a co-founder of the Channel Islands Section of the Mercedes-Benz Club of America, its first vice president and its second president. Luckily, Bob's wife, Charlene, shares her husband's interest.

During their years as 450SL owners, other Mercedes cars have come and gone; a 190SL, a 280SE, a 250SE Coupe, a 300SEL 6.3 . . . They have now purchased a beautifully restored 220SEb Coupe. It is going to be their show car. The 450SL will remain their roadcar.

We reach the summit now and begin to roll down the other side of the mountain, the road still undulating, the view now displaying another green paradise of orange groves, and, in the distance, the soft outline of Anacapa Island, its blue-gray contour floating heavy on the fuzzy horizon of the Pacific. We both sit quietly, enjoying the downhill rush, the slow gyration, the flowing wind . . .

"I can understand why you want to keep this one for your road car!" I say. "Few cars I have driven would have felt so good going down this hill!"

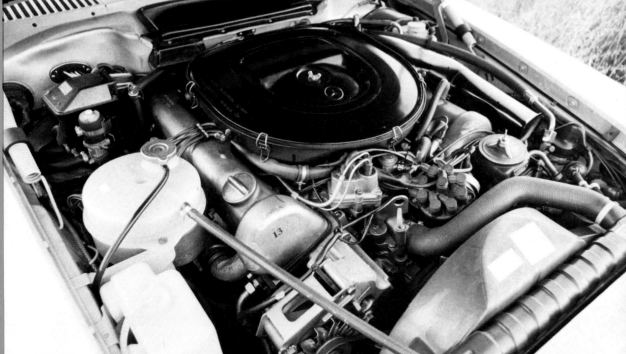

"Mercedes for the Road,"
eighth in The Survivor Series, was
photographed, written and designed
by Henry Rasmussen. The technical
specifications, the brief history and
the notes on collectability were
compiled by Gene Babow. All black
and white photographs, unless
otherwise indicated, were obtained
from **Road & Track**, mainly from their
Studio Wörner Collection. Librarian
Otis Meyer provided valuable help in
locating the material. Assistant
designer was Walt Woesner. Copy
editor was Barbara Harold.
Typesetting was supplied by Tintype
Graphic Arts of San Luis Obispo,
California. The color separations
were produced by South China
Printing Company of Hong Kong,
which was responsible for printing
and binding as well. Liaison man with
the printer was Peter Lawrence of
New York City.

Special acknowledgements go to
Jose Harth and his family of Caracas,
Venezuela, for making the author's
stay there an unforgettable
experience; to Bill Kosfeld of
Motorbooks International for his
pleasant handling of day-to-day
contacts connected with publishing.
The author is also indebted to Tom
Warth of Motorbooks International,
whose continued support made yet
another title in this series possible.

The author finally wishes to thank
the following contributors: Frank
Barrett, editor and publisher of **The
Star** magazine, Charles Brahms,
Paul Dexler, Bob Esbensen, Jobst
Heemeyer, John Harrington, Bruce
Meyer, Ena Rasmussen, Robert
Reinfried, Shirley Rusch, Paul
Russell of the Gullwing Service
Company, Topsfield, Massachusetts,
John Sheetz, Frank Skinner and
Kenneth Smith.

# Porsches For The Road

## Henry Rasmussen

# PORSCHES F(

First published in 1981 as
*Porsches For The Road*

OR THE ROAD

Porsche and racing are synonymous. Professor Ferdinand Porsche learned early that racing victories meant free publicity. The House of Porsche never forgot that. By 1953, the factory realized that the stock 356 and the 1.5-liter push-rod engine would not satisfy future racing plans. Enter the 550 Spyder. Karosserie Wendler of Reutlingen built the aluminum body to Porsche's specifications. The design originated with the Glöckler specials, but the final styling was by Erwin Komenda. Dr. Ernst Fuhrmann designed the four-cam engine single-handedly; 1498 cc, 110 DIN hp (125 SAE) at 7500 rpm, with a Hirth roller bearing crank. It was willing and able: 0-60 under ten seconds. But that didn't win races; balance was the key word, and power: top speed 140 mph with flexibility. And handling: one road tester said the center of gravity was below the ground. And brakes: big, finned drums, with stock sixteen-inch 356 wheels and slightly wider tires aft. The engine was mounted ahead of the rear axle with the four-speed synchromesh transmission behind it. Weight was just 1,250 pounds, wheelbase 82.7 inches, and price $6,800. The ladder frame was changed to a tubular one in late 1955 and the model name was changed to 550A. There were changes made right to the end of the Spyder series in 1962. About two hundred examples were made. While Porsche built a strong, reliable touring car in the 356, it was the Spyder that gave it the reputation of a winner. And Porsche sold what it raced. But naturally, the factory was always a little ahead of the purchaser in development.

Affectionately known as the bathtub, the Speedster captured the spirit of Porsche in the United States. It was the idea of Max Hoffman, United States distributor for Porsche, to have a stark price leader. When introduced, the tag was $2,995 in New York City, with some standard equipment at extra cost. This was Hoffman's idea; for Porsche, it was in a sense a step backward. The cabriolet had a padded top and roll-up windows; the Speedster had just a simple canvas top and side curtains. Vision was terrible with the top up. But, with the four-cylinder, air-cooled, push-rod engine, the Speedster was reliable and fast. Fast is relative, but point-to-point distances were covered amazingly quickly. Racing proved this. With the Super 1600 cc engine (actually 1588 cc), power was 75 DIN hp (88 SAE) at 5000 rpm; 0-60 in 10.5 seconds and a top speed just over 100 mph. The car was solid, unlike other sports cars, because of the platform frame with unit body. If a rattle developed, it was something the owner put in or on the car. Each wheel was independently suspended. Wheelbase was 82.7 inches, weight about 1,850 pounds and in 1958 there was also the normal engine, 60 DIN hp (70 SAE) at 4500 rpm and the four-cam engine with plain bearings known as the Carrera. The four-speed, synchromesh transmission was a delight. Braking was through big drums, with a swept area greater than most luxury sedans. The Speedster is raced in vintage racing as well as current SCCA racing. It can win either variety. With ancestors like the Auto Union Grand Prix car and the Volkswagen, how can it miss?

# 550 Spyder

# 356A Speedster

Porsche usually made its engines to fit in a racing classification. The original 1086 cc engine fit in the 1100 cc class; the 1582 engine of the later 356s fit into the 1600 cc class. The four-cam engine won races in the 1100 cc, 1500 cc and in the largest version, the 2000 cc class. This four-cam engine was detuned and placed in the 356 series. The 1966 cc version engine with plain bearings was put in the B-series and labeled the 356B/2000GS, but was called and labeled the Carrera 2. Homologation called for 100 units, but 320 B-series and 126 C-series cars were actually built. Power was 110 DIN hp (130 SAE) at 6200 rpm. A 0-60 time of 8.7 seconds and a top speed of 125 mph was easily possible. For the added power, disc brakes were fitted all around. Price in the United States was $7,595. Bodies were by Reutter, made with the usual precision. The engine was available in both the coupe and cabriolet. Weight of the coupe was 2,200 pounds. An identifying feature was the skirt under the rear bumper with the twin exhaust pipes protruding. The front grilles, next to the parking lights, were generally omitted. The usual rear engine location with four-speed transmission just in front of the engine was continued. Wheelbase remained 82.7 inches. With the extra power, the Porsche balance remained with the disc brakes. Handling was still tops. The larger four-cam engine now provided more low end torque without any loss of power to maximum revs. It became an ideal Gran Turismo auto for point-to-point driving or racing.

After fifteen years of production in Stuttgart/Zuffenhausen, the 1965 356C was about as different from the 1950 356 as a facelift on a one-year-old Detroit model. The engine was enlarged from 1086 cc to 1582 cc, disc brakes replaced the drums, a fully synchromesh transmission replaced the crash box and the headlights and bumpers were a little higher. However, the car looked similar, had the same platform frame with unit body, retained the 82.7-inch wheelbase, and kept the rear engine with the four-speed transmission in the front of the engine. Only two body styles were available — the coupe and the cabriolet — and just two engines — the 70 DIN hp (88 SAE) at 5000 rpm or the 95 DIN hp (107 SAE) at 5500 rpm. Actually, the 126 Carrera 2 models should be included here, but with 16,668 356Cs produced, their number was almost insignificant. The 95 DIN hp was designated the 356SC and performance was 0-60 in eleven seconds and a top speed of 115 mph. Karosserie Reutter was now absorbed by Porsche. Since 1960 Reutter couldn't keep up with the demand; therefore Karmann complemented production. The cars were still made by hand, more so than any other production auto. The price of the cabriolet was $4,200 in the United States. In the finest European tradition, it still had a padded top with bows covered by a headliner and was very snug. It was not a fussy car, still able to thread a needle in traffic; fast, yet economical. It didn't need 300 hp to attain 100 mph nor did it need power steering or even power brakes.

# 356B Carrera 2

# 356 SC Cabriolet

A fiberglass Porsche for street and racing! With a steel-box frame which was strengthened by bonding to the body, many say the 904 was the most beautiful Porsche made. Styling was by Ferdinand (Butzi) Porsche III and the body was made by Ernst Heinkel Flugzeugbau. Fiberglass was chosen for lower weight and the small production run planned. While 100 units were needed for homologation, 110 cars were actually made. The body came in three sections: the hood, the tail and the cockpit. The engine compartment was planned for the six-cylinder racing engine. It wasn't ready in time, so the Fuhrmann four-cylinder, four-cam engine went in. Two stages were available — for the street, 155 hp at 6400 rpm; for racing, 180 hp at 7200 rpm. Displacement was the same as the Carrera 2 at 1966 cc. Engine placement was right behind the seat, midship. The five-speed transmission was aft, a repeat of all racing cars from Porsche. The racing engine would propel the 904 from 0-60 in 5.6 seconds and a top speed of 160 mph. Price at the factory was $7,425. The 904 was only 41.9 inches high and weighed 1,430 pounds. Braking was by four-wheel discs. The light alloy, five-inch-wide rims were mounted with Dunlop SP 165x15 radials. Wheelbase was 90.6 inches. Most 904s were sold in racing form. The factory raced some 904s with six-cylinder engines, and some with eights. Some 904s were seen in open versions, but the long, clean silver coupe with the bobbed tail was the usual version. In 1964, the Carrera GTS took first and second places at the Targa Florio. Many other victories followed.

Actually, Porsche Design 912 was the engine for the fabulous 917 race car. The road car called 912 just happened to be the number after 911. Porsche Design 901 was actually the new six-cylinder engine. But Peugeot held the rights to use combinations where the middle number was a zero, causing Porsche to change to 911. The 912 was the 911 with the old four-cylinder push-rod 1588 cc engine producing 90 DIN hp (102 SAE). Obviously, it was not as fast as the 911 — as a matter of fact it was slow: 0-60 in 11.5 seconds and a top speed of 115 mph. Disc brakes were used all around and it had a wheelbase of 89.3 inches on the 1969 model. The car was available as a coupe or Targa model. The 912 occupied the lowest step on the price ladder. In 1965, the United States price started at $4,745 and by 1969 it had gone up to $5,200 — base price for the coupe. About 30,000 912s were made. Styling was by Butzi Porsche. It retained the basic look of the 356 but had more room for passengers and luggage. Although Reutter had since been absorbed by Porsche, and the factory built the 911 bodies, the 912 was usually built by Karosserie Karmann. The 911 was sold for a year before the first 912 became available. The first few 912s had a painted dashboard with only three instruments, just like the 356C. With the built-in flexibility of a Porsche, the 912 could still gobble up the miles rapidly. On club tours, the 911 would only be able to pull away if there was a long straightaway. The 912 kept a lot of people driving Porsches who couldn't have afforded a 911. That was one of its purposes.

# 904 Carrera GTS

# 912

"You can't win them all," stated a Porsche ad for the 914/6. It listed eleven wins out of twelve starts in C Production SCCA racing. The 914 was the low-priced Porsche, replacing the 912. The 914/6 was the expensive 914. The car was made in arrangement with Volkswagen. Karosserie Karmann made the 96.5-inch wheelbase body, based on a design by Gugelot Design of Neu-Ulm. Most bodies received the VW Type IV engine; however, a small number of bodies went to Stuttgart/Zuffenhausen to receive 911 engines and running gear. The 1969 911T 1991 cc engine was placed midship. With two triple-throat Weber carburetors, the engine produced 110 DIN hp (125 SAE) at 5800 rpm. The 914/6 had four-wheel disc brakes, a five-speed synchromesh transmission and weighed 2,250 pounds. Externally, small script on the rear panel and five-lug wheels were the clues to the 914/6. The fourteen-inch Fuchs alloy wheels were usually fitted. As delivered, it would do 0-60 in 8.2 seconds and top out at 125 mph. The price in the United States was $6,000, just a few dollars shy of the 2.2-liter 911T. Because of that, sales were disappointing. The 914/6GT with larger engine and mean-looking fender flares didn't help sales. Even a planned series of 916s — a fixed-head coupe, with new nose and rear panels — got no further than eleven cars. Demand dwindled and production faded in 1971 just after 3,362 914/6s had been made. Sales continued until 1972. A funny thing happened: With no more new 914/6s available, they became more popular. The mid-engined, four-cylinder 914 lasted until 1976.

The cost of racing the potent 917 was tremendous; however, the publicity of winning races justified that cost. Still, Ernst Fuhrmann, the new president of Porsche, looked for a less expensive route. He saw that with a little magic, the ten-year-old 911 could become a winner. The result was the Carrera RS — a production-based car. Take one six-cylinder 911 and increase the engine size to 2687 cc and the power to 210 DIN hp (230 SAE), add the 911E/S front spoiler and a ducktail rear spoiler, reduce the weight and build five hundred examples to qualify for homologation. It was that simple; actually, sales topped 1,800 units, even without the United States market, which was eliminated due to emission regulations. The sales impetus allowed its inclusion in Group 4 racing as well as the planned Group 3 racing. In February 1973, an RSR was the overall Daytona winner. The Carrera RS used the platform frame and unit body resting on an 89.3-inch wheelbase, and it weighed 2,000 pounds. Suspension, in Porsche tradition, was all-independent. The rear spoiler actually worked — it reduced rear lift from 320 pounds at 150 mph to just 93 pounds, with a plus of increasing airflow in the engine compartment. Performance — how about 0-60 in 5.5 seconds and top speed of 150 mph? Wheel width was six inches with four-wheel disc brakes. Price, about $12,500. Of note are the graphics. Decals weigh nothing; red or blue ones on a white car spelled out Carrera, in reverse lettering. Matching color Fuchs alloy wheels completed the effect.

# 914-6

# 911 Carrera RS

Would you consider rare, a model that was produced in only 174 units? In 1975, that's the total number of 911 Carrera Targas. Only thirty-six were painted gold on black. The 911 Carrera was a mean-looking machine, with the larger wheels, fender flares and that big "whale-tail." In the United States, the Carrera was the top of the line. The plain 911 was dropped, and lowest-priced 911 became the 911S. For once, the two models had the same engine (in the United States). Both were rated at 157 SAE hp (152 in California) at 5800 rpm. Performance was 0-60 in 8.4 seconds and a top speed of 137 mph, just 134 for the 911S due to the whale-tail. Gone was the usual Porsche separation of models by horsepower. The Carrera in the United States was a trim option: standard was five-speed transmission, front and rear spoiler, flared fenders, seven-inch front and eight-inch rear, painted alloys, black trim including the roll bar, leather seats and velour carpeting. It still kept the twelve-year-old body, with an 89.4-inch wheelbase, unit construction, and weighing about 2,370 pounds. The Targa, named after numerous victories in the Sicilian Targa Florio, was introduced in 1967. At that time, it had a roll bar, removable top and plastic rear window. There were four possibilities: closed, top off, rear window down, and top off and rear window down. Later, the plastic rear window was replaced by a glass window. Sales of the 1975 Porsche 911 didn't slacken, even with the gas crunch, higher prices and the rumor of a new liquid-cooled, front-engined Porsche.

It seems like turbocharging was invented by Porsche. Actually, the principle goes back to 1905, when a patent was given to Swiss engineer Alfred Buchi; ten years later he got another patent more in keeping with the current application. In World War II, aircraft engines used the turbo; then came the Indianapolis-type race cars in the fifties. In 1962, Oldsmobile introduced a turbo V-8. Porsche's first turbo was the 917-10 Can Am car in 1972. Turbocharging made a championship car, the 917, a terror. After 1973, Porsche developed the turbo for the 911 engine. Turbocharging is simply routing the exhaust gases back into the engine. The wastegate bypasses the gases around the turbine, thus limiting boost. The good, old 911 received a shot in the tail with the turbo. By 1979, the last year the 930 was sold by Porsche in the United States, the 3299 cc six-cylinder engine was putting out 261 SAE hp at 5500 rpm. Performance was 0-60 in about six seconds and a top speed of 155 mph. The car could be like a little lamb, very docile and even a little old lady would have no trouble driving it. The tiger in it required only a heavy foot. Where the regular 911S would run out of horsepower, the Turbo merely slammed you back in the seat. Only four speeds were necessary. Production never exceeded six hundred units a year. The last fifty 930 Turbos brought into the United States had special plaques with Ferry Porsche's signature. They were called "signature edition." Porsche still makes the 930, but not for United States consumption. The 930 Turbo is the ultimate Porsche, still maintaining balance, precision and technology.

# 911 Carrera Targa

# 930 Turbo

The 928 started life on a clean sheet of paper. It was targeted for the mature buyer who was weaned on sports cars. The front-mounted, liquid-cooled engine displaces 4473 cc, has a single overhead cam, is a V-8 and produces 219 SAE hp at 5250 rpm. Performance is very pleasing: 0-60 in seven seconds and a top speed of 138 mph. The rear transaxle can be ordered with either five-speed manual or fully automatic transmission. The rear axle is special; it is called the Weissach axle and aids the driver by actually turning into the corner. Weight distribution is 50/50. Handling is superior to the 911. Wheelbase is 98.3 inches and the weight is 3,410 pounds. Tony Lapine, an American who heads the styling studio at Porsche, and his staff styled the body. It is built at the factory. In Europe, the 928 was named "Car of the Year" when introduced. In the United States, the car was originally priced at $26,000. Porsche has chosen to keep secret how good the 928 really is. A drive in the car is sheer delight. The front and rear sections have an aluminum substructure covered by polyurethane, painted to match the body. The biggest, heaviest, most luxurious Porsche retains the intricate balance that is Porsche's. It may be the best Porsche yet. Keeping with tradition, a 928S has been introduced in Europe, featuring increased power and improved handling. There's even a vestigial spoiler below the rear window. Porsche owners have always asked for more power and the factory has always responded. Can homologation and racing of the 928 be far away? And how about a turbo version?

The 924, presented in late 1976, was a totally new Porsche. It broke the tradition of rear-engined, air-cooled cars with a bang. Porsche stated that the price was "not inexpensive." It was, nevertheless, the least expensive Porsche. In a sense, it is like the 356 made in Gmünd, Austria; it uses production parts from other automobiles, the VW and the Audi. The transaxle is similar to one Professor Porsche designed for Mercedes-Benz. Since Butzi Porsche had left the factory, the styling of the car was in the hands of Tony Lapine. The 924 uses a front-mounted, four-cylinder, single overhead cam engine, also used by Audi. In turbo form, it displaces 1984 cc, puts out 154 SAE hp at 5500 rpm and tops out at 130 mph, with a 0-60 time of 9.2 seconds. Wheelbase is 94.5 inches and weight is 2,850 pounds. Judged by numbers made, the 924 is the most successful Porsche; production has already topped 100,000 units. Cost of the Turbo is $21,500, base price, United States. Besides the Turbo series, there have been several special versions offered, each with special colors and options: the Championship Edition in white with red and blue striping, celebrating the double World Championship in 1976; the Limited Edition in gray; the Sebring Edition in red, copying the Sebring pace car; the Weissach Edition in platinum; and the Carrera GT series. In the now-familiar required number of production units for homologation, four hundred Carrera GTs were made, but are not for sale in the United States. In the future, maybe the polyurethane fenders from the Carrera GT will be used on a new production version.

# 928

# 924 Turbo

# Essence of a Sports Car

Most enthusiasts agree on what makes a car a sports car. Sure, there are extreme opinions. Yes, there are some who would only consider the most exotic. And there are those who would accept anything that moves fast and lacks a muffler.

Yes, there are extremes. But the majority agree that a sports car should be relatively small, have an intimate cockpit, should be fast, fun to drive, handle well, should be low and beautiful in a sensuous way — and have a sound to match.

One winter night, I think it was in 1953 — I was still a teenager in Sweden then — a major rally passed not far from where I lived. I was, of course, among the spectators, watching the cars negotiate a ninety-degree curve at the top of a hill. The road was icy and they needed speed to get to the top, but not too much, or they would overshoot the turn and end up in a deep ravine. I watched the cars all night as they passed in a steady stream, exploding the stillness of the night, sliding sideways through the curve with roaring engines and spinning wheels, the roof-mounted searchlights exploring what lay ahead, the falling snow looking contrastingly peaceful as it was caught in the quick-moving beams. That was the first time I saw and heard Porsches in action, and I was impressed by their newness, uniqueness and effectiveness.

Yes, I knew then that a Porsche had all it took to make it a true sports car, and more. And it was accomplished in such clever ways; it was rear-engined, air-cooled and aerodynamic. Yes, the Porsche was unique, sensible and honest in every way. It not only matched the definition of a sports car, it exceeded it; a sports car should now also be economical, dependable and comfortable.

It was this concept that quickly earned Porsche a place at the top — a concept that, enthusiasts agree, captures the essence of a sports car.

**P**orsche's second-generation steering wheel, the first of its own design and introduced on the 1953 models, decorates a 1958 Speedster, right. Ivory color gave a distinctive look and two spokes allowed a perfect view of the instruments. The third generation, introduced in 1959, was inspired by emerging concern for safety; it was now concave, black and had three spokes. A horn ring was optional, as seen on a 1965 SC Cabriolet, left. A Les Lester wheel fit snugly in the 904 cockpit, above. Spokes were engine-turned, and a wood rim represented the classic racing look of the period.

**E**arly Porsches did not carry the coat of arms that has since become such a famous symbol. Not until 1953 did the crests of the state of Baden-Wuerttemberg and the city of Stuttgart supply the staghorns and the rampant horse for a design that from then on adorned every Porsche. Here it can be seen applied to a variety of surfaces: the chromed deck-lid handle of an A-series 356, the forged alloy wheel of a 924 Turbo and the shining paint surface of a 911. The scripts on the opposite page, found on the front fenders of two famous Porsche models, represent motoring pleasure in its purest form.

**P**rimitive charm characterizes the cockpit of the 1955 550 Spyder, above, and the 1958 356 Speedster, left. The Spyder's low-cut, beautifully curved racing windshield and the Speedster's flimsy, minimal, no-frills side curtains recreate the open-air pleasures of the aviators and race drivers of the pioneer days. The interiors of the 1975 Carrera Targa, right, and the 1978 928, upper right, on the other hand, create a total contrast, expressing the ultimate in electronic refinement and upholstered luxury, encapsulating their occupants in an environment of relaxing comfort.

**S**hiny surfaces create the setting for this study of lights. The classic simplicity of the 356-series is represented by the close-up of a 1958 Speedster, above right; by the telephoto facia of a 1963 Carrera 2, far right; and by the wide-angle shot of a 1965 Cabriolet, above, its beehive lenses serving both as parking lights and blinkers. To the right, the much-developed 911 theme in the form of a 1979 930 Turbo, shows a beautiful solution to the same function. Far right, the exciting lines of a 928 is further proof that good design can prevail in the face of ever more complicating regulations.

**S**poilers didn't spoil anything, although purists initially felt they did – visually. But, as with so many successful designs, the spoiler was based on a functional concept. Its first road-car application came on the 1973 Carrera RS, right, nicknamed "ducktail." It increased rear wheel grip by as much as 20 percent at top speed and also had several other positive effects on stability and handling. Further refinement came on the 1975 Carrera, above. Now enlarged, rubber-rimmed and horizontal, it was called a "whaletail." The final form is seen on the 1979 930 Turbo, left, with its large louvered area funneling air to the intercooler.

First used in 1952, Porsche's ventilated disc wheel was available painted, or as on the 1958 Speedster to the left, chromed. The hubcap was plain, but in 1959, with the arrival of the B-series, it carried the crest. Far left, Porsche's famous Fuchs forged alloy wheel, first available on the 911. On this 1973 Carrera RS, it was painted to match the Carrera script on the body side-panel. Above left, the cast alloy wheel of the 928 is not only distinctive, it also allows superb ventilation. Above, one of the best-looking wheel designs ever, Porsche's new forged alloy wheel, here fitted to a 1981 924 Turbo.

F our Porsche power units, all engineering masterpieces in their own rights, display their features on these pages. The basis was, of course, the development of Ferdinand Porsche's air-cooled push-rod engine for Volkswagen. In the 1958 1600 S Speedster, above, his engineering milestone produces 75 hp. Pictured to the right, the famous four-cam engine, designed by Ernst Fuhrmann. Here, mounted in the street version of the 1955 550 Spyder, it generated 110 hp. To the left, the ultimate development of the 911 power unit; the 1979 3.3-litre US-specification 930 Turbo has an output of 261 hp. To the far left, the latest creation from the Porsche engineers, the all-aluminum, liquid-cooled, fuel-injected V-8 of the 1978 928. It produces 219 hp, but was designed with much room for further development.

# Chronology of Production

## By Gene Babow

Ferdinand Anton Porsche, born in 1875 in Maffersdorf, Bohemia, was a genius. His detractors, may they rest in peace, said that he could scarcely draw a line. They forgot that genius extends to picking associates who can translate the ideas of the master.

He was wholeheartedly devoted to the pursuit of these ideas. It was not unusual for him to have a sandwich in his pocket, so that he could have a meal while working. He would often sleep for a brief moment in the most unexpected places. He valued time. He once said he intended to live to be one hundred because he felt he had so much left to do.

Ferdinand Porsche was a pioneer in the areas of front-wheel drive, four-wheel drive, four-wheel brakes, automatic transmissions, streamlining and mid-engined Grand Prix cars. With a flick of the pen he would design the Auto Union Grand Prix racer with sixteen cylinders, 545 hp and weighing 1,500 pounds; or the Volkswagen, using the same principles as the Auto Union, but placing them in a practical perspective.

He was full of dreams and worked hard for their realization. He was never satisfied with his designs; he always saw possibilities for their improvement, hence there were always changes in production. His view was: "Through sporting successes, we shall popularize our marque and thus we shall sell considerable numbers of vehicles." The Porsche as we know it today is living proof of the validity of this theory.

Porsche went to electro-technical school against his father's wishes. His father had wanted him to take over the family tin shop. At just eighteen, Porsche built a light-station in his father's home. At twenty-five, he had

Even though the first car to carry the Porsche name was born in humble circumstances, it built on the accomplishments of a giant among automotive engineers – Ferdinand Porsche. To the left, father and son, Ferry, supervise testing of the pre-war Auto Union – a creation of the Porsche engineering firm. Above, driving impressions are discussed with racing-ace Bernd Rosemeyer. After the father's death in 1951, development of the Porsche car rested on the shoulders of Ferry Porsche, to the right seen describing its virtues to a journalist. (Photos Studio Woerner, courtesy Road & Track.)

already designed the front-wheel drive Lohner-Porsche. This vehicle had electric motors mounted in the front wheel hubs. Remember, the year was 1900! See if this sounds familiar: To prove the capabilities of the machine, he increased the power, applied a measure of streamlining and drove the Lohner-Porsche in record time up the Semmering Pass in Austria.

Thinking ahead, however, he saw the limitations in range and power of this type of vehicle. True, he tried the motors in the rear wheels, then in all four wheels and then, finally, he used a gas engine to provide energy to power the electric motors. But, he was now ready for new challenges. He left Lohner to start with Austro-Daimler. During this time he also won a competition event in another car he had designed — the Prince Henry model. Furthermore, he designed a small 1100 cc car called the Sascha, which won its class at the Targa Florio. One of his mechanics was a man who later gained prominence as Yugoslavia's premier and president, Marshall Tito. And one of his drivers was Alfred Neubauer. Later, Porsche would introduce Neubauer at Mercedes, where he would lead the competition department to numerous victories. Porsche himself also moved to Mercedes, where he was responsible for the fantastic S series Mercedes, including the S, SS, SSK and SSKL. After his sojourn with Mercedes he returned to Austria to work for Steyr; and later, he again joined Austro-Daimler.

The time is now 1930 and Porsche was tired of working for others. In a rented house on Kronenstrasse, in Stuttgart, Germany he started his own firm — offering consultation as well as complete designs of engines and vehicles. The House of Porsche began. The numbering system of Porsche designs started here. Not wanting his first client to think that it was the first design, Porsche started with number seven.

This first design, Type 7, was a small vehicle for the firm Wanderer. Type 12 was a Zündapp vehicle for the well-known motorcycle firm. Type 22 was the Grand Prix Auto Union. Type 60 was the Volkswagen. Type 82 was a jeep-like derivative of the VW, known as the Kubelwagen. Type 101 was the Tiger tank. Type 128 was the water-going VW, known as the Schwimmwagen. Type 356 — we'll get to that shortly.

Porche's associates in the new firm included his son Ferdinand Anton Porsche II, nicknamed Ferry; Erwin Komenda, who would execute the styling of the 356 as well as the 550 Spyder; Karl Rabe, chief designer and responsible for the torsion bar suspension; Franz Reimpeiss, who presented the first study of the platform design of the VW; Karl Frohlich, an expert in gearboxes; Josef Kales, aero-engine designer; Josef Mickl, a computer specialist before there were computers; and Joseph Zahradnick, specialist in steering and front suspension. A formidable list of talents.

While Porsche had long thought of a car bearing his name, the first attempt toward this goal was the car developed for the 1939 Berlin-Rome Race. The race never occurred because of World War II. Another design study, the Type 64, was meant to have been a sports-type vehicle on the VW theme. The state-owned VW firm, however, would have nothing to do with that kind of thinking. But, publicity gained through winning a race was a different matter. Porsche convinced the men in power that a VW-based car would be good for this purpose. This car, known as the Type 60K10, was built at Karosserie Reutter in Stuttgart.

One of the three Berlin-Rome cars built remained in Professor Porsche's possession. The car was purchased from him just after the war by Otto Mathé of Innsbruck, Austria. Porsche needed the money to start production of the Type 356. The prototype was built as a mid-engined car and based mostly on VW parts, so a contract with VW was needed at this time. The contract prevented Porsche from designing a competitor to the VW; a sizeable sum of money accompanied the agreement — this money also came in handy in the development of the Porsche sports car.

A small series of fifty cars were planned. They would be made in Gmünd, Austria. Based on the VW, but with modifications for the sporting aspect, the series would be made of aluminum. (Otto Mathé bought two of the Gmünd coupes; he still has them.) The acceptance of the Porsche was gratifying. A move back to Stuttgart was finally possible.

In Stuttgart, space was rented from Reutter. Tradition had to start someplace, and this was the place. Quality was to be first and foremost. The fit of the doors, hood and trunk required handwork to maintain a minimum space between the openings. The last digits of the car's serial number were stamped on each part. The surface of the body was also hand-finished. Zero flaws ensured quality. The car was assembled for fit, then disassembled for painting. All parts were painted at once, in an area which was surgically clean.

In 1951, Professor Porsche died, partially as a result of his war-related imprisonment in France. He did not live to be one hundred, and he still had many things to do. But his son, Ferry, carried on in a manner that the master would have been proud of.

By 1954, 5,000 of the Type 356 models had been made. The Porsche philosophy continued: The factory

**S**hape of things to come! Created for the 1939 Berlin-Rome race, this aerodynamic coupe introduced the concept that would later form the basis for the first Porsche. The war forced cancellation of the race, so the three cars built were never put to their true test. Of the three, one was wrecked during the war, another was vandalized by occupation forces, and the third still survives in the hands of Austrian race driver Otto Mathé who purchased it from Porsche right after the war and raced it very successfully. These pictures, by Gene Babow, show the way it looks today in Mathé's garage – still basically original.

raced cars but also encouraged private owners to race them. Class wins in races and rallies were now commonplace. Starting in 1951, Porsche won its class at Le Mans. Looking ahead, however, it was readily apparent that the 356 was too heavy and the VW-based four-cylinder push-rod engine was near its limit of development for racing use.

In Frankfurt, the family Glöckler raced a special lightweight Porsche. It did well. Erwin Komenda improved the styling and the Type 550 took shape. The new engine, Type 547, was designed almost totally by Dr. Ernst Fuhrmann. It was a four-cam, four-cylinder, air-cooled unit. It was right from the beginning. The initial goal of 100 hp/liter was achieved just a few years later. Fuhrmann kept the outside dimensions of the engine similar to the push-rod one. It was obvious it was meant for the street as well as for the track.

Perhaps this is a good time to go into nomenclature, especially as it relates to the Type 356. The Stuttgart production Porsche 356 lasted from 1950-1965. There were four major subspecies: the 356, from 1950-1955; the 356A, from 1956-1959; the 356B, from 1960-1963; the 356C from 1964-1965. These are considered model years. In true Porsche tradition, continual changes abounded, year by year.

No complications should arise in trying to comprehend the different body styles. True, they transgressed the subspecies, but the two basic ones were constant; the coupe was always available, from 1950-1965, as was the cabriolet — a fancy convertible with roll-up windows, a padded top and headliner.

In 1952 and 1953, the America Roadster was produced in limited numbers by Heuer Body Works in Weiden. It was the Type 540. Only sixteen were made before another roadster, which it inspired, made its entrance — the Speedster.

Max Hoffman, the early distributor for Porsche in the United States, wanted an inexpensive leader to sell. A special series called the America (not to be confused with the Type 540 roadster, same name) coupe and cabriolet was sold. It had no identification on the outside and is known by very few. It was stripped of the rear seat and other niceties and sold for about $3,300. By late 1954, the name was changed to "Continental." Although not a catalog model from the factory, magazine ads from Hoffman show this model. Some cars even had the name on the front fenders. A threatened law suit from Ford Motor Company, because they were planning to reintroduce the Continental MK II, caused a third name, "European," to be used. By 1956, model designation reverted to simply 1600 and 1600Super within the 356A Series.

Probably the most recognized early Porsche, the Speedster, was introduced in 1954 and continued into 1959. The Convertible D (for Drauz, the coachbuilder) was a 1959 model only, carrying the Speedster body, but now with a higher windshield and roll-up windows. By now, the demand for Porsches outstripped the capacity of Reutter to build them. Karmann of Osnabruk was called on to supplement the production. In 1960, with the introduction of the B-Series, the D became the Roadster. In 1961, production of that Roadster shifted to D'Ieteren Fréres in Belgium. Karmann produced a notchback coupe that looked like the cabriolet with a hardtop, called simply the Karmann coupe.

The complication in nomenclature was caused by the various displacements of the engines. Rounded-off displacement numbers identified the engines. The push-rod engine of 1950 displaced 1086 cc; it was called the 1100, and so on. There were engines of 1300, 1500 and 1600 designations. Again in true Porsche tradition, there was a more powerful S designation in the 1300, 1500 and 1600 types. In 1961, an even more powerful engine was introduced — it was called the Super 90. It put out 90 DIN hp. From 1955 on the four-cam engines were also used in the 356 series and they were then usually called Carreras. They displaced from 1500 to 2000 cc.

Up until the 356C series, nomenclature was simple. For instance, you might have a 1961 356B with a normal 1600 engine in a coupe. In 1964, the normal engine was dropped and the 1600S engine would be designated the 356C and the Super 90 engine would be known as the 356SC. Either could be had in the coupe or cabriolet. Now, that wasn't hard, was it?

Now for the curve ball — the four-cam-engined cars: 1500GS, GS/GT, Carrera 2, 2000GS/GT and 904. These were all road and race cars of the Type 356, (except for the 904) powered by the Fuhrmann four-cam engine. This fabulous engine, a veritable giant-killer, would power Porsche road and race cars for a decade in rapid fashion. Even today, they power the vintage racers in winning style. In sizes from 1100 cc to 2000 cc, they made a racing name of Porsche.

Nomenclature aside, the Porsche was meant to be driven. It brought a new dimension to sports car driving. The car challenged the driver to join forces and operate as one. The famous auto writer, Ken Purdy, said, "You almost never see a bored Porsche driver." The balance of this car was something new — power, handling and brakes complemented each other. Steering was light and quick, gearbox was smooth with

*Porsche Number One saw light in 1948. These pictures were taken in a converted sawmill in Gmünd, Austria, temporary home of the Porsche engineering firm. Top, the wooden buck used to check the fit of the hand-hammered body panels. Above, workmen attending to details of the still unpainted body. Left, the engine was a Volkswagen, although it now sported dual carburetors and modified cylinder heads. Right bottom, Porsche Number One, a roadster, resting behind Porsche Number Two, a coupe, its front shown above. (Photographs by Porsche Werkfoto, courtesy Ray Stewart.)*

hand-picked ratios and the car could slice through holes that didn't exist for other cars. Even the 1600 normal could go point-to-point with a 300 hp opponent and often be there first. The more curves, the more likely it was that it would be first. More important, the driver would be wearing a big smile and be relaxed enough to do it again.

A little out of order, the Type 904 is included here. It still had the four-cam engine. It was both a road and race car. Different power was available for each owner option. To reduce weight, a fiberglass body was utilized that was made by Heinkel, the aircraft manufacturer. The frame was box steel, to which the body was bolted and bonded. The car was designed by Ferdinand Porsche III, also known as Butzi.

Around 1960, a new touring car was being formulated. It would be a continuation of the Type 356, but faster and roomier. The engine, designated Type 901, would be a six-cylinder, air-cooled unit, displacing two liters and producing 130 DIN hp at 6200 rpm. The new model was introduced at the Frankfurt Auto Show in 1963. The body was styled by Butzi Porsche. Because a French automaker held the rights to all three-digit numbers with a zero in the middle, the new model identification had to be changed from 901 to 911. Deliveries of the new car started in late 1964. In 1965, the old four-cylinder engine was installed in a lower-priced version called the 912.

Back to nomenclature. The 912 stayed as the 912 from 1965-1969. The 911 transversed an alphabet soup of letters that still continues. The 911 added an S in 1967. Right, more power and the new alloy wheels by Fuchs! In 1968, the S was joined by the letters T and L. T was for touring, the lower-priced 911; L was for luxury, replacing the S in the United States because of emission regulations. In 1969, the L was dropped and replaced by an E, for Einspritzung or fuel injection. The S was reinstated in the United States. There was also an R, but that was a lightweight racing model in 1968. The T, E and S continued until 1973. In 1974, the T was dropped completely. The E became the lower-priced model and reverted to the plain 911.

A small series of fast cars were made in 1973, and were only available in Europe, where they were called the Carrera RS. In 1974, the engine was toned down and became the Carrera, now available in the United States. In 1975, the plain 911 was dropped, and the 911S and Carrera remained. In 1975, a 25th Anniversary model of the 911 was sold. These 750 special silver cars carried a numbered plaque with Ferry Porsche's signature. Next year, the Carrera was turbocharged and became the 930. The designation 912E appeared — it was a 911 body with the Type IV VW engine. It covered the period from the end of the 914 until introduction of the 924. In 1978, the S designation was dropped and became the 911SC.

The 911 is still going strong after eighteen years. The design is still in style and time has not affected the looks of the car. Flares on the fenders and the choice of either coupe or Targa still satisfies owners in spite of the fact that the 1964 price of $6,000 has increased to more than $30,000, for various and sundry reasons.

Backtracking a little, the mid-engined 914 was introduced as a 1970 model. The VW 1700 cc engine was used. The body was manufactured by Karmann. The introductory price in the United States was $3,595. The 914/6 was completed at the Porsche factory and outfitted with the 1969 911T engine, displacing 2000 cc. The 911 for 1970 displaced 2200 cc. The 914/6 was dropped in 1972 and replaced in 1973 by the 914/2.0, which had a more powerful four-cylinder engine than that of the original 914 version. The 914 lasted until 1976.

The 914 was as much a Porsche as was the Type 356. What's wrong with using VW parts? Many manufacturers wish they could. The handling of the 914 was delightful. The Targa-type roof and the two trunks were popular. A derivative of the 914, the 916, was planned. It would have the 2.4-liter 911 engine, and be quite expensive. The latter stopped production at just a handful. It could also have become too much of a competitor to the 911, which it would easily have surpassed in handling and performance.

Let's return to the Turbo. The 930 Turbo has to be the ultimate Porsche. It signifies all that Professor Porsche could have foreseen, except that he would probably have improvements already in motion and it would still be sold in the United States — it was not after 1979.

What would Professor Porsche have said about the 924 and 928? Both are complete turn-arounds for Porsche. They are liquid-cooled and front-engined.

In reference to the 924, he would be happy that in four years, more than 100,000 have been sold. Would he have changed anything on the car? He did design a similar trans-axle for Mercedes; it was used in the Mercedes Grand Prix cars in the thirties.

The 928 would probably be in his garage, next to the 930 Turbo. Both would be used. He would appreciate the luxury of the 928. It may be the best Porsche yet. Following Porsche tradition, there is now a 928S. He would appreciate that model and also have something in mind for future development. He would be disenchanted with the sales of the 928 and the way it is

**N**ow finally back in Stuttgart, where Porsche's engineering firm had been located before the war, 1950 saw the beginning of serious production of the Porsche car. Reutter, the coachbuilder, made a small area available to Porsche in its Zuffenhausen facility and also supplied bodies, above and left. Above, the engine receives final touches. Now could also begin all the activities necessary to launch a new make: Porsche tested on the Autobahn, Porsche taking part in Concours d'Elegance, Porsche posed in snow, Porsche competing in races. (Photos by Studio Woerner, courtesy Road & Track.)

advertised. He would have been pushing hard for a competition version to get sales rolling.

He would look at Dr. Ing. h. c. F. Porsche AG and be proud. The factory in the outskirts of Stuttgart/Zuffenhausen has grown immensely from the rented space at Reutter's. He would note that Reutter had been taken over by Porsche in the early sixties. (Speaking of Reutter, the firm now builds seats for Porsche and other companies under the name Recaro. Recaro is actually an anacronym taken from the first two letters of Reutter and letters from Karosserie.)

Financially, the small firm of Porsche has not had one year of red ink; it has always been in the black. In effect, the racing was paid for by the resulting increase in sales. More black ink came, and comes, from designing and consulting for outside firms. In 1947, after the war, Porsche had as much money coming in from this source as it had before the war started.

This black ink is all the more amazing when you look at the history of automobile manufacturers. Of the 5,000 makes started over the almost one hundred years of automobile production, only a handful still survive. Even this handful is not secure, some are teetering now. Try to name some manufacturers who have started since 1948 and are still in business. It is much easier to name those who have failed since 1948.

The future of current road cars from Porsche has to be speculative. However, it is said by Porsche officials that the 911 series will last as long as buyers will purchase them. This could be changed by increased smog requirements, especially in the United States.

The 924 will remain, but the engine will probably be all Porsche. At Le Mans this year (1981) a 924 took seventh place overall. It was powered by the 2.5 liter half of the 928 engine. It will be called the Porsche 944. The 928 will stay as is. The more powerful 928S will not meet United States smog regulations.

More than 500,000 Porsches have been made. It is still a small company; remember, Chevy can produce that many in six months, but they are just Chevys.

When Dr. Ernst Fuhrmann was president of Porsche, he said, "The president of Volkswagen, a big firm, drives a Volkswagen; the president of Opel, a big firm, drives an Opel; I am president of Porsche, a small firm, I drive a Porsche 928S."

May Porsche always stay that way. They build a car that demands to be driven hard; a car that is conceived with controls at the fingertips, built to last with a minimum of servicing, gets a respectable number of miles per gallon and still performs as you would expect a sports car to perform.

# 550 SPYDER

# Long Live The Spyders!

Like an individual, an automobile also has a destiny. And the two are often intertwined. Sometimes, at best, they are destined to become loved, pampered and treated with respect. Other times, most of the time, they are destined to just roll along, without any special significance, ending up in some forgotten place. And sometimes they are headed straight for disaster, destined for a short, dramatic life, ending in tragedy.

I look across the vast, gold-colored territory that surrounds me. To the north, to the south, to the east, there is not a house to be seen, not a tree, not a bush. The vastness begins at the roadside where I stand, expands uninterrupted, rolls gently along the contours of the valley floor, rises into hills, covers them with gold, monotonous gold, and continues on until it meets blue sky, monotonous blue.

To the east, the dark gray of a road, thin in the beginning, like a string, cuts through the hills and widens gradually as it runs on across the valley. To the northeast, another road, another string, widens, runs on, straight as a cutting-edge, finally meeting up with that first road, exactly where I stand. The two roads, joined in one, continues behind me, curves, passes a group of buildings, and travels on westbound.

There is an eerie stillness here. Nothing moves. Not even the cows seem to move, grazing in the distance, looking like black dots sprinkled among the gold. And there is an eerie silence. It makes me aware of what once took place here. I bend down by the roadside, looking for crumbled pieces of aluminum.

Suddenly, the silence is broken by the distant sound of an engine. As it nears, I can hear that it comes from a truck. But on that day, September 30, 1955, it was not a Mack, nor was it a Kenworth approaching the point where the two roads meet. No, on that day, long ago, it was a Porsche 550 Spyder. Its silver-colored, low-slung, aerodymanic body penetrated the air like a bullet, shooting toward that crucial intersection with a speed of eighty-five miles an hour. Its young, famous-faced driver, sunglasses shielding his eyes, speed-

The 550 Spyder was inspired by a series of Porsche-powered cars built and raced by Walter Glöckler as early as 1950. To the left, the first of these, driven by Heinz Brendel, is on its way to a class win in the 1952 Eifelrennen. Above, Hans Herrmann and Herbert Linge, in the cockpit of one of the prototype Spyders, return from a practice run at the factory. They later drove the same car to a class win in the 1954 Mille Miglia. Johnny von Neumann successfully campaigned another prototype in the United States. Pictured to the upper right, he is preparing for a start in Bakersfield. The photographs in the lower right show two production version Spyders, one sporting a plexiglas bubble at Hockenheim, the other being guided through a curve by German driver Theo Helfrich.

wind tugging at his hair, a content smile curving his lips, suddenly noticed a black Ford, facing him, slowing down, preparing to turn onto the road running in a northeasterly direction.

The famous-faced young driver expected the Ford to stop before it turned. Normally it would have. By law it should have. But on that day, it did not stop, and then, realizing it was his moment of truth, he saw that it was too late to correct his speed and direction.

The heavy, strong-built Ford caught the light, thin-skinned race car exactly at the point where the driver sat. The Porsche skidded on, came to a rest up against a fence, a twisted heap of aluminum, the passenger thrown clear, the driver's legs caught between steering wheel and pedals, his body hanging out across the door, his neck broken.

James Dean, twenty-four, actor, race driver, was fatally injured, and later, dead in the ambulance.

I walk over to my car, parked by the roadside. On the way back I again look for crumbled aluminum pieces, ridiculous, of course, since every bit and piece must long since have disappeared. I drive the short distance to the buildings. They turn out to be a village by the name of Cholame, population sixty-five, barely visible on my California map. I stop for gas.

Sure, Glen, the manager of the station, remembers. He was playing basketball over by the school when it happened. Later, that same evening, he saw the wreck himself. It was sitting there in front of the garage. Right there, Glen points.

Some time after the accident, the engine was sold and installed in another race car. The transmission was also sold. The body was obtained by the traffic safety people who displayed it all over the country to show what happens when you drive too fast. The last time the wreck was seen it was on a train back from Florida. When the train arrived at its destination, the wreck was not on it. Some say it was stolen and cut up in small pieces, sold as souvenirs.

James Dean's Spyder was a mid-run chassis number of the first series. All in all there were about two hundred built. Of these, only ninety were of the first series. This was the destiny of one of them.

Chassis number 061 had a different destiny. It was delivered on September 2, 1955, in Butte, Montana, about the same time as James Dean took possession of his Spyder. It is known that 061 was raced extensively. It was seen on tracks all over the Pacific Northwest. When the original four-cam engine blew, a Corvair engine was installed. Later a supercharged
*(continued on overleaf)*

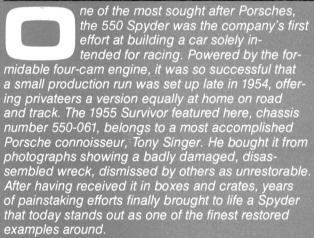

O ne of the most sought after Porsches, the 550 Spyder was the company's first effort at building a car solely intended for racing. Powered by the formidable four-cam engine, it was so successful that a small production run was set up late in 1954, offering privateers a version equally at home on road and track. The 1955 Survivor featured here, chassis number 550-061, belongs to a most accomplished Porsche connoisseur, Tony Singer. He bought it from photographs showing a badly damaged, disassembled wreck, dismissed by others as unrestorable. After having received it in boxes and crates, years of painstaking efforts finally brought to life a Spyder that today stands out as one of the finest restored examples around.

engine was fitted. The car went through a succession of eight owners, all adding to it and subtracting from it, until it finally was left sitting in the corner of a garage, the original engine and transmission in boxes, the body panels apart and demolished, separated from the frame, dry-rotting, wasting away. The owner had at first thought it would be possible to restore it but he finally gave up on that idea and decided to sell it. His ad appeared in Auto Week.

Tony Singer of Long Island, New York, was turned into a Porsche enthusiast after he had bought a 1963 Super 90 in 1971. By 1974 he also owned a 904 and happened to see a red Spyder in a showroom on Long Island. It was for sale. Until then he had been unaware that such a Porsche existed. Now, seeing it, discovering it, he thought the beautiful styling and the honest engineering made it the ultimate Porsche. He decided to sell the 904, but by then, the Spyder was gone. Tony Singer did not give up. About a year later he found an ad in Auto Week.

It took another year before he was able to close the deal and take delivery of 061. At that time he had still only seen photographs of it. And they had not looked encouraging. Everyone he had showed them to had thought it would be next to impossible to restore it. No one had ever put a Spyder body back on its frame since it was done at the factory more than twenty years earlier. But Tony Singer did not give up.

He assigned the restoration to Grand Prix SSR of Setauket, New York. Tony Dutton was responsible for the day-to-day work. Tony Singer was keeping himself occupied with research for authenticity and acquisition of missing parts. He even went out and bought two more Spyders, chassis numbers 059 and 089, so they could be studied for clues of how the 550 originally was put together. When it was found that they were not fully authentic, he managed to borrow 090, the last one built and still perfectly unaltered.

After 2,300 man-hours and two-and-a-half years, the Spyder finally stood ready for its premier showing at the 1978 Porsche Parade in Aspen, Colorado. It was awarded the coveted Judges Choice.

The Stradivarius violin, a masterpiece, is now on it's third century. Its course of destiny has been varied. The Porsche Spyder, another masterpiece, is only going on its fourth decade. No one knows what destiny has in store. We know Tony Singer's is in good hands. And who knows, preposterously, of course, maybe right now someone is quietly buying up all the small pieces of James Dean's Spyder, attempting to put it all back together. Who knows?

Pictured to the left, top, a line-up of production version 550 Spyders. These are works-prepared cars with the one closest to the camera possibly a Le Mans competitor. Bottom, the Spyder and the Jagdwagen, both in limited production, shared the same space at the Porsche factory. Above, top, one of the photographs of chassis number 061 that Tony Singer saw before he bought it. The picture clearly shows the deplorable state of the car. Bottom, Tony's Spyder takes shape in the workshop at Grand Prix SSR. To the right, top, the tubular ladder-type frame of the production version 550. Bottom, 550A Spyders under construction at the Weidenhausen coachworks in Frankfurt in 1956. Note the new space-type frame.

# 356A SPEEDSTER

# Top Down and Flat Out!

We've just raised the top on Rudy Binkele's Speedster, parked outside his home in the hillside outskirts of San Luis Obispo. It's a very simple operation to raise that top. And it looks very good with those two bows set far back, pushing up like on a tent, the canvas tight like a drumskin, and with that long, unsuspended stretch of canvas falling off dramatically to meet with that super-low windshield.

"I've noticed that people look with more excitement at the Speedster when the top is up!" Rudy says. "It must be because it's so outrageously low. Another reason is that they can't see the driver. All they can see is a shoulder and a pair of hands holding the steering wheel. Unless you lean forward, you've no vision at all to the sides, especially if you're six-foot-three, like I am. No vision at all!"

"I guess that top is just for looking at!" I say.

"Yes, that's about all it's good for. You don't really need it when you drive in the rain. It shoots right over your head anyway."

"You have to keep on driving forever." I say. "But you can't do that when you're held up by a red light. Or when you get the gate at a railroad crossing, or when you've the road blocked by cattle."

"That's when you reach behind the seats and pull the top up. You don't fasten it because you want to let it down again as soon as you're ready to go!"

"You don't happen to have a yardstick or something else to measure with, do you?" I ask. "I'd like to see how low that windshield actually is. In inches!"

"I'll go get something!" Rudy says and walks off toward the house, turning his head, glancing at the Speedster, sitting there, looking fat and round.

"Looks like a tank!" he says and disappears.

When Rudy Binkele first saw a Speedster — that was in Santa Barbara in the mid-fifties — he thought it was the ugliest thing he had ever seen. Compared to his own Chevy it was, of course, strange looking. But after he had seen what the Speedster could do on a racetrack, he was completely sold.

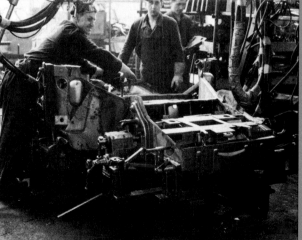

*The unique photographs on these pages were taken in the mid-Fifties. At this point, Porsche employed around six hundred workers, who turned out an average of seventeen cars a day. Pictured above, a portion of the assembly hall; a Speedster body is hanging from its travers in the foreground, a worker is in the process of lining up brake drums, and mufflers are being brought up on a cart. Pictured to the left, the chassis is being manufactured with the help of a special jig. To the right, top, a Speedster body, painted and trimmed, is ready to be mated to its chassis. To the right, bottom, a lineup of half-finished bodies, Speedsters in the foreground, Coupes in the background.*

It would take almost twenty-five years and eight different Porsches before he finally got this Speedster. He traded his 1959 RSK Spyder to get it. The RSK had been drastically modified. It had eight-inch tires and flared fenders and a 912 engine instead of the original four-cam. He had driven it in club-level competition and had also shown it successfully, but with his restaurant business taking more and more time, the RSK ended up collecting dust. He found himself looking for a car he could drive anytime, anywhere — an exciting road-machine like the Speedster. The one he got was perfectly restored to original specifications. It was so good, in fact, that he won several firsts in shows. But that wasn't what he really had in mind for it. You can't have a Speedster sitting there, just to look at. So nowadays, he drives it often and hard on a loop of his favorite back-country roads.

Rudy drove the loop just this morning. I was a passenger. The California sun was already so hot, in spite of the speed-wind, that we had to get back to the house for something to drink. Soon its my turn to take the Speedster out on the loop.

While I'm waiting for Rudy I open the lid to the engine compartment. It's all so simple and clean and understandable in there. There's the generator. There are the carburetors. There's the oil filter. And so on. It's almost simple enough for me to think that I could do some work on it myself. Maybe.

I walk around to the front lid and open it. The battery, the spare wheel and the jack are located all the way up front — to counteract the weight of the engine in the rear. The fuel tank is set up against the back of the dashboard. In front of it is a space, about fourteen inches deep. A pouch, holding the side-curtains, fits precisely in that space. I take them out and place them on the car, fitting the pins in their holes, and pulling down the leather straps over the small pins on the inside of the door. It gives me a strange sensation, like preparing for a mission of some kind.

Rudy comes back with a seamstress' measuring tape dangling from around his neck, looking like a tailor, and looking like a bartender too, with a glass of Coke and ice in each hand. Between sips, I measure the windshield. Vertically, the area of vision is nine inches. I measure the side-curtains too. The vision area is only six inches.

"Not to look through. To look at!" I say.

I'm behind the steering wheel now. It was sixteen inches across, by the way. Rudy sits in the passenger seat, looking calmer than he probably is. We're ac-

*(continued on overleaf)*

From any angle, the Speedster is a most appealing and exciting design, as unique today as it was when introduced in 1954. Its round, slippery forms were developed without the aid of a wind tunnel, and it is a credit to stylist Erwin Komenda's concepts. Later testing has proven the original 356 shape to be one of the most aerodynamically efficient designs. The early-morning, fog-swept beach proves as fitting a location for this 1958 1600 S Speedster, chassis number 84300, and its enthusiast-owner Rudy Binkele, as their normal habitats of country roads, racetracks and car shows.

celerating through the gears now, the stick feeling loose and flimsy, just as I had expected, remembering my experiences with Volkswagens, and needing long movements, the speed-wind flowing noisily across the top of the windshield, bugs splashing onto it. The car is doing close to eighty now, in fourth, the road straight but narrow, dropping off, and ahead, curving sharply to the left.

"Don't let up yet!" I hear Rudy shouting over the engine, busy sounding in its characteristic hammering, whining, rushing way. "You don't have to brake until you hit that 25-mph sign up there. Now! Shift!"

I down-shift to third, brake, and nudge the car carefully over to the left, cutting grass, a little on edge because I've heard stories about how easy the backend goes; but the Speedster sticks to the road like it was glued, and I steer it back to the right and accelerate, throwing it in fourth, the road going slightly uphill now, and turning to the right further ahead. I relax for a moment, feeling how tightly the seat holds me. I push back in it, realizing then how upright the driver sits compared to today's lay-down racing position.

"Don't let up!" I hear Rudy shout again. "That's another 60-mph curve up there! Go close to the telephone pole on the right. But don't go too close!"

I down-shift and go through that one too. It's a repeat of the first. The road is running uphill now. I keep it in third until I reach the crest, then accelerate and put it in fourth, calmly pressing the gas pedal to the floor. The road is straight, running downhill, and bumpy, and I feel the suspension working. It's not as stiff as I had expected. In fact, it's not stiff at all. The speed is increasing now, the wind becoming aggressive, the needle closing up on one hundred. Golden hills are rushing by on both sides, and barbed wire fences, and cows and horses and sheep, and telephone poles, and Keep-Out signs, and No-Hunting-Posted signs, and windmills, and mailboxes, and hay freshly cut, and hay uncut. I feel in control. The cockpit is the center of it all. Just in front of me I see the top of the low curving windshield, and the curving dashboard, so simple and beautiful, and beyond it the curving hood and fenders, it all being curvy and round and sensuous; behind me, the engine is working hard and enjoying it, enjoying it like a racehorse stretching out on the straightaway to win.

"Now you know why they call it a Speedster!" I hear Rudy shouting, and turning my head quickly I see him smiling, calm as ever. He can't be as calm as he looks, I think to myself. I decide to keep that pedal nailed to the floor for as long as I can . . .

Pictured in this spread are various 356-series dashboards. Above, a 1950 Cabriolet. It used the Petra steering wheel, and did not yet have a crest on its horn button. Left, a Coupe from the same period. The 1951 photograph focuses on the reclining passenger seat. To the near right, top, a 1953 model, now sporting both a new steering wheel and a crest. Notice also the eye-lids above the two large gauges. Center, a 1954 Speedster. It has two large dials and a small center-mounted one. Later models had three of equal size. Bottom, the dash of an A-series Coupe. Three equally-sized gauges is now the style. Far right, top, the interior of a B-series Coupe with a new steering wheel, but basically the same layout. Bottom, the B-series Roadster. (Photos courtesy Road & Track).

# 356B CARRERA 2

# Carrera Nostalgia

You can talk Porsche anywhere. Al Hansen and I talk Porsche as we park his Carrera 2 in front of the Bella Union Saloon in Jacksonville on this slow-paced, off-work, sun-bright Saturday morning. First time we've seen the sun in two months, Al says. Jacksonville was once the capitol of Oregon. It was a center of gold mining, but it didn't die like so many other gold-rush towns. It lived on, thanks to its gold. Even during the depression, they lived off of the gold they dug out from tunnels under their houses. Al tells me all this. But we're really talking Porsche.

We open the doors to the Saloon and walk across the planks that make you think you see bullet holes in them from all the gunfights you imagine must have taken place in here. We pick a window table so we can keep an eye on Al's Carrera. Al orders the omelette with onions and cheese. I know it's still breakfast, Miss, but I must have the warm German sausage, lovingly simmered in dark beer, as the menu reads, and served with sauerkraut. I must, Miss. Goes with our Porsche talk, I say.

You know, Al says, the young-generation Porsche enthusiasts, they probably have no idea where the Carrera name comes from, do they? They probably think the Porsche sales people grabbed it from out of thin air, like Detroit would do. Don't you think? But you and I know that it comes from one of the most fantastic road races ever put on. Carrera Panamericana, I say. Really has a ring to it, doesn't it?

Wasn't it first run in 1950, I ask? Yes, I think an Olds won it that year. The Mexicans put the race on to promote their new Panamerican Highway, you know. It started just south of El Paso on the United States border and ran all the way to the Guatemalan border. But there were no Porsches in it that first year.

I think the first time was 1953, wasn't it? I don't think any Porsches ran it in 1951. But in 1952, one came in eighth. And in 1953, two Guatemalans ran the two 550 prototypes. I know that. One broke down, but the other won its class. At the end there were only two

*In this spread the camera has captured for posterity some of the activities of those rare Gmünd Coupes. In the two photographs at the top of this page, Johnny von Neumann, California Porsche pioneer, rounds the hay bales during a race at Pebble Beach. Later, the same car was raced with its roof cut off. Above, a picturesque scene from the 1951 record-run at Monthlery. Wearing a mustache and scarf is Porsche's competition boss, Huschke von Hanstein. To the left, the Coupe is frozen by the flash during the evening portion of the run. The first Porsche victory at Le Mans came in 1951; Veuillet and Mouche drove their Coupe to a class win. Right, top, their #46 car gets some well-earned juice. Bottom, the same drivers repeated their Le Mans win the following year. (Photos courtesy Road & Track and Gene Babow.)*

cars left in the class. The other was a stock 356.

But, of course, they didn't have the four-cammer in those cars, did they? No, they first used the four-cammer in 1954, when Hans Herrmann won the class and placed third overall. Yes, that was the last year of the race and the year of the big Porsche win. Just think about that. At the finish, after five days of flat-out racing, the one-and-a-half-liter Porsche was still right up there among those big four-and-a-half- and five-liter Ferraris. Just think about that. Yes, 1954 was the year of Porsche's big Carrera win. The next year, in 1955, they put the four-cammer in the 356 body and called it Carrera.

1955, I think to myself, chewing on the natural casing of those German sausages while Al is working on the last of his omelette, yes, 1955 was a good year. I saw Hammarlund win at Skarpnack that year, in Sweden, on that monotonous, curve-straightaway-curve-straightaway airport circuit outside Stockholm. Yes, I can still see him coming up on that hairpin turn in his silver Carrera, braking for all he's worth, tires smoking, down-shifting quickly, the four-cammer rumbling and coughing and spitting fire, the whole car tilting heavily on its springs as it rounds the corner, the right side of the front skirt almost scraping the track, the tires screaming, and then, that slippery silver shape shooting out of the turn, passing all the other cars, accelerating down the straightaway, now with that fully open, fully unleashed four-cammer sound loud and throaty, and every time he's shifting, the backend of that low-slung body sinking even lower, the rear wheels flexing wide, a puff of blue smoke shooting out from that fat exhaust pipe, and finally, the Carrera getting smaller and smaller while the other cars are still in second gear. Yes, 1955 was a good year.

Say, Al, your Carrera is a 1963, right? Any racing history? Yes, it was raced in France, Al says. The owner's manual is in French. Doesn't do me any good because I can't read it, but it shows that the car was delivered in France. Also, the speedometer is in kilometers. From France the car went to Germany. Frank Hunt of Minneapolis brought it over and restored it. Did a very good job.

I look out through the window at the Carrera 2. It looks just like a regular B-series coupe, doesn't it, I say, except for that louvered skirt below the rear bumper. Right, Al says, and minus the grilles over the openings below the headlights. The Carrera 2 has oil coolers there, and they need all the ventilation they can get. But let's have a ride in it now, Al says. Yes, (continued on overleaf)

**H**ere is what the uninitiated would call a typical early Porsche, but it's actually not the earliest style. The B- and C-series coupes, with their raised bumpers, lights and fenders, differed slightly from the original 356. The Survivor featured here, chassis number 122214, belonging to restorer and collector Al Hansen, also differs in another important way. As an expert would recognize, the lack of horn grills below the headlights shows that it is a 2000 GS Carrera 2. It has the potent four-cam engine on board, capable of catapulting this B-series 1963 classic from 0-60 in less than nine seconds, thus making it the fastest of all 356-series road Porsches.

let's I say. I'm ready for it. Thank you, Miss. Those German sausages sure worked wonders for our conversation. Thank you very much, Miss.

Al wants me to drive. I don't mind. Be sure to keep the revs up, he says, or else the plugs will foul. The four-cammer is famous for that. Keep it over twenty-five hundred to be on the safe side. But don't run it up above four thousand. It's still being run in.

When that like-nothing-else sound starts pouring out through the dual pipes, even though it's muffled, sidewalk car enthusiasts turn their heads. A Porsche? Doesn't sound like one. Is it really? I keep the revs up, find the catching point of the clutch, let it out, and get off and away in a fairly decent fashion, keeping the revs up at the proper level. That low, guttural note comes willingly from somewhere deep inside.

You don't want to have to clean the plugs on this one, I say, talking louder now. They are pretty hard to get to, aren't they? You bet, Al says, shaking his head, smiling, looking like he knows from experience. It's a very complicated engine from whatever way you look at it. It's difficult to work on unless you really know what you're doing. But it's beautiful and unique.

I have the open road ahead of me now. I run it up to four thousand in second, then shift to third, run it up to four thousand again, and let it float there. I'm feeling the beauty of it now. I give it more foot, feeling the car surging forward, hearing the sound opening up, and then, as the four-cammer reaches fifty-two hundred, sensing a vibration of power spreading through the floor and seat, reaching for my spine, and I know that's the way it should be.

Yes, Al says with a forgiving smile as I take my foot off and let the tach needle sink to four thousand, yes, that four-cammer sure is a beautiful machine. You should see the way the parts are made. Hand finished. Hand assembled. You should understand how everything works and why. What I know about the German people I have learned from Porsches; solid values, sound thinking and planning.

We cruise comfortably fast now, on a narrow road, curving in and out between fields and farms, mountains on both sides. Applegate Valley, Al says. You know what I like about old Porsches? I like that they are old. And I like that in spite of the fact that they are old they are still modern, he says. Yes, that's a very fine analysis, I say, as I down-shift, preparing for a hairpin curve, going in fast, keeping the revs correct, braking now. Yes, a very fine analysis.

You can talk Porsche anywhere, but it's especially good in an old Carrera.

*The various Porsche Coupe models is the subject of this picture spread. On the opposite page, first column, top to bottom, the Gmünd model is first. Notice its peaked roof and high windshield. Next, the 1950 model with its split windshield. Next, the 1951 model which had a solid windshield, but retained the crease. On this page, above, the A-series. It now had the bumper separate from its body, and in this case, over-riders for the United States market. Back to the opposite page, second column, first, an A-series with detachable hardtop. Next, a photograph showing the effect of the 1959 re-styling; an A to the right, and a B to the left. Finally, the Karmann Coupe. To the left, the Roto Hoist, conceived and manufactured by Al Hansen of Medford, Oregon. (Photos courtesy Road & Track.)*

# 356 SC CABRIOLET

# A Topless Review

Somewhere in Denver, there's a one-story brick building. There's no sign above the door, and there's nothing interesting about the outside of it. On the inside, is where it gets interesting. Bill Jackson keeps his Porsche collection in this building. Lined up along the walls are rows of cars, all under covers.

It's interesting just to guess what's hiding beneath those covers. But you have to know your models well, because there are things you may never have heard of. What about a Schwimmwagen? Or a Jagdwagen? Or a Porsche marine engine?

How about this one? I see familiar fender forms and part of an air dam below the cover. An RSR? Yes. One of the early Peter Gregg cars. And this? Another RSR. Yes. One of the three Martini prototype cars. Raced by the factory in 1973 and 1974. How did you ever manage to get that one? Bought it directly from them, Bill says without blinking.

This one should be easy, Bill says smiling, uncovering the 1965 SC Cabriolet I've come to photograph. Freshly polished and detailed, its champagne lacquer is shining, its black interior spotless. Lynne, my girlfriend, and I, Bill says, drove it to the Porsche Parade in Seattle. It's probably the best all-around Porsche you can own. It's quick. It handles well. It's economical. It's comfortable. And it's an open car! But the top is padded so it stays warm in the winter. And — it has the classic Porsche look!

It takes an hour to complete the tour. By then Bill is called away to other duties. I'll try to be back by three, he says. We'll shoot it at Red Rocks, all right? Perfect, I say, but don't rush! I knew I would find enough in the sanctuary to keep me occupied even if he should happen to be gone for a month.

The sanctuary is a suite of two rooms built within another large room in Bill Jackson's building. The literature collection is kept here. The shelves are full of books and magazines, folders, holders and envelopes. I decide to do some research on the open Porsche models while I wait.

*Featured on these pages, the earliest open Porsches. On the left-hand page, Porsche Number One, on a street in Zurich, Switzerland. At this point, certain changes are being done; the bumpers have been removed and the wheel cut-outs have been given a flowing, more elegant line. The cockpit and the engine compartment are clearly visible in the picture to the right. On this page, top, the Beutler Cabriolet. This is one of two with a more sculptured rear and it is on display at the Swiss Museum of Transportation in Luzern. Beside it, one of two Gmünd Cabriolets, this one on display at the German Automuseum in Schloss Landesburg. The two pictures above show the America Roadster belonging to Robert Hicks of Oregon. (Photos courtesy Road & Track and Gene Babow.)*

I see photographs from a place called Gmünd, in Austria, where the first Porsches were made. The buildings look like they were old already then; the plank walls appear weathered and cracked; the windows have panes missing and broken; the driveway is full of potholes and the grass is growing wild. Porsche had to move here in 1944 when allied bombing made Stuttgart too dangerous.

I see pictures of the first car. It is 1948. They show a strange-looking creation with a rear deck that's too long. But the characteristic sloping Porsche front is already there. It was a true roadster, with a flimsy top and without roll-up windows. There was only one copy made — in aluminum. Enter: Style 1.

Before this car was completed, work had begun on another, much improved and changed version. This was the coupe. All in all, less than sixty came out of the Gmünd production, all aluminum-bodied. Bill Jackson, naturally, has one of them — a coupe.

Six of these, in chassis form, were sent to Switzerland where convertible aluminum bodies were fitted by Beutler. The Porsche front is there, but on two of them, the rear had become more pronounced. The Beutler Cabriolet was Porsche's first true cabriolet, with a padded top and roll-up windows. Enter: Style 2. Bill is keeping one under surveilance.

In 1949, two convertibles were produced by Porsche themselves in Gmünd. These look like the later production Cabriolet, but have a different windshield and an aluminum body. Let's call it the Gmünd Cabriolet. Enter: Style 3.

The year is 1950. Porsche has moved back to Stuttgart, where production finally starts in a serious way. Now comes the 356 Cabriolet, its styling derived directly from the coupe, built by Reutter in steel, with padded top and roll-up windows. More than five thousand would be sold between 1951 and 1959, its body style basically unchanged. Enter: Style 4.

By now Porsche was trying for the American market. Max Hoffman, an independent dealer in New York, spearheaded this effort. He had strong feelings about price and styling. As a result, another open car was drawn up and built by Heuer, a sometimes supplier of cabriolet bodies to Porsche. The America Roadster, named after its intended market, retained the Porsche front but sported a new fender line, sweeping low at the cockpit, rising again above the rear wheel. I see pictures and it strikes me that the design of the cockpit area must have been strongly influenced by Jaguar's XK120. I look at the windshield

*(continued on overleaf)*

**F**inal version of the faithful 356! And many Porsche enthusiasts would agree: The finest in sensible sports car motoring! The C-series was the result of fifteen years of refinement in the areas of handling, braking, dependability, performance, and finish – and in the case of the Cabriolet, it was topped off, so to speak, with an all-weather, fully padded top, made according to classic traditions. The 1965 model featured on these pages, chassis number 160909, belongs to Bill Jackson. An accomplished collector of all Porsches – not many models are missing in his stable – he still appreciates the basic, honest pleasures of driving his Cabriolet – last of a breed.

and the upholstery, the way it has been wrapped around the edges of the cockpit. The resemblance is even more evident in a picture showing the America Roadster with the top up. I feel sure Hoffman had told Porsche what a formidable competitor Jaguar was in the United States, especially coming in at a price of $3,300. I think Hoffman wanted a car with those features, and he got it, but he didn't get the price. The America Roadster came with a $4,600 price tag. Only sixteen were built between 1952 and 1953. This was due to Heuer's financial troubles, but also due to the fact that there was a new roadster under development — the Speedster. The America Roadster was aluminum-bodied and had a simple top and side curtains — a true roadster. Enter: Style 5. And, correct, Bill Jackson has one of these also!

The Speedster came in 1954. In this car Porsche and Hoffman had a price leader, at just below $3,000, as well as a style leader that was uniquely Porsche. It opened the United States market in grand style. The bodies were made by Reutter, in steel — except for a few aluminum Carreras — and it was a true roadster. Altogether close to five thousand Speedsters were made between 1954 and 1958. Enter: Style 6. Bill Jackson has three, right!

In 1958 Porsche gave in to dealers who felt that the Speedster was too primitive. It got a higher windshield and roll-up windows. Now called the D-Convertible — for Drauz, the builder — it was no longer a true roadster, although it still had an unpadded top. This steel-bodied version was made in 1,330 copies between 1958 and 1959. Enter: Style 7.

The basic 356 style was slightly reshaped in 1959. The top and window of the D-Cabriolet were applied to this new body. Around three thousand were made between 1959 and 1961, now bodied by the Belgian coachbuilder D'Ieteren. Although it was not a true roadster it was called the Roadster. Enter: Style 8.

The new body also came in the classic Cabriolet version. There were no exterior differences between the B- and C-series, except for the hubcaps. The steel bodies were made by Reutter in almost ten thousand examples between 1959 and 1965. Enter: Style 9.

As I write this, several months later, the phone rings. A reliable source confirms what another had told me: The Porsche people are definitely working on a new, true Cabriolet, based on the 911 and soon to be introduced in rendering form. Enter: Style 10.

The shooting at Red Rocks? Just barely made it, getting the usable shots of the Cabriolet on the last four frames of the last roll of film!

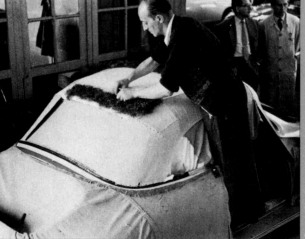

*Porsche's series-produced open cars is the subject of this spread. The photograph above shows the 1961 assembly-line manufacture of Roadsters at the Belgian coachbuilder D'Ieteren in Brussels. To the left, a padded top is being expertly attended to by a craftsman at Reutters in Stuttgart. On the opposite page, first column, top, the 1950 356 Cabriolet, with its split windshield and flush bumper. Below it, compare the rounded windshield frame of the Speedster with the sharp-angled one of its successor, the D-Convertible, pictured at the bottom of the first column. Second column, top, the B-type Cabriolet. Exterior difference between this and the C-type was the hubcap. Next, a Speedster in action. At the bottom of the page, the 1960 Roadster with its simple top and roll-up windows. (Photos courtesy Road & Track.)*

# 904 CARRERA GTS

# The Last Road Racer

There's something about the styling of the 904 that makes it appear so light and delicate. It's the most strikingly beautiful of all Porsche road cars.

The 904 was a truly dual-purpose car. It was conceived that way not only to qualify it for racing — rules required one hundred to be built — but also to help pay for its development. It was the last time Porsche could offer a car that looked the same when raced in world class competition as it did on the road.

The 904 was styled with aerodynamics in mind, although, as a matter of interest it was developed without the aid of a wind tunnel. Later tests have shown it to have the very low drag coefficient of 0.33. What marks the 904 as a work of art is the harmony between the various elements of the body, the execution of the details and the overall expression of balance, power, speed and aggressiveness. It all reveals the highly developed artistic sense of the stylist — none other than Butzi Porsche, the son of Ferry Porsche and the grandson of Ferdinand Porsche.

While both Ferdinand and Ferry had chosen the field of engineering as their specialty, Butzi chose industrial design. He was appointed the head of the Styling Department when it was organized in the early sixties. Thanks to the infancy of this department and the urgency with which the 904 was needed, Butzi worked out the styling of the 904 virtually single-handedly. Without the often hampering effect of staff and committees, Butzi succeeded in creating a masterpiece — one that will always have a place among the great automotive designs.

But styling was only one aspect of the 904. What was hidden beneath its beautiful skin was more important on the racetrack. The 904 had originally been conceived for the new six-cylinder engine. But it wasn't ready in time for the 1964 season; the decade-old, well-proven four-cam engine was instead fitted behind the cockpit.

The combination of low weight — the fiberglass body weighed only 180 pounds — high-power output

*The fiberglass bodies for the 904 were built by the aircraft manufacturer Heinkel, and delivered painted and detailed. The picture above shows the engine and suspension being mated to the body at the Porsche factory. To the left, the snug and functional cockpit. The seats were not adjustable, instead both pedals and steering wheel were. The steering wheel shown in the photograph was replaced by an English-made Les Lester, wood-rimmed wheel in the production version. The engine, to the right, was the Fuhrmann four-cam unit in its biggest-bore form, just under two liters, and was very accessible once the tail portion of the body was removed. Above, right, the beautiful and efficient profile of Butzi Porsche's masterpiece. (Photos courtesy Road & Track.)*

and low drag coefficient made the 904 a winner. During its two major seasons, it showed its superiority in all forms of endurance events. 904s unexpectedly took first and second overall in the 1964 Targa Florio. 904s placed first, second, fourth, fifth and sixth in class at Le Mans that same year. The next year, a 904 again took first in class. Also in 1965, a 904 surprised everyone by placing second in that year's grueling Monte Carlo Rally.

One of the first outings on United States soil was the twelve-hour Sebring. Five cars had been entered, but there was also a sixth present in the pits. It was chassis number 904019, belonging to Dutch privateer Count Carel de Beaufort. This 904 was his backup car. It took part in practice, but never raced.

Another newcomer on the track was Alfa's GTZ. One of the factory team drivers was Chuck Stoddard. That time at Sebring was his first encounter with the 904s, and he had an excellent opportunity to judge them in their true element, dueling with them for twelve hours. Three of the five 904s crossed the finish line, Briggs Cunningham taking fifth overall and first in the 2000cc class. Chuck was thirteenth overall and the winner of the 1600cc class.

Chuck grew up with cars. At the age of fourteen, living in Connecticut, his home was too far from school to qualify for bus service, so he bought an old Ford, parking it behind a barn since he didn't have a license. During his teenage years he bought, fixed and sold cars. In 1948, after having seen his first MG, he discovered that the world didn't consist of Fords alone. The MG awakened his interest in European sports cars. In college, he majored in automotive engineering, graduating from Boston's MIT. He was obviously preparing for an automotive career.

In 1952, he took up racing, over the years campaigning everything from a TD, a Jaguar, a Siata and an MGA to an Alfa Giulietta, an AC Ace and a Porsche 550 Spyder. In 1957, he opened a dealership in Willoughby, Ohio. He represented just about every obscure make you can name, as well as Porsche and Mercedes. He continued to be active in racing, adding national SCCA championships in G, D, and C production to his accomplishments. In 1964, he also captured the National United States Road Racing Championship for under two litres.

By 1965, his racing involvement had become so serious that the next step would have been to turn professional. It was that or the business. Luckily for Porsche enthusiasts, he chose the business. After
*(continued on overleaf)*

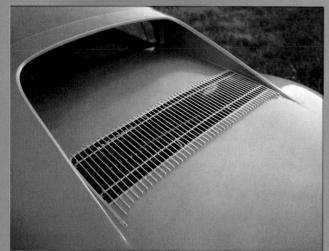

**S**eldom has a more potent race car been available for the road than the 904 Carrera GS. Porsche had a tradition to live up to – the 550 of a decade earlier. Again, the engine was ahead of the rear axle. Again, it was the famous four-cammer, now refined and enlarged, producing 155 hp. The body was of fiberglass – a Porsche first – and styled by Butzi Porsche. The ultimate package moved from 0-60 in less than six seconds! This 1965 Survivor, chassis number 904019, is restored and owned by Chuck Stoddard – Porsche race driver, Porsche dealer, Porsche collector, Porsche connoisseur extraordinaire!

having gradually phased out all other makes, he concentrated on Porsche. Today, his impressive facilities stand as a monument to dedication, organization and the quest for perfection. It must be one of the most complete Porsche organizations of its kind in the world. There's a new and used car dealership, complete with showroom, service and parts departments. There's also a restoration facility with engine and machine shop, body and paint shop and even an upholstery shop. There's a mail-order organization, with a 124-page catalog distributed worldwide, that specializes in parts and accessories for Porsches of all ages. Many of the older parts are remanufactured, carefully matching the original specifications. The stock of parts occupies a 2,000 square-foot area and consists of about 15,000 items. There's also a collection of vintage Porsches, the latest addition being an America Roadster, immaculately restored. A Gmünd Coupe is waiting in the wings. In addition to all his other duties, Chuck also served as president of the Porsche Club of America in 1979 and 1980.

It was in the early seventies that Chuck began to realize that all those historic Porsches would not be around forever, and if he wanted to own them, he better get them while they were still available. One of the models he had always wanted was the 904. Destiny arranged it so that the one he found, chassis number 904019, was one of the cars he had encountered at Sebring in 1964. Today, the 904 is immaculately restored, the work of Chuck's own hands.

We spent a most enjoyable afternoon together in the outskirts of Willoughby, the 904 resting quietly in a field of dandelions, waiting for the last afternoon sun to illuminate its silver body in just the right way. Chuck and I, in the meantime, discussed old Porsches, new Porsches, restoration and racing, and with those subjects out of the way, the drawbacks of socialism and the attractiveness of cats.

After the shooting, I was offered a ride in the 904 — I had to take my shoes off to fit — and discovered another of its aspects, besides the fact that it was very small. Its sound! When Chuck gave it full throttle, on the street in front of his dealership of all places, there was only one word that came to my mind — obscene! It was a sound that was in total contrast with the lightness, delicateness and beauty of that body. It was a sound that turned all heads. I felt like I was standing in the middle of Times Square during the rush hour, dressed only in my shorts.

I tried other words, but there was only one that could describe that sound — obscene!

904 prototypes were shown to the press at the Solitude circuit during the latter part of 1963, with prospective buyers also invited. In a short two-week period after this event, almost the entire planned production had been spoken for. The photograph at the top of the opposite page shows that the weather did not cooperate as willingly as the buyers. Above, the 904 looked good from any angle, but the three-quarter frontal aspect was especially flattering, focusing on the long nose and the beautifully shaped headlight covers. Left, bottom, notice the air intake for brake ventilation just behind the side window. On the production version, this was replaced by a scoop, visible on the 904 at speed in the picture to the right. The area hasn't yet been painted. (Photos courtesy Road & Track.)

# Bit By the Porsche Bug

"Yes, Ray, you were definitely bitten by the Porsche Bug that time. Even though it took so long for it to break out, it was still the occasion when you got the affliction you're suffering from now!"

"You mean that time in Germany?"

"Yes, it has a tendency to affect you many years later. You're never safe. If you have the disposition, a bite like that will usually get you sooner or later!"

Here I am lecturing Ray Stewart, a doctor of medicine, on the effects of bites by the Porsche Bug! Presumptuous, perhaps, but we all know that doctors don't have the answers to everything. And I am, after all, well-qualified to give advice in this field, having myself suffered from the affliction for many years.

Ray has just told me about his first encounter with a Porsche. It took place in Bamberg, Bavaria. The year was 1956. He was fourteen then and lived in that German town with his mother and father, a United States Army officer. It was a family habit to go on an outing every Sunday after church. On this particular Sunday, as so many times before, they went to Schloss Bamberg, the old castle that had given the town its name. There, besides the beauty of the surrounding scenery and the intrigue of the medieval architecture, Ray's father could enjoy his favorite beer — the Bamberger Hofbrau — served cold in the Schloss Keller. At that age, Ray was, of course, only allowed a sip. Just a little for his education.

But it wasn't the Bug of German Beer that bit him that time, nor was it the Bug of Medieval Castles. No, it was the Porsche Bug. Yes, the dreaded Porsche Bug in the form of a low, smooth, streamlined 356, parked under the branches of some birch trees, resting innocently beside a cobblestone driveway, its round surfaces silvery in the summer sun.

Ray was impressed by the Porsche. But he didn't feel an immediate attraction. It was too different. He did sense that it was a car meant to be driven fast. Why else would they have made it so streamlined? It was as if they had not cared about fashion or what people liked. They had only made it look the way it

*A replacement for the 356, first intended as an improved version of the aging classic, then becoming a totally redesigned vehicle, started its drawing board existence already in 1956. The engine was new, the transmission was new, the suspension was new, and so was the styling. It was the work of Butzi Porsche and his staff, and although the new style was fresh, slim and functional, the family resemblance was unmistakable. These photographs were taken during its premier showing at the Frankfurt Auto Show in September of 1963. It would take an entire year before customers were able to own one. Notice the small Porsche script and the twin exhaust pipes in the picture to the right. (Photo courtesy Road & Track.)*

*had* to look in order to glide smoothly though the air. And he did sense that it was meant for the pleasure of driving. Why else would there be so little room in it? Ray also remembers that he was surprised when his father told him the engine was in the rear. Yes, the Porsche was too different for Ray's taste.

But, that was all it took. It was the first bite! Oh, yes, there was one more thing. Ray's father thought it would be a good idea to preserve the occasion for the future. Perhaps he sensed the importance of the moment. In the viewfinder of his camera he saw a unique sports car, sleepy-looking with its aftermarket eyelids, and he saw a young man, wearing a tie, his jacket a size too large so he could grow into it, his blond hair crew-cut, his hand resting on the door handle with a blend of pride and embarrassment — a young man just bitten by the Porsche Bug.

It was the summer before he went to Eugene, Oregon, as a freshman in college, that he had finally managed to save up enough money to buy the car he thought was his dream car — a brand new 1963 Corvette. But his best friend arrived at school in a new Porsche. And, to his own dismay, Ray found himself wanting to swap cars with him. As often as he managed to talk his friend into it, he took the Porsche for a drive, sometimes borrowing it for the entire weekend. Ray remembers how he felt that he could drive as fast with the Porsche as he could with the Corvette, perhaps faster, especially over the winding roads of McKenzie River Pass.

When the new-generation Porsche, the 911, arrived in 1965, Ray was disappointed to see that the price had risen to way beyond his means. But, when the 912 appeared soon afterward, his hopes of owning a Porsche returned. If it hadn't been for the fact that after having graduated from dentistry school, he immediately went back to school, this time to study medicine, he would have bought a 912 right away. Now, he had to wait until 1969. He still had to practice dentistry on weekends to pay for the Porsche.

Twelve years later Ray and I are looking at that same 912. He still owns it. We've just completed the shooting session. I had hoped for rain; it would have been decorative, and for a while the clouds looked very dark, but nothing came of it. The 912 is resting on the bottom of a dried-out riverbed, somewhere in the eastern outskirts of California's San Bernardino National Forest, just where the desert is attempting to take over from the mountains.

*(continued on overleaf)*

**P**orsche's second generation, the 911, was an all-new car with an all-new six-cylinder engine and a price tag to match. This made room for a less expensive version: the 912. It had the old economical four-cylinder engine, now further refined. The styling and handling were the same as the new generation. It was just what Ray Stewart, original owner of this 1969 912, chassis number 129023289, had been waiting for. Today, although having expanded his palate to include even the most expensive Porsches, he is still as pleased with his 912, still keeping it as it was when new – right down to the tires.

It's getting dark now and the horizontal rays of the sun are illuminating the familiar forms of the second-generation Porsche. I have always been impressed by the skill with which the stylists, under the direction of Butzi Porsche, managed to transfer the look of the old 356 to the totally redesigned 911. The old roundness was gone, a new sleekness was there instead. The front was flatter, the nose more drawn out, the roof sloping less, ending in a longer rear. The key to the shape of the entire design was evident in the shape of the side windows with its smooth, yet disciplined curve. The bumpers were well-integrated with the body, looking somewhat like the early 356. The blinkers and position lights were combined with the horn grill into a pleasing wraparound design that gave the car much of its fresh appearance; the same approach was also used for the rear blinkers and brake light combination. The new 911 was a far cry from the old 356. Yet, there was never any question of heritage.

Ray maneuvered the 912 out of the riverbed and I took over the wheel for a sunset test drive. The steering was quick. The front felt a little too light for my taste, but it stuck nicely in the curves, even when you pressed it. It was leaning a little low, and the front wheels were bouncing; Ray admitted that it might be time for new shocks. The shifting was a definite improvement over the 356, although with the five-gear layout I always ended-up going from first directly to third. The stick was shorter than on the 356 and had a more precise feel as well as a nicely shaped knob. With its less-powerful 356 engine on board, the 912 was definitely no racecar. But the sporty feel was there, and the looks — and economy too!

As we turn on the headlights, the sun now sinking behind the mountains, and swing the nose toward home, Ray turns to me.

"I think there's definitely something to that Porsche Bug theory of yours!" he says.

He tells me of how he has by now owned over twenty Porsches; everything from Speedsters to a 910 race car that raced at Le Mans. He tells me about a corporation he has just organized which offers to convert 928s to turbo-charged roadsters. And he tells me about another venture, just about to be started; the remanufacturing of the 904. It's going to be a faithful copy of the real thing, so good owners of 904s are going to be able to buy spare body panels. It's going to be available both as a kit and as a complete car.

"The bad thing about this affliction," I say, getting in a last word of encouragement. "The bad thing is that there's no cure. You just have to live with it!"

On these pages is a sampling from the first decade of 911 history. Left-hand page, top, a pre-production car. Notice the stubby look; the longer wheelbase did not come until 1968. Bottom, far left, the experimental engine in the Frankfurt showcar. Left, the production version. Left, center, the 1970 model – entering the period of the classic 911 look. They had the longer wheelbase, giving them that perfect visual balance; they had the forged alloy wheels, light and distinctively beautiful; and they still had the uncluttered bumper arrangement. To the right, bottom, the 1973 model, now with a front air-dam and new, less distinctive cast alloy wheels. Above, the early interior, here seen on a 1968 model. Above, right, the interior of the 1973 model, virtually unchanged. (Photos courtesy Road & Track.)

914-6

# Road Testing For Real

1977 was a big year for Sam Cabiglio. He went to Europe three times, bringing more than fifty cars back to California. Eight of them were 930 Turbos.

One particular day in June of that year, we find Sam in Italy. We see him as he makes his way through heavy afternoon traffic in Milan, patiently maneuvering a big-winged, wide-flared 930 Turbo he had picked up at the factory a few days earlier. It is raining.

We see him as he turns into Via Frua, a street lined with mature, gray-trunked trees and century-old apartment buildings. Shops occupy the street level. Cafés sprawl on the sidewalks. They lay abandoned now as the heavy rain comes down with full force.

From habit, Sam's well-trained, all-seeing eyes scan every car he passes. Suddenly, he picks up the blue silhouette of a 914, parked in front of one of the shops. It is the five-spoked Fuchs alloy wheels that trigger his reaction. It must be a Six! Sam knows that those wheels came only on the Sixes! He also knows that very few Sixes were made. He slows down, turns around, and makes another pass. Sure enough. It is a Six! He finds a parking space, opens his umbrella, and ventures out for a dash across the street.

Sam looks the car over while the rain plays the drums on the tightly stretched fabric of the umbrella. The Six is very well preserved. And it is a 1971! Only about four hundred were made that year. Sam can tell that it is a 1971 from looking at the vinyl on the seats. This car has the smooth, leather-grained kind, as opposed to the waffle-perforated version used in 1970. He reaches for his red notebook, rips out a page and scribbles a message on it — all with difficulty, because of the rain and the umbrella — and leans over the car to fasten the note under a windshield wiper. Just then, the owner emerges from one of the shops. He approaches, his face wearing an expression of intrigue and suspicion. What is wrong?

"Per caso, la verebbe vendere?" Sam asks, holding
*(continued on overleaf)*

*The 914 was obviously targeted to the young and beautiful, as evidenced by the publicity photograph above. Although the 914 did not have much room in its cockpit, it could boast of two luggage compartments. The removable roof-panel was another popular feature. When not in use, it was stored in the rear compartment and took very little space. The picture to the far right shows the sporty look of the cockpit – seats almost flush with the floor and steering wheel with a nice vertical angle. The 914 was also a potent racing machine. Left, one of the two 914-6s that came in second and fifth in the 1970 1000 kilometer race at Nürburgring. To the right, Dwight Mitchell behind the wheel of the Northern California Porsche+Audi Dealer's 914 in 1973. (Photos courtesy Road & Track.)*

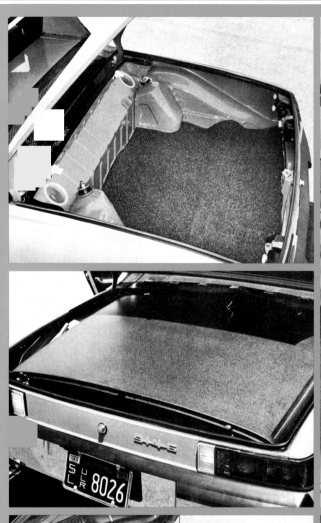

**H**andling was the primary strength of the 914; the location of the engine, ahead of the rear axle, gave it a nearly ideal weight distribution. When Porsche's six-cylinder, 110 hp 911T unit was installed, creating the 914-6 – it got power to match! Sam Cabiglio, purveyor of exotic Porsches, knew from his experience with a 914-6 in club racing the superiority of this combination. He found his 1971 914-6, chassis number 6420234, in Milan, Italy. Driving it to the limit across the Alps to Switzerland – the ultimate road test – further convinced him of its outstanding virtues.

up the palm of his hand in a calming gesture. "Is the car by chance for sale?"

"Forcé!" comes the surprised reply. "Maybe!"

Sam was five years old when he and his parents moved to California in 1951. Cars were always the all-overshadowing interest during his childhood. But he had to wait until he turned seventeen before he could buy one. It was a Porsche Speedster, and it cost him two hundred dollars at the local junkyard. It came without an engine, but Sam soon took care of that problem, later selling the restored Speedster and using the handsome profit to buy a late model Coupe. He soon traded the Coupe for another Speedster, this one in perfect condition. He soon sold this Speedster too. Now the profit not only bought one, but two Coupes. A pattern was emerging!

In 1966, Sam earned a place in the spotlight when he put a Porsche engine in a Fiat 600. The combination worked so well that the promoters of the now defunct Lion's Dragstrip in Long Beach paid him to compete in a well-publicized run-off with a record-breaking Dodge. To everyone's surprise, Sam won! This resulted in a write-up in Hot Rod Magazine.

In the early part of the following year, Sam left for the first of his many buying trips to Europe. Among other cars, he picked up a brand-new 911S at the factory. On the desk of the man in charge of the delivery was a copy of the same issue of Hot Rod Magazine! It turned out to be the perfect introduction, and that first visit formed a basis for a continuing relationship with the people at the Porsche factory.

During the boom period that lasted from the late Sixties to the mid-Seventies, when certain models of great demand in California were still plentiful and cheap on the Continent, Sam perfected the pattern that he had developed as a teenager.

We return to Sam in Milan. Later in the afternoon, he reaches an agreement with the owner of the Six, and the deal is quickly consummated. Sam and his friend Mike leave for Stuttgart that same evening, where the cars bought on the trip will be assembled for later transport to California. It is agreed that Mike will drive the Turbo, while Sam will take the Six. Nothing is said about a duel. Nothing had to be said.

Their route to Stuttgart first takes them to Como, just north of Milan, where Sam was born. A short stop is necessary here to bid relatives farewell. From Como, they cut across to Lecco. The pace quickens as they race north along the shores of Lago di Como. Sam has a hard time keeping up with Mike here, but he knows, once they pass Chiavenna, his chance will

come. From there the road will shoot up into the mountains, winding, snaking, zig-zagging its way up the steep hillsides, cutting through the Splügen Pass and crossing into Switzerland.

The rain that had started in Milan follows them as they race on to the north. The higher they climb, the colder it gets. The rain finally turns into snow. But this proves to be the favorite playground of the Six.

Once on the mountainous section of the road, as Sam had expected, he is able to take over, passing the Turbo and holding onto the lead without difficulty. He is particularly impressed by the high-speed stability of the Six, noting it with special gratitude every time he comes shooting out from the dry tunnels onto the icy wetness of the uncovered roads. And in the curves, the Six really proves its racing heritage.

After Splügen, when the road again becomes wider and straighter, Sam has to give up the lead to Mike. They traverse Switzerland, passing through Chur and Buchs. Sam still in hot pursuit, they cross the border to Austria at Feldkirch, leave Austria at Lindau, race on along the eastern shore of the Bodensee, and continue on northbound to Stuttgart, where they arrive just before midnight, five hours after they left Milan.

I visit Sam Cabiglio at his place of operation in Long Beach. The building has a sign, but it is effectively hidden by the broad branches of a palm tree. It doesn't matter, because the people who count always know where to find him. Inside, you see a constantly varying assortment of Porsches — everything from racecars to road cars, from classics to the latest, unimported models. And everything from parts and customizing to advice and enthusiasm.

We drive the blue Six to the Palos Verdes Peninsula, where I had found a beach full of pebbles. We have to do the shooting in the morning in order to avoid the high tide.

The sun comes up behind hazy morning clouds, just as I had ordered. By the time the shooting is done, the sun breaks through and it turns out to be another one of those perfect Southern California days. As we get back on the coast road, ready to do some testing, a marvelously curvy beach nymph needs a ride to Manhattan Beach. Sure, we can take that route. No problem. The European version of the 914 has a cushion between the two seats, making room for a second passenger. A thorough test requires everything to be checked out. And I can now honestly report that there is enough room between the seats to make it pleasant. There is one thing though, that seemed to pose a problem — the shifting.

*The 916, if built in quantity, would have been the fastest production Porsche in 1972. The most expensive as well! Calculations showed that it would have had to be priced fifty percent higher than the most expensive 911. So, unfortunately, the eleven prototypes were the only ones built. The 911S engine developed 190 hp and gave the lighter car a top speed of 145 mph and a 0-60 time of less than seven seconds. To make room for the seven-inch wheels, the fenders had to be flared. Fiberglass panels took the place of the bumpers, giving the front and rear a very clean look. The frontal view shows a nice integration of driving lights and oil cooler air intake. The roof was made of steel and welded on for increased stiffness. (Photos by Bill Warner, courtesy Road & Track.)*

# 911 CARRERA RS

# The Champion Mechanic

Mention the name Vasek Polak to an experienced Porsche enthusiast and he will respond with a word of admiration, a smile at the recollection of an exciting race, or maybe even with an anecdote.

To the Southern California Porsche owner, Vasek Polak may be the man he bought his first Porsche from back in the fifties. It may be the dealership where he has purchased his subsequent Porsches. It may be the place where he has been going just to see what was new on the horizon.

To the serious Porsche restorer, Vasek Polak is a name he is well acquainted with. It doesn't matter in which part of the world he lives, if he is restoring a vintage Porsche racing machine, he sooner or later has had to talk to Vasek Polak about that brake drum or this crankshaft or those other hard-to-find parts.

To the observer of the Porsche racing scene, Vasek Polak is a name associated with the great drivers and the great races and the great victories. He will connect Vasek Polak with names like Bonnier, Behra, Miles, Ickx, Redman, Donohue, Schechter and many others. And he will recall the successes in SCCA, Can Am and Trans Am racing. So if you are a Porsche enthusiast, the name Vasek Polak will have been mentioned often. But it has not always been that way.

The unknown part of Vasek Polak's story begins in Prague, Czechoslovakia, where he was born in 1914. Racing and racing machinery was his main diet already in the late thirties; he operated his own machine shop, specializing in cylinder grinding; in his spare time he raced motorcycles. Photographs of the young Vasek show him on his four-valve Rudge, negotiating a curve with elegant style, leaning fearlessly, and after the race, wearing the victor's laurel around his neck with a proud smile, his leather jacket zipped open, his blond hair ruffled and unconstrictable.

In 1949, we find Vasek Polak in West Germany. He was first the maintenance manager for a United States Army repair depot, then ran a mixed machine shop in Munich. A brief visit to the United States in

*The first 911 Carrera to be marketed in the United States was introduced as the flagship of the 1974 model line-up. It had the ducktail, which improved stability during high speed as well as during cornering. But it was optional, as was the Carrera script on the body side panels. Also in 1974 came the new, higher and wider bumper design, necessitated by stricter impact laws. The accordian rubber joints became a visual eyemark of this change. The engine, as used in the Carrera, was still mechanically fuel injected, as opposed to the other 911 models, which came with the Jetronic system. The restyled interior featured new, lighter seats with integrated headrests, new door panels with larger, covered pockets, and a new, smaller, three-spoked steering wheel. (Photos courtesy Road & Track.)*

1951 gave him an idea of where he wanted to settle. But it took another four years before a major obstacle had been overcome: that of getting his family out of Czechoslovakia. During those years he became involved with Porsches — a union of destiny. From then on he also knew how he would like to earn his living: He wanted his own Porsche dealership.

Vasek Polak and his family arrived in New York in 1956. A job awaited him with the Porsche distributor Max Hoffman. It did not take long before he invested in a car — his first on American soil. It was a Ford, and he paid twenty-five dollars for it. Of course, the Ford was for family transportation. For racing he had his eyes on a 550 Spyder. With his connections, he was soon able to buy one. In 1957, he took the Ford, the Spyder and the family and went west, like so many before him, settling in the Southern California community of Manhattan Beach. Soon afterward he was appointed the Porsche dealer there. His two immediate goals had been accomplished. The next phase could begin; the one that would make Vasek Polak a household word among Porsche people.

I open the heavy glass doors to Vasek Polak's Porsche showroom. It occupies an entire city block along the Pacific Coast Highway. To the right and straight ahead, I see rows of shiny new Porsches; 911s, 924s, 928s, as well as choice examples of used ones. To the left, lined up along the glass facade, their aerodynamic front ends facing that never-ending stream of vehicles passing on the highway, I see the cars that are not for sale at any price — the racing machines. This is only a small portion of a collection that has grown, not so much because of deliberate acquisition, but because Vasek could not give up his beloved race cars.

Vasek Polak was the name that came to my mind when I searched for a 2.7 Carrera RS to feature in this book. The model was not imported to the United States, so it is very hard to find one here. When I spoke to Mister Polak on the phone, he needed a few seconds to think, then he confirmed that he indeed had an RS sitting in one of his private garages. He had taken it in trade some years ago and had tested it himself at Willow Springs and found it both clean and strong. Ja, it is white like they all were. Ja, it has red wheels and red Carrera script on the sides. Ja, ja, it is okay to photograph it.

To interview Vasek Polak is no simple thing. First of all, he is nowhere and everywhere at the same time. And, when he does show up, unexpectedly from
*(continued on overleaf)*

**D**ramatic looks was just one of the reasons behind the appeal of the Carrera RS. True, the Carrera script and the color-matched wheels were visual effects, but the front air dam and the rear spoiler were functional, and together with the lightened body and the enlarged engine, responsible for the Carrera's exciting performance – sixty could be reached in less than six seconds. This Europe-only, touring-equipped 1973 2.7 Carrera RS, chassis number 9113600845 belongs to Vasek Polak, for more than two decades a name synonymous with outstanding accomplishments in the sales, service and racing of Porsches.

nowhere, you discover that there are at least three engines turning inside his head, all operating independently, all at the same time. One is working on the problem of the proper preparation of a particular race car. Another is wrestling with details of negotiations with a visitor from Stuttgart. The third, if you are lucky, is concentrating on you, unless the phone rings.

The interviewer gets in a few questions between phone calls in German, Slovak and inimitable English. The interviewer is trying to form a picture of a career that is so vast that it is hard to know where to begin. Who is Vasek Polak? What kind of man is he? Is he a businessman? An administrator? With an organization that employs more than one hundred people, and has been in operation for twenty-four years, he must be a very good businessman. But what else?

Vasek Polak makes an effort to cut out the phone calls. He leaves his chair, comes around his desk to sit in a chair beside the interviewer. He is stocky in body, strong-faced, shirt-sleeved, his blond hair from the old photograph, gray now, but still unconstrictable. I ask him what, during all these years, was best. At once, the other engines stop. He starts talking faster than I can take notes. Let the phone ring.

Best was Nassau Speed Week 1958. Graf Trips was driving special RSK for Johnny von Neumann. I was waiting in Nassau for car to come on ship from factory. When it came, I prepared at the Volkswagen dealership. After first practice, problem with engine. Could not be fixed. Airship another engine. Came night before race. Worked all night. How did you stay awake? Coffee? No, do not need drink or eat when you are excited. Where did you stay? Do not remember. Not important. Graf Trips had permission to drive two laps to check how everything worked. But no practice. In race, worked like a clock. Won overall. And at trophy presentation, everyone standing around, microphones, loudspeakers, Graf Trips stopped everything, took microphone, told everyone that Vasek here, without him it would never have worked. Then he presented me his trophy. Still have it. Then a pause and a smile: That was best. Yes, all that was best! That is the answer.

The interview was over. Sorry. Phone calls in German, Slovak, and inimitable English. But the interviewer was pleased. He had received insight. He knows what kind of a man Vasek Polak is. He knows there is a great heart behind that facade of invincibility. A heart that beats for great drivers and great machines. Vasek Polak — champion mechanic of champion race cars.

The Carrera RS was the first phase in Porsche's production car racing program, started in 1972. The RS was based on the 911S, and one of the first concerns was to save weight. This was accomplished mainly by removing the rear seats, by making the body of thinner steel, and by using fiberglass bumpers. Another concern was to improve aerodymanics and handling, and this is where the ducktail and front air-dam played important roles. The engine, also from the 911S, was enlarged to produce 210 hp. Another element of the racing image was the Carrera lettering on the side panels. The first style can be seen on the prototype, pictured to the right, top. Before the premier showing at the 1972 Paris Auto Salon, the script was redesigned. Although only five hundred cars had to be built to qualify the Carrera for racing, slightly more than one thousand were completed and sold. Of these, approximately fifty were brought up to full racing specifications and called RSR. Pictured above, a racing-prepared 911S is shadowing a racing-prepared 911 Carrera RS. To the right, bottom, George Follmer in an RS at Daytona. To the left, Peter Gregg behind the wheel of one of his successful RSRs. (Photo courtesy Road & Track.)

# Modern Day Outlaws

Try to create a picture in your mind of the representative Porsche owner. Early thirties. Successful businessman. Knows what is fashionable in art. In dress. In lifestyle. Knows how to enjoy it. You got it! That's Greg Jahn! But, while a man fitting this description usually owns one Porsche, Greg owns four!

Greg was always a sports car enthusiast. As a kid, he built models. As a teenager, he drove Triumphs. In college, he drove Corvettes. All this before he finally came to his senses and settled on Porsches. Greg lives in Cherry Hill, an affluent satellite-city of Philadelphia. His cars are maintained by Cherry Hill Classic Cars. Tom Hessert is the owner of this establishment, John Nelson the trusted associate.

Greg, Tom, John and I are seated around the best table at the best restaurant in the area. Greg knows how to pick 'em. Goes with the image. And it really is a very nice place. White table cloths. Matching napkins. Waiters with accents. And a menu so full of French it's tempting to just close your eyes and point. But Greg knows what it all means. Goes with the image. After the Coquilles St. Jacques is ordered, and after the Boeuf à la Maison, and after Baron Philippe's Mouton-Cadet 1976, after that, we get down to the business at hand. Porsches. I already know that Greg has an SC Cabriolet, a Carrera 2, a Carrera Targa and a Turbo. And I know that they're all sitting there in his garage. But I haven't seen them yet.

I'd think you'd have a hard time making up your mind which one to drive, I say. Well, in a way, Greg answers. I like 'em all, you know. But they all have their different purposes. Take the Cabriolet, for instance. That was my first Porsche. I drove it very much in the beginning. Then I spent a lot of money and time to restore it. It became a showcar. And then I couldn't drive it anymore. I got tired of that, so now I drive it again. I got the Carrera 2. Now I'm restoring that one to become a showcar. The Carbriolet is a car for that pure old-time, fast-but-comfortable pleasure-

*Porsches last for a long time! The 356 was in production for a decade-and-a-half. The 911 has been around for nearly two decades, and is still going strong. Featured on these pages is the 911-look for the early Eighties. The 1980 SC, to the right, sporting both fender flares and safety bumpers, still has the basic look of the 1963 original. Above, the interior of the SC, with its three-spoked steering wheel. Left, the engine compartment. Right, top, the 1980 Weissach Coupe, a limited edition. Basically an SC equipped with front and rear spoilers, wide alloy wheels and sportier shock absorbers, the Weissach came in two versions, Platinum Metallic and Black Metallic. The interior was light beige with burgundy piping and burgundy carpets. (Photos courtesy Road & Track.)*

drive, that open-air, Sunday-afternoon-type cruising. It doesn't demand anything from you. But it can do all you want it to do under those kind of driving circumstances. With the Turbo, it's totally different. True, it can be driven slow and without spirit, but I'd like to meet a sports car enthusiast who can resist all that power. So when you drive the Turbo, you find yourself occupied with the car. It demands so much from the driver. You can do so much with it. But you can also easily overdo it. Frankly, the Turbo scares me. I think that's a healthy attitude, though. You have to be a professional driver to really extend that Turbo to its limits. What about the Carrera? Now, the Carrera is something in-between the two, It's very fast. It's very comfortable. It doesn't scare you. In fact, it's a very forgiving car. And it looks great! It has it all. Let's go over it point for point, I say. Now we're all contributing to the discussion. We're all talking. Between bites.

First the tires. Right. They're seven inches wide in the front and eight inches in the back. On a regular Porsche they're six inches front and back. Right. The wider tires, of course, improve the traction and cornering. I use Dunlop Super Sports. They're squealy and noisy, but I like to hear it when I go through the curve. Good. And the wide wheels look nice too. Let's not forget that! Okay. Then the wheels. Right. They're the forged alloys by Fuchs. Just about half as heavy as the steel wheels on the 356. On the 1975 Carrera they're painted to match the color of that Carrera script on the side of the body. That looks very good. Okay. The flares next. Yes. They have to do with the wheels. You need those flares to make room for the wider tires. And they look good too. Then we have the air dam. Right. But we have to talk about the dam together with the spoiler. You can't have a car with only one of them, you know. Spoils the balance. Right. The dam keeps the air from slipping under the car. Keeps it from lifting. The spoiler keeps the air pushing down on the rear. Right. It all works together to hold the car down at high speed. And the side-wind stability becomes better too. The spoiler reduces top speed slightly, they say. But it looks good, right? Right. Let's not forget that. It's the trademark of the Carrera and the Turbo. And what's next? The Targa top. Right. That's very nice to have. That's the link to the Cabriolet. Not quite as nice as a real convertible. But safer. And you don't get as much wind. And it's unusual. There were only 172 Carrera Targas built in 1975. What's next? Are we running out? No. The black trim. Right. That became available in 1974.

*(continued on overleaf)*

**U**nique would be a keyword in a description of the Porsche on these pages: It's a Carrera, it's a Targa and it's gold on black. Only 36 were made! Owner Greg Jahn, a Porsche aficionado with a taste for the exotic, saw one flashing by during a visit to Hollywood, California. He knew instantly it was a car he had to have. It took phone calls to Porsche dealers all over North America to locate this 1975 model, chassis number 9115410024, in Florida. With its gold wheels and lettering, all-black trim, Targa top, spoiler, wide tires and flares, it has all the striking attributes of the breed.

Looks very good. Especially on a black car, like yours. I have seen Ralph Lauren's car and it's all black. Even has blacked-out windows. Looks really good. And the black with gold trim is very unusual. Only thirty-six of them built in 1975. Now we're running out of things, right? What about the all-leather seats with the waist supports? Right. They're very nice. And that fat, small steering wheel? Nice. Very nice.

Consuming the Boeuf à la Maison keeps us quiet for a while now. But we're soon at it again.

What about the police? Do you have any trouble? Yes, you almost have to be an outlaw to enjoy these cars to their fullest capacity. Right, modern-day outlaws. I remember one time when I was on my way home. On the turnpike. Was doing 120 in fifth. Cruising along. It was two o'clock in the morning. You know you're not causing another oil embargo just from going full speed for an hour or so. And you know you're not taking any chances in the middle of the night. No traffic. Straight road. No fog. No moisture. I was cruising along, doing 120. Suddenly, I passed a trooper. He must have been half asleep beside the road there. It must really have shook him awake to see me speeding by like that. But what could I do? It was too late to brake. So I just kept going. I knew he couldn't catch up with me. After about ten minutes I came to the tollbooths. They were all full of red lights and all kinds of officials were out there flagging me down. The trooper had called ahead on his radio. I just stayed in the car. About five minutes later, the trooper comes along, his lights and face about the same color. He said I was under arrest. And the car was impounded. They would get a tow-truck he said. Of course, I knew what a tow-truck would do to the Porsche. It would tear up the under-carriage. So I refused to get out of the car. It was all right to arrest me, I said. And it was all right to impound the car, I said. But I won't have my car damaged, I said. If you get a flat-bed, fine, but no regular tow-truck. We were arguing back and forth, the trooper getting madder than you know what. Then they were all trying to call for a flat-bed. Have you tried to get a flat-bed in the middle of the night? After about two hours, the trooper came back to the car. Just leave, he said, and make sure I never see you again. Just leave, he said. Yeah, it makes you some kind of an outlaw, doesn't it?

Well, gentlemen. Are we ready to inspect the monster? Yes, I am. Yeah, me too. Let's go. This was good food. Thank you. Yes, thank you very much. We feel like musketeers. Just the right mood for driving a Porsche Carrera.

*The Targa was introduced in 1965. It was styled by Butzi Porsche. The two photographs above show the pre-production version. Notice that the roll-bar carries the Porsche crest rather than, as later, the Targa script. Deliveries of the new model began in the spring of 1967. At first, the roof-panel was collapsible and the rear window soft, allowing four different variations on the open-air theme. The fixed glass window and the ventilation slots on the roll-bar came with the 1968 models. The 1967 promotional picture to the left shows an attractive way of demonstrating the strength of the roll-bar. Above right, a 1973 Targa, seen from a three-quarter angle. Lower right, the side-view of a 1975 Targa. Far right, a 1979 Targa featuring the black roll-bar. (Photos courtesy Road & Track.)*

930 TURBO

# Too Hot To Handle!

The things I had *read* about the 930 Turbo intrigued me: The ultimate 911. The ultimate Porsche. An engineering masterpiece. The most practical of the supercars.

The things I had *heard* about the 930 Turbo intrigued me even more: Most owners don't know how to drive them. A very demanding car. An inexperienced driver who tries to drive it to the limit is a fool.

I was certainly most eager to form my own opinions about the 930 Turbo. But I knew I wasn't enough of a driver to give it a valid shake-down. Luckily, I knew the man who was: Pete Smith.

The Porsche dealership in Hollywood is located on Cahuenga, just a block off Hollywood Boulevard. A few years ago, when I first had a chance to visit the dealership's warehouse in the back, I saw Steve McQueen's Speedster in there. Last year, I saw Paul Newman's 928. Two weeks ago, I saw Robert Redford's 930 Turbo, brought all the way from Utah for scheduled maintenance. But this time, I was here for a pure and honorable reason — not to see star cars — to find out the truth about the 930 Turbo.

Pete Smith has automobiles in his blood. His grandfather was one of the first Chevrolet dealers in San Francisco. In 1939, his grandfather moved south to Glendale, where he took over a Dodge/Plymouth dealership. Pete's father inherited the business. In the early Sixties, he bought Johnny Von Neuman's Competition Motors, Porsche's early California stronghold, getting the Volkswagen dealership with it. Pete arrived on the scene in 1964. In 1969, when the Porsche/Audi union took place, more room was needed. The responsibilities were split between the two Smith brothers, Pete moving across the street to a new facility — housing Porsche/Audi — his brother concentrating on the original Volkswagen set-up.

But, being a Porsche dealer doesn't in itself make a man equipped to extract the full potential from a 930 Turbo. It takes more. Pete's career in racing began

*The Turbo was first seen at the Paris Auto Show in the fall of 1974. The new "whale tail" spoiler had already been put to use on that year's three-liter Carrera RS, to the left captured during testing in Germany. Fifty of them were turned into full-fledged race cars: the RSR. In the beginning, the Turbo also had a three-liter engine, but in 1978, it was fitted with the three-point-three liter unit. The pictures on this page feature the 1976 version, its exciting profile seen above. With the introduction of the enlarged engine, the spoiler became higher and more squared-off. The picture to the right, of the Turbo's rear seats, is proof of the luxurious appointments. Above, a close-up of the Turbo's tachometer with its turbo boost gauge. (Photos courtesy Road & Track.)*

rather innocently. He entered his Speedster in the first Historic Races at Monterey. He did so well there, capturing a first in class, that his appetite was whetted.

In 1977, he found himself the owner of a Porsche 908. It was the car Vic Elford had driven to a second overall in the 1969 Targa Florio. Pete restored it and decided to enter SCCA Group A sports racing. After having won seven out of nine races, he captured the championship in the Southern Pacific Region. So far in the 1981 racing season, his successes include a first in class in the twelve-hour Sebring. He was the co-driver of the 1976 Porsche Carrera RSR. He was also the co-driver of the same car in the twenty-four-hour Daytona, placing second in class. Le Mans is the next goal. Pete races for the enjoyment of it, he says. For the exhilaration of speed. For the satisfaction of the accomplishment. For the pleasure of having completed that perfect lap, when everything went smooth, fast and safe. To him, he says, the most demanding element of endurance racing is concentration.

Pete and I walk together through the service department, reaching the warehouse in the back. The Turbo is parked immediately inside the doors, in the front row, ready for action. The first thing I notice is the exquisite color. A metallic gray-blue. I ask Pete about it. Yes, he says, I specified that. It's actually a Mercedes color. The Porsche blue has too much blue in it, in my opinion, he says. I agree, I say, the silver with a touch of blue gets rid of that sweet, baby-blue effect. Makes it very classy and crisp.

Next, we open the doors and are overcome by that intoxicating aroma of leather. Yes, says Pete, I ordered it all in leather. Dash, door panels, armrests — everything. This leather is in the Porsche catalog. It's a tan-brown. The car is also equipped with electric sun roof, electric windows, air conditioning and stereo. Pete pushes in a tape — out comes Bach. Truth: The 930 Turbo is a luxury car. The fit, the finish, the amenities — not plush and fluffy — it's real, tasteful, meaningful luxury.

Pete gets in behind the wheel. He starts the engine. It fires up right away. It's quiet. Maybe disappointingly so. Even when we get out on the street and Pete gives it a little more throttle, it's quiet. There's a whistling sound when the turbo cuts in, but that too is hardly noticeable. That's characteristic, Pete says. Even as a race car on the track, the Turbo is quiet.

In traffic now, we're moving without any stalling, overheating, spitting, coughing or other typicals associated with high-performance machines. Anyone

*(continued on overleaf)*

**U**ltimate Porsche road machine! The 930 Turbo is the extension – to a seemingly impossible degree – of the original Porsche concept which combined sportiness, comfort and dependability. In the 930 Turbo, Porsche engineers mix their most advanced racing technology with their most innovative comfort features, creating a car so docile you can use it for everyday city driving, yet so powerful, a touch of your toe makes it leap from 0-60 in about six seconds! Pete Smith – race driver, Porsche dealer, enthusiast – is the owner of this immaculate 1979 Turbo, chassis number 9309801130.

can drive this car, Pete says, anywhere, anytime, as long as he doesn't try anything exotic. It's so docile, it's incredible! We're out on the freeway now, going north on 101. But watch now, Pete says. And I watch his foot as he puts the accelerator to the floor. Nothing much happens. It takes a second or so, and then suddenly, I'm thrown back in the seat, for the first time feeling the tingling sensation in my legs from the G-force. We slow down. We were passing cars left and right, like we had been shot out of a cannon. That's a danger, Pete says, the other drivers on the road don't expect a car they saw in their rearview mirror three seconds ago to be passing them, so they may change a lane or make another maneuver that causes trouble. Truth: The 930 Turbo is a tame street car, but it's also a wild race car. In the wrong hands, it can be a lethal weapon. The incredible acceleration that takes place when the turbo cuts in and the seeming effortlessness and quietness with which it does it, can easily get you in a lot of trouble.

We turn off the freeway now and onto Mulholland Drive, with all its sharp curves, winding picturesquely around the hillsides above Hollywood. Pete accelerates, approaches a curve, then brakes hard and turns on the power on the way out of the curve. He repeats it again and again. That's how you do it, he says. Slow in — fast out. If you don't brake enough before the curve, you'll have to steer your way around it.

·If you lose the rear, and you're experienced, you counter with the steering wheel and let the car sort itself out. If you're inexperienced, you'll let up on the throttle and then the rear will throw the other way, swinging from side to side — a situation that's almost impossible for the novice to control. The turbo engine doesn't have much braking power, so you have to rely on the brakes, not the engine, to slow you down before a curve. That's also why the 930 Turbo is equipped with the 917 racing brakes. Truth: The 930 Turbo is a demanding car. It demands that the driver has the capacity to handle it.

So, is the 930 Turbo the ultimate 911? Yes, most likely. It's hard to imagine that further development will take place. Is the 930 Turbo the ultimate Porsche? It depends. If you believe that a Porsche isn't a Porsche unless it has the engine in the rear — then, yes. But the rear location of the engine and the semi-trailing-arm rear suspension do have inherent problems not even the magic of the Porsche engineers can get rid of. Truth: With these basic problems corrected in the new generation, the stage is set for even greater things from Porsche.

*Famous turbo-powered racing machines is the subject of these pages. To the right, top, the impressive rear view of the two-point-one liter unit used in the Turbo RSR. This version was not built on the 930, but rather influenced its development. Far right, two views of an RSR. They were raced in the 1974 Manufacturers Championship racing for prototypes and sponsored by Martini & Rossi. Above, the 934 prototype. This machine was built on the 930 Turbo, as can clearly be seen, and competed in Group 4 GT racing. The 934s of teams such as Kremer's, left, dominated the 1976 Championship scene in Europe. Right, bottom, the ultimate 930 development: the final version of the 935, competing in Group 5 GT racing. (Photos courtesy Road & Track.)*

928

# Eye of the Beholder

Just as I had expected, the location was perfect. The rough brutality of the dirty, blue-grey walls of coal, rising like mountains on three sides, obscuring sky and horizon, was a stark contrast to the smooth, clean silver shape of the 928. The Porsche represented the ultimate in technology, art and lifestyle on our planet, while the crater-like surroundings represented the outer-space-like void of life and beauty.

"It's perfect!" I tell Roger Gallet, owner of the 928, as I complete my first circle around the car, looking at it only through the viewfinder of my camera. For a long time, I have been intrigued by the prospect of photographing the 928. To see an object like a car through the lens of a camera is like seeing it again for the first time. And you're always curious to find out how it will look and what kind of effects you can create by choice of angles, lenses, light and location.

"Are you disappointed?" I ask Roger.

"No. Not at all. But I must admit that I was hesitant at first, when you suggested a mine. I had thought more along the lines of a golf course or a park. But I see it now. It's like the ugliness of the surroundings make the car look even more beautiful!"

Roger's 928 is the only one in Uniontown. The city is an old center of Pennsylvania's coal mining district, and people here have always lived a simple, close-to-earth life — a life far from luxuries like exotic cars. Roger's 928 is really an attention-getter.

The sun is having a hard time breaking through. At times, it looks like it's going to rain. But for now, the clouds, dark blue-gray like the coal, are keeping the rain to themselves. There's a barely noticeable shadow. I load the camera with a roll of 64 ASA Kodak EPR.

My initial reaction when I first saw the 928 was one of relief. Finally, the monopoly of "the Italian school of design" had been broken. Not that I didn't appreciate their creations, but it got a little monotonous when all you saw were sharp edges and wedge shapes. I was pleasantly surprised to see the roundness of the 928.

*Moving at a pace slow enough to ensure the highest level of quality, the new 928 assembly line put out twenty-eight cars a day at the time these photographs were taken. It is a study in precision and a showcase of the latest assembly line innovations. While the 911 line moves from station to station at seven-minute intervals, the 928 line moves when the job is done. The facilities are surgically clean and the noise level is so low that visitors and workers can communicate in a normal tone of voice. To the left, the impressive power unit ready for its mating with the chassis. Above, a partial view of the assembly hall. To the right, top, a 928 body fresh out of the paint shop. To the right, bottom, the half-finished interior. Notice the electronic "brain" on the floor of the passenger side. (Photos Gene Babow.)*

It was as much a step backward as it was a step forward. There was an obvious connection with the cars of the Fifties, and most significant, a connection with the ancestor of the 928 — the 356. The width, the swelling forms, the sloping front and rear profiles — all reminded me of the classic Porsche. It was a modern interpretation of the same concept.

"How do you like the headlights?" I ask Roger.

"I like them. By the way, they aren't unique, you know. The Lamborghini Miura has them too!"

"That's right. But I think it was an ingenious move to incorporate them on the 928. They strengthen the tie-in with the 356. Remember that flat, flounder-fish look of those early Porsches? Peering up at you with a slightly embarrassed expression? The 928 has that same look!"

"Yes. You're right! Never thought of that before. Those lights also give the front life. Most of the modern sports cars are too plain. I miss the expression of the headlights. You can't get that same feeling from grilles and air scoops alone."

Roger walks over to the 928, opens the door, turns on the lights and returns to our observation point. As they rise, they create a periscope-up feeling; or they remind you of an awakening monster.

"Here's another thing about that design. Thanks to the lights being exposed like that, they can open forward, which allows them to be round and aerodynamic, leaving only a minimal area out there in the speed-wind. Normally, you know, the lights are attached to rectangular flaps, which means they have to open backward, leaving those flaps in place during driving, looking ugly and catching wind.

The Porsche engineers handed the stylists a very wide engine. In order to keep it low, they had to make it wide. This created a visual problem. True, it was easier to make the front low, but to disguise the width took some doing. They solved it beautifully, letting the wheel wells swell out from sharp edges on each side of the car, those edges becoming the focusing points for the eye's judgment of the width. The stylists weren't as successful in hiding the bulk of the rear. Another, in my opinion, questionable solution is the shape of the wheel cutouts. Throughout the history of automotive design, we have seen that the most beautiful and aerodynamically effective approaches were the ones that closely followed the circle of the wheel. In the rear, where on the 928 the cutout is lower than in the front, it looks all right. But in the front, the shape of the cutouts leave large openings on either side of

*(continued on overleaf)*

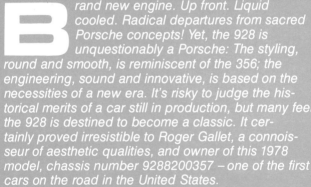

**B**rand new engine. Up front. Liquid cooled. Radical departures from sacred Porsche concepts! Yet, the 928 is unquestionably a Porsche: The styling, round and smooth, is reminiscent of the 356; the engineering, sound and innovative, is based on the necessities of a new era. It's risky to judge the historical merits of a car still in production, but many feel the 928 is destined to become a classic. It certainly proved irresistible to Roger Gallet, a connoisseur of aesthetic qualities, and owner of this 1978 model, chassis number 9288200357 – one of the first cars on the road in the United States.

the wheel, exposing parts of the chassis and suspension to the eye.

"It's perfect from the three-quarter front angle!"

"And it's perfect from straight on, too!"

"And from straight behind!"

"But not so good from the three-quarter rear angle. A little too bulky!"

"What about from the side?"

"I would have liked to move the greenhouse back visually, by having the wide panel between the windows slightly further back and slightly more upright. But we're playing a game. There are too many unknowns for us to suggest changes!"

"I know what you mean! It's like trying to pick apart the smile of Mona-Lisa. Every slight little change would upset the whole beautiful effect."

"But the rear light assembly is a real masterpiece. Totally unique, functional and beautiful!"

"But, of course, one of the most important innovations are the fully integrated bumpers. Can you imagine getting rid of those ugly bumpers that have destroyed designs for the past decade?"

"Yes, that's a relief. Remember the look of those early Gmünd cars, when they were raced without bumpers, and you could see all of those beautiful, round shapes? And remember the rear of the Abarth? The 928 has much of that same look! But I'm getting nostalgic now. Better get some shooting done!"

The sun still has a hard time breaking through the clouds. But it's lower now. And it creates a diffused light source so strong it erases some thin branches of dead trees that cling to the edge of the crater. This light is perfect. The right moment is now. I'm not saving film. Two hundred frames take less than half an hour. I'm shooting until the light is gone.

Somehow, news of our presence in the crater has spread. There's a small group of spectators; workers from the mine, boys on bicycles, and two old ladies. Roger has been keeping them happy by answering questions. Is it for *Life* magazine? No, Ma'am, this is a book about Porsches! About what? Porsches! Is it going to be on television? No, it's for a book! How much does this machine cost? Forty thousand!

"Why would anyone in their right mind pay forty thousand for that monster? Looks like a flying saucer!"

"Don't you like it, Ma'am?"

"Like it? I think it's ugly as sin!"

Beauty is in the eye of the beholder, as Toulouse-Lautrec put it when a viewer was offended by one of his paintings showing a lightly dressed female. Yes, beauty certainly is in the eyes of the beholder.

The 928, without question, represents a new level of accomplishment when it comes to a mass-produced sports car. It is outstanding in the area of technology as well as in the area of styling. The photographs featured here are ample evidence of the latter. The picture above, left, clearly shows the two sharp creases running down each side of the front fenders, camouflaging the massive width that was required to house the wide engine. Above, the 928's most flattering angle is this three-quarter frontal one. To the right, the driver's view. To the far right, a very successful Cabriolet conversion offered by Ray Stewart of Long Beach, California. The prototype conversion is the work of Gene Winfield of Canoga Park, California. (Photos courtesy Road & Track and Ray Stewart.)

# 924 TURBO

# The Magic Show is On!

I had tried to get out by creating a rocking motion, quickly shifting from first to reverse and back to first. But I had only dug myself in deeper. Steam had been pouring out from under the car as the engine rubbed its hot belly in the mud. I had finally turned it off and stepped outside to survey the situation. The conclusion had been easily arrived at: I was stuck!

The 924 Turbo is brand new, swiped off the showroom floor at Carlsen's in Redwood City. I'm at the southern end of San Francisco Bay, where an intriguing-looking wasteland is reigned over by marshy fields and garbage dumps. I have taken all my shots. The sun is setting. I had chosen a different spot, closer to the water, but the Rangers chased me away from there. As if that wasn't enough, now I'm stuck. That's what I get for choosing exotic locations.

There was no traffic at all on the road. But there was a dump station about half-a-mile away. I had walked there to call for a tow truck. Now I'm back, sitting here behind the wheel of the 924 Turbo, waiting, the orange hazard lights blinking like the neon signs in a second-rate private-eye movie.

I lean back in the seat, trying to be positive, remembering the pleasant driving experience with the Turbo earlier in the afternoon. It sure stuck to the road. Those P7s are fantastic. They do make the ride hard and noisy, but the grip is great. And the turbo power feels good. Enough to have a reserve when needed. And enough to have a good time when wanted. Of course, it's not as dramatically aggressive as the 930 Turbo. Not by far. But it's not bad. The same whistling sound from the turbo is there. I'm not a test driver. But I know what I like. And I like to drive the 924 Turbo. But I don't like the finish of the interior. Not good enough for a $20,000 car.

My thoughts drift into the history of the 924. It's sure had a tough life. First of all, the Porsche engineers had to work with components available inside the Volkswagen/Audi group. It was the only way to keep

*(continued on overleaf)*

*The 924, and variations on that theme, is the subject of the photographs on the right-hand page. In the first row, top to bottom, three views of the basic 924. In the second row, top, the 924 Sebring. A total of 1300 units were produced of this limited edition. It was brought out to commemorate the choice of a 924 as the pacecar of the 1979 twelve-hour race at Sebring. They were all painted a bright red, with black, white and gold striping – the colors of the Porsche crest. Pictured below it, the 1981 924 Weissach. A total of four hundred were made of this limited edition. They were all painted two-tone Platinum Metallic. Below this, a 924 Turbo at speed, and to the left, its interior. Above, one of the first publicity shots of the new 944. (Photos courtesy Road & Track and Porsche Public Relations.)*

**D**rag coefficient: among the best. Handling: among the best. Performance: among the worst. But with the introduction in 1979 of the Turbo, the 924 finally got the power to match its other attributes. It now produced 154 hp, reached a top speed of 130 and sported a 0-60 time just above nine seconds. Exterior give-aways were subtle: A small rear spoiler, two rows of louvers below the front bumper, air intakes (one on the hood and a row of four up front) and, optionally, the new forged alloy wheels with P7 Pirellis. This 1981 version, chassis number 93A0152125, belongs to Porsche dealer and avid Porsche enthusiast Charlie Burton.

the cost down. And then, when the 924 was ready on the drawing board, the Volkswagen people wanted it for themselves. It would then have been marketed as a Volkswagen or an Audi. But in the end, Porsche got it. Part of the agreement was that it should be manufactured at the Volkswagen plant in Neckarsulm. But Porsche would have full control. Well, on top of this zig-zagging birth process, when the 924 was finally introduced, it had a hard time coming across as a Porsche. Having a water-cooled, front-mounted Audi engine, and being assembled by Volkswagen, the skepticism of the Porsche purist was understandable.

But it couldn't be denied, the 924 had been designed by Porsche. And as such it had some basic things going for it. It had the engine up front and the transmission and gearbox in the rear, accomplishing ideal weight distribution. With the assistance of the new suspension, it all combined into one of the best handling machines in the business. The 924 also had that well-designed, moderately exciting, aerodynamically super-effective body going for it. Now, all it needed was some more of the Porsche magic — the same magic that had added another decade to the lifespan of the 911. The first number in Porsche's magic show was the 924 Turbo.

Another number was the D-production kit-racer. Introduced briefly into the 1979 SCCA season, it blossomed in the 1980 season, capturing fifteen regional wins and one divisional championship. This meant a much needed face-lift of the 924's anemic features.

But that wasn't all. The good old Carrera name was called upon again, effectively tying the 924 to the Porsche heritage. The prototype was first seen at the 1979 Frankfurt show. It looked great. I was especially attracted by the new interior. The idea was to build a car based on the 924 Turbo that would open the doors to Group 4 racing when the new FIA regulations became effective in 1982. With minor changes to the hood scoop and the rear fenders, and minus that good-looking interior, the four hundred cars needed for homologation were sold as the 924 Carrera GT; unfortunately, only available in Europe.

And as if the GT wasn't enough, soon came the GTS. A further lightened and refined version, still road going, the GTS produced 245 hp and was made in fifty copies. The racing version, the Carrera RSR, produced 375 hp the way it ran at Le Mans 1981, coming in sixth overall.

In that same race, another RSR came in seventh, powered by a new, four-cylinder engine. This unit, basically one-half of the 928 engine, produced 410 hp.

*On these pages, a sampling of 924 derivatives for the benefit of increased adrenaline production. To the lower right, the prototype of the 924 SCCA D-production racer. To the upper right, the 924 Turbo Le Mans, a full-blown racing development of the 924 Carrera GTS. To the left, a 924 Carrera GT. This turbo-charged version was made in four hundred copies, unfortunately only available in Europe. Above, the extremely attractive Automotion Club Racer. This 924 Turbo derivative is the brainchild of Tom Green of Santa Clara, California. A fiberglas fender and spoiler kit makes it look good, and a suspension kit makes it handle as well as it looks. (Photos courtesy Road & Track, Gene Babow and Automotion.)*

In its normal, un-turbocharged state, it's scheduled to power a new Porsche model — the 944. The 924 Turbo will be eliminated when the 944 arrives in the United States in the fall of 1982. But later, naturally, there will be a 944 Turbo, probably with an output of around 200 hp. And then? Well, Porsche's Magic Show is on! Who knows what's next?

The sun is gone now. I'm getting cold. And still no tow truck. Do some more thinking! Keep the spirit up! I remember the visit earlier in the day with Tom and Marjorie Green at Automotion. They offer yet another 924 alternative.

The Greens have been involved with Porsches since 1970, when they first prepared their Convertible D for club racing. The hobby soon grew into a business. In 1973, they started Automotion, specializing in Porsche parts and accessories, offering their wares through a mail-order catalog with worldwide distribution. There are now fourteen employees at the Santa Clara headquarters. That's where I went to see the 924 Automotion Club Racer.

It consists of kit components especially designed to make a 924 look and perform like a race car. It enables the enthusiast to prepare his 924 for auto crosses and time trials. The components are developed and designed by Automotion and manufactured to their specifications. The fender kit costs about $2,500, while the suspension kit runs about $1,500. This would bring a 924 up to the limit allowed by club rules. The prototype, where all the components are tested and developed, looks very good. Unfortunately, it had a run-in with a beside-the-road object the day before my visit, so it was temporarily out of commission. But Tom promised me a future test drive.

I'm extracted from my thoughts by the lights of an approaching car. As it comes closer, to my disappointment, I see it's not the tow truck. As it comes to a stop, four over-sized farmhands get out, moving slowly, looking like marauders, approaching the Turbo, probably hoping to find it abandoned. They look disappointed when I roll down the window, and even more disappointed when I ask them if they would help me get the car out. After a couple of half-hearted efforts, the Turbo is still stuck. I look in my pocket and fish out four twenty-dollar bills. Holding them out through the window like a carrot on a stick, I promise them one each when the car is free.

The experience returned my confidence in the buying power of the dollar. The Turbo was virtually lifted out of the mud hole. Naturally, I met the tow truck after only a few hundred yards.

"Porsches For The Road," sixth in the Survivors Series, was photographed, written and designed by Henry Rasmussen. The technical specifications in the content section were compiled and researched by Gene Babow. Assistant designer was Walt Woesner. Copy editor was Barbara Harold. Typesetting was supplied by Tintype Graphic Arts of San Luis Obispo. The color separations were produced by Graphic Arts Systems of Burbank. Zellerbach Paper Company supplied the 100-pound Flokote stock, manufactured by S. D. Warren. The special inks were formulated by Spectrum Ink Company of Los Angeles. Litho-Craft of Anaheim printed the book, under supervision of Brad Thurman. The binding was provided by National Bindery of Pomona.

In addition to the skilled craftsmen associated with the above mentioned firms, the author also

wishes to thank the owners of the featured cars for their invaluable cooperation.

Special acknowledgements go to Gene Babow of Kentfield, California, Sam Cabiglio and Ray Stewart, both of Long Beach, California, Pete Smith of Hollywood, California and Chuck Stoddard of Willoughby, Ohio, for sharing so generously of their knowledge, earned over many years of involvement with Porsches. The author is also indebted to Tom Warth of Motorbooks International for his support, without which this book would not have been produced.

The author finally wishes to thank the following contributors: David Barr, Bruce Baker, Warren Eads, Gary Ellidge, Sepp Grinbold, Tom Hessert, Bruce Meyer, Otis Meyer, John Nelson, Rich Pasquali, Jim Perrin, Bob Raucher, Brad Riple, Joe Riva, Shirley Rusch and Carl Thompson.